Children and young people

substance misuse services

the substance of young needs

COMMISSIONING AND PROVIDING SERVICES FOR CHILDREN AND YOUNG PEOPLE WHO USE AND MISUSE SUBSTANCES

London HMSO

ISBN 0 11 321934 2

Published by HMSO and available from:

HMSO Publications Centre
(Mail, fax and telephone orders only)
PO Box 276, London SW8 5DT
Telephone orders 0171-873 9090
General enquiries 0171-873 0011
(queuing system in operation for both numbers)
Fax orders 0171-873 8200

HMSO Bookshops
49 High Holborn, London WC1V 6HB
0171-873 0011 Fax 0171-831 1326 (counter service only)
68-69 Bull Street, Birmingham B4 6AD
0121-236 9696 Fax 0121-236 9699
33 Wine Street, Bristol BS1 2BQ
0117-926 4306 Fax 0117 9294515
9-21 Princess Street, Manchester M60 8AS
0161-834 7201 Fax 0161-833 0634
16 Arthur Street, Belfast BT1 4GD
01232 238451 Fax 01232 235401
71 Lothian Road, Edinburgh EH3 9AZ
0131-228 4181 Fax 0131-229 2734
The HMSO Oriel Bookshop,
The Friary, Cardiff CF1 4AA
01222 395548 Fax 01222 384347

HMSO's Accredited Agents
(see Yellow Pages)

and through good booksellers

CHAPTER 1   The Director's Introduction   1
CHAPTER 2   Executive Summary   7
CHAPTER 3   A Guide to this Report   15

PART A - THE BACKGROUND
CHAPTER 4   Influences, Definitions and Associated Problems   17
CHAPTER 5   Education and Prevention   35
CHAPTER 6   The Current Position   51

PART B - A STRATEGY FOR THE FUTURE
CHAPTER 7   A Summary of Key Concepts and Challenges   63
CHAPTER 8   A Strategic Approach to Services for Children and
             Adolescents who Misuse Substances   67

PART C - COMMISSIONING AND PURCHASING SERVICES
FOR CHILDREN AND ADOLESCENTS
CHAPTER 9   Commissioning Services for Children and
             Adolescents who Misuse Substances   77
CHAPTER 10   A Commissioning Action Plan   87

PART D - KEY ISSUES EFFECTING THE DESIGN AND DELIVERY
OF SERVICES
CHAPTER 11   Legal Issues   91
CHAPTER 12   The Principles of Good Practice in Service Delivery   97
CHAPTER 13   Training   115

PART E - THE IMPLICATIONS FOR THE PROVIDERS OF
SERVICES
CHAPTER 14   Towards Comprehensive Services For Young
             People   123
CHAPTER 15   A Summary of Advice for Specific Providers of
             Services   137
CHAPTER 16   Service Evaluation and Performance Management   141

PART F - CHECKLISTS AND REFERENCES
CHAPTER 17   Checklists   145
CHAPTER 18   References and Bibliography   167

PART G - THE ANNEXES
ANNEX A   The Methodology of the Review   179
ANNEX B   Policy, Guidance and Funding Arrangements   183
ANNEX C   The Editors and Authors   195
ANNEX D   The Steering Committee   199
ANNEX E   Participants in a Seminar on Children, Adolescents
             and Substance Misuse   203

THE SUBSTANCE OF YOUNG NEEDS

**Commissioning and Providing Services for
Children and Young People who Use and Misuse Substances**

THE EDITORS

Senior Editor

Dr Richard Williams

Expert Editors

Ms Jane Christian

Dr Martyn Gay

Dr Eilish Gilvarry

HAS Headquarters Editors

Ms Kina Avebury

Mr Giles Emerson

Mrs Zena Muth

PRINCIPAL AUTHORS

Ms Kina Avebury

Ms Jane Christian

Dr Martyn Gay

Dr Eilish Gilvarry

Dr Richard Williams

CONTRIBUTING AUTHORS

Mr Niall Coggans

Mr Mike Farrar

Mr Finlay Graham

Mr Richard White

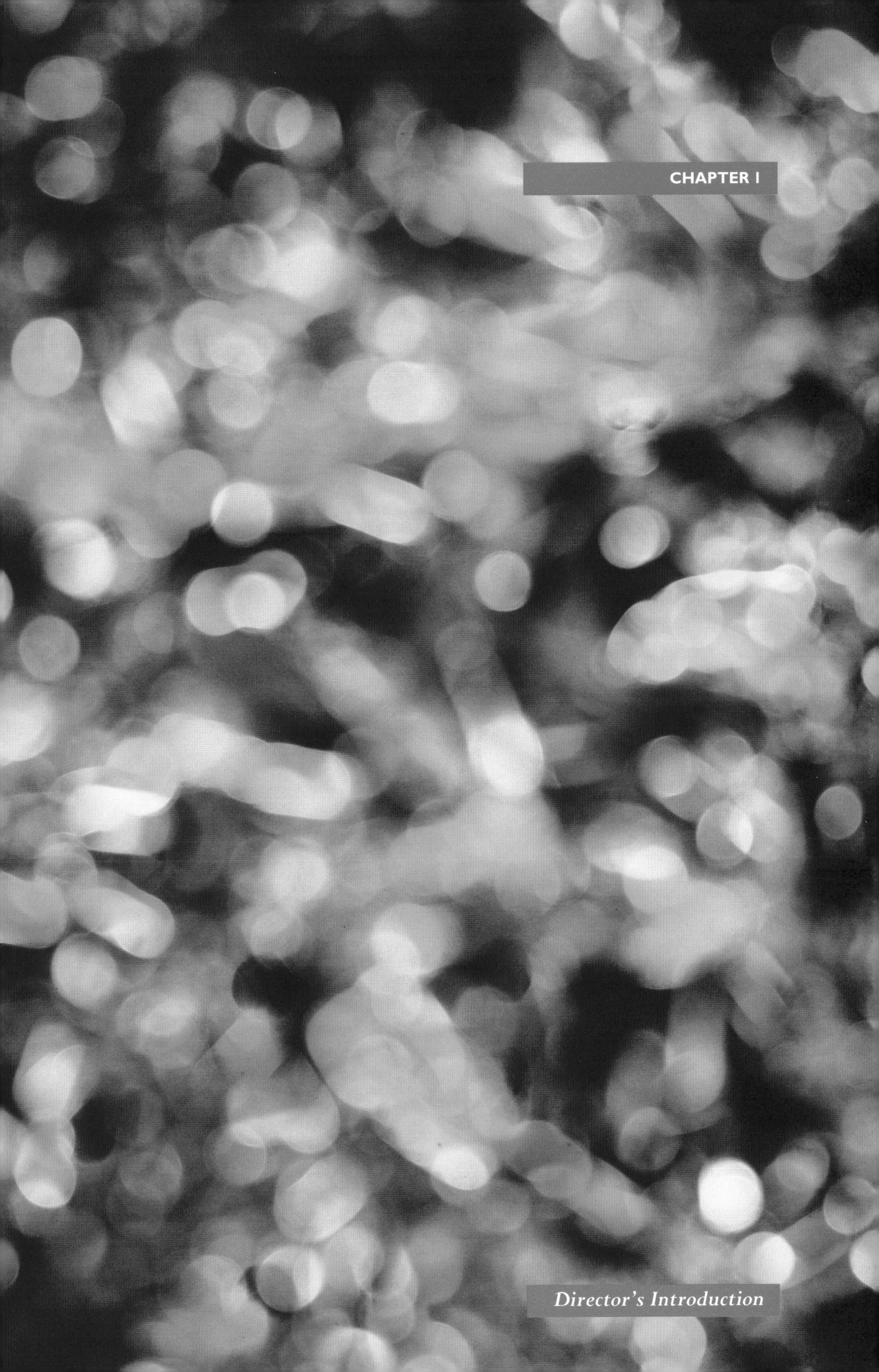

CHAPTER 1

Director's Introduction

THE WHAT OF WHAT

"When we asked Pooh what the opposite of an Introduction was, he said "The what of a what?" which didn't help us as much as we had hoped, but luckily Owl kept his head and told us that the Opposite of an Introduction, my dear Pooh, was a Contradiction; and, as he is very good at long words, I am sure that that's what it is.

The House at Pooh Corner, A. A. Milne.

My intention, is that this chapter should outline for readers *"The what of...(the)...what..."* or, in other words, introduce the complex subject matter and the many themes raised in the course of undertaking this review.

This thematic review of services for children and adolescents who misuse substances, which refers particularly to the misuse of alcohol and drugs, is one of a series of thematic reviews conducted by the NHS Health Advisory Service (HAS) on related, parallel and overlapping topics. The series includes important documents on suicide prevention *(Suicide Prevention - The Challenge Confronted, 1994)* and the commissioning, role and management of child and adolescent mental health services *(Together We Stand, 1995)*.

Chapter 11 of *Suicide Prevention - The Challenge Confronted,* concerns adolescents. It highlights the strong influence of alcohol and substance use and misuse on young people who commit suicide and on those young people who deliberately harm themselves.

Together We Stand (chapter six, paragraph 130), reviewed progress made by the NHS and local authorities in commissioning the broad spread of mental health services required by children and adolescents. It records that 75% of health authorities had, by 1993, put forward proposals for alcohol and substance misuse services which could include provision for young people. The same review highlighted the significance of substance use and misuse for the mental health problems and disorders experienced by this population.

The word *substance* in this report is used to cover a wide range of materials. Alcohol, still the favourite drug for adolescents, is included as are drugs and other volatile substances. Much of the research work has been carried out on services, and their clients, that offer intervention with a more restricted range of materials - commonly alcohol and drugs. So, these words are used advisedly in places. Elsewhere, the term *substance* has been deliberately chosen to reflect the position espoused by the NHS Health Advisory Service (HAS) which is that services for young people should be developed with the capacity to deal with alcohol, drugs and other substances within the same framework.

The HAS has adopted the terms **use** and **misuse.** We acknowledge that clear distinctions between *use,* often styled as *experimental or recreational use,* and *misuse* are hard to draw. *Use* of most drugs is also illegal and some who experiment may experience problems consequent on intoxication. Experience indicates that, while the trend towards increasing use of drugs and alcohol by young people is undesirable because of their increased exposure to the potential dangers of social, psychological and physical problems, experimentation alone cannot be seen as indicative of personal disorder. In this report, *misuse* is defined as use that is harmful (see paragraph 25), dependent use, or use of substances as part of a wider spectrum of problematic or harmful behaviour. In these terms, young people who misuse substances may also have significant problems with their psycho-social development.

Although the preferred terms of this text relating to the consumption of substances are substance *use* and *misuse*, the term *abuse* appears in some paragraphs. This reflects the use of that term in the original material and research from which evidence is being drawn in this report.

Despite the existence of all the information that the HAS brings together now, the field of substance use and misuse is a confusing one. It is associated in the minds of many people with uncertainty, moral issues, concern about the very fabric of family life and society and, not to put too fine a point on it, the whole arena has become invested with prejudice and stigma. Increasingly, this is the case when we consider the use of substances - alcohol, drugs and other compounds - by young people.

For some of us, this very subject conjures images of a dangerous and decadent youth culture that is a long way in its mores from their parent's generation. Yet this report shows just how wide of the mark these views can be. This is not to doubt the high levels of experimental and recreational use of a wide variety of substances by young people (these matters are considered fully in this document) but what also emerges is a picture of a considerable number of disadvantaged or vulnerable young people who are more prone to using substances in worrying and dangerous ways, and misusing substances, than their peers. These are young people who, all too often, come from backgrounds that put them at risk and who show patterns of problem behaviour within which substance use or misuse is a component.

FINDING THE WAY FORWARD

"But, Eeyore," said Pooh in distress, "what can we - I mean, how shall we - do you think if we -" "Yes," said Eeyore. "One of those would be just the thing. Thank you, Pooh."

The House at Pooh Corner, A. A. Milne.

The world that I introduce is an uncertain one which is, in part, a consequence of the controversial nature of the field. The uncertainty also reflects a genuine lack of knowledge although there is more researched information to guide our way than might at first appear to be the case.

Sadly, the current state of services dedicated to the needs of children and adolescents who use and misuse substances of all kinds is parlous, particularly in the statutory sector. Most innovation and many of the few existing services are to be found in the non-statutory sectors - with, of course, some notable exceptions.

But young people are served, albeit in essentially unplanned and sporadic ways, and the credit for much of what is being done should fall to some dedicated personalities in the field. These are professional people who have interpreted their roles widely and who have had the fortune to work for agencies and other personalities who have let them develop the lead they have shown. I have been fortunate in being able to gather a number of these leaders together in undertaking this thematic review. The information collated in this report, and the advice which stems from it, is grounded in evaluated research and the hard-won experience of clinical practice. Therefore, this report is as authoritative as present knowledge and wisdom will allow.

LEADING THE WAY

"For if the trumpet give an uncertain sound, who shall prepare himself to the battle?"

I Corinthians xiv, 8

This verse aptly summarises one of the reasons for the poor level of development of substance misuse services for children and adolescents and pinpoints an important lesson for the future. What is needed now in developing services is leadership provided by commissioners, purchasers and providers from a range of agencies who are willing to consider the evidence of need presented here and then move forward to inspire the creative development of services. Much could be achieved by bringing together those elements of service that are already being deployed by a variety of different services, though in more explicit and recognised ways.

This report paints a picture of younger people who have fallen between existing services. Perhaps this is because these services still have large agendas of their own. But this situation also reflects a lack of ownership among services of the problems presented by the substance use and misuse of children and adolescents. This does not deny that the vigorous development of services may require new resources. But NHS and local authority commissioners, working in close conjunction with one another and with the purchasers of services, including GP fundholders, are now in a position to take an overview and, where necessary, to re-align the distribution and structures of services to achieve a more even balance of care. Again, leadership within commissioning, purchasing and providing organisations is required alongside ownership of the challenges required to achieve more for this client group. Our experience indicates that collaborative partnerships between commissioners, purchasers and providers are vital in ensuring the effective development of appropriate services.

THE WORLDS OF CHILDREN

The quotations in this introduction that are taken from *The House At Pooh Corner* could be viewed as patronising or denigrating both to adolescents and to readers but, most definitely, this is not their intention. Rather, they have been selected to make the points they do and to emphasise a matter of key importance in commissioning and providing services for this client group. This is the need to base the design of services and their front-line delivery on an understanding of the world as seen by young people of different ages; and on clear knowledge of their emotional and physical development. Much more is known about the latter than can be rehearsed in this report and the former can only be approached by meeting and talking to children and adolescents.

This report is concerned with children and adolescents of all ages. Not surprisingly, much of what is contained refers to adolescents and this reflects the current pattern of drug use by minors.

Nonetheless, it is important to understand how many young people make important decisions about their openness or otherwise the use of substances quite early in their adolescence. Discussions with older teenagers suggest that they would welcome information, advice and support at around 13 years of age and afterwards, even if they might not say so at the time. Evidently, giving information first to post 16 year-olds is just too late and older adolescents and young adults may require a different profile of services presented in different ways that reflect their intervening development. In this, we see the all important interaction between family background, the balance between risk and protective factors, child and adolescent developmental pathways and the use and misuse of substances.

The point made recurrently in this review is that the staff of services that are appropriately orientated require a working knowledge of all these matters and that this should be a potent influence on their training - a vital matter that is also dealt with in this review.

A STRATEGIC FRAMEWORK FOR SERVICE DEVELOPMENT

This review considers the current level and styles of services available to children and adolescents who use and misuse substances. It draws on a critique of these services to identify some lessons for the future. Others are derived from theory and research and can be described as *evidence-based.*

What is clear is that commissioners, purchasers and providers require a strategic template upon which to base their understanding, needs assessments, and the consequent design and delivery patterns for services. Earlier in 1995, the HAS published its parallel review of mental health services for children and adolescents. Understandably, there is much overlap between these two reviews as they deal with the same client group. In its report on that review, the HAS put forward a *4 Tier Strategic Framework* for services. This approach was developed in parallel and together with a number of key players in the field and it has received support from a wide range of the professions as providing an effective way forward. Importantly, it has been very well received by managers and professionals in local services. Thus, the HAS has taken the opportunity to develop and extend this model to cover services for young people who use and misuse substances.

ACKNOWLEDGEMENTS

The Editors and Authors

My special thanks are due to the editors and authors of this document (see Annex D). They have led in the preparation of this report with great dedication and attention to detail and they have worked hard to meet exacting deadlines. They have responded positively to my requests for further information and fresh drafts. They are all busy people and I am all the more grateful to them for the volume of their own private time that they have invested in this review over a period of two and a half years. Also, I am grateful to their professional colleagues and to the managers of the services employing these people for their forbearance and for enabling the authors to take leave of absence to conduct this review.

From within this group, I must select four people for particular attention. Jane Christian, Martyn Gay and Eilish Gilvarry have been the backbone of the review. They have done most of the thinking and much of the fieldwork and they have contributed the lion's share of the drafting. Without them, this thematic review would not have been done.

Martyn Gay led the review and I take this opportunity to offer him special thanks - not just for this job, which he has conducted with his usual personal flair, but also for a professional friendship which has spanned the entirety of my consultant career. I value his wisdom highly.

The authors and I offer our special thanks to Mrs Annette Young and Dr Anthony Thorley both of the Department of Health. They sat as observers on the steering committee and were members of a working group that was established by the leader of this thematic review. The expertise and experience of Mrs Young and Dr Thorley were invalauble. They assisted Ms Christian, Dr Gay and Dr Gilvarry, who formed the core group, to formulate their thinking at the outset of the review and were particularly helpful sources of knowldege and advice when the initial drafts that led to this report were written.

Finally, I would like to thank Kina Avebury. She joined the core team in its final stages to contribute her experience from a previous review to the arduous drafting and editing processes. She has done much in bringing this report to its final form.

The Steering Committee

When the two thematic reviews began that have led to *Together We Stand* and to this report, I established a single steering committee to advise me on the work. The core teams which undertook each were drawn from this body. The biographies of the members appear in Annex D. Once again, this review has benefited considerably from their wisdom and dedication. They have ensured that this review has received guidance from an appropriately broad perspective. I thank them all most sincerely, and particularly so as their work comes to a close.

CONCLUDING COMMENTS

The intentions of the thematic review and of this report are to offer information and guidance to commissioners, purchasers and providers on services for children and adolescents who use and/or misuse substances. Much of it is addressed to NHS managers but, as we show, the field is a multi-sectoral one in which the statutory health and local authority and non-statutory sectors should combine in well rehearsed but innovative ways to ensure the delivery of services for a vulnerable and needy client group. Again, as identified in *Together We Stand,* collaboration and co-ordination are the key processes. The strategic framework proposed here espouses these concepts and provides a rational basis for their development.

The White Paper, *Tackling Drugs Together,* puts considerable emphasis on:

*   reducing the acceptability and availability of drugs to young people;

*   reducing the health risks and other damage related to drug misuse; and

*   increasing the safety of communities from drug-related crime.

The White Paper's publication in 1995 provides a vital impetus to authorities in taking initiatives to provide better services for children and adolescents. The Welsh Office consultation document, *Forward Together,* presages a similar initiative in Wales. I hope this report will provide the knowledge-base that will enable commissioners, purchasers and providers to move forward with confidence and a clear purpose.

Dr Richard Williams
Director
The NHS Health Advisory Service

November 1995

I   The use and misuse of drugs and alcohol by children and adolescents is a
     matter of increasing concern. For some, experimental and recreational use
     does not represent a long-term problem for the individuals concerned or
     for their families. But more sustained substance use and, in some cases, only
     relatively limited exposure to substances, can lead to problems for young
     people. These children and adolescents require interventions not only
     from the health services but from social services and education
     departments, the police, and the probation and criminal justice services.
     The non-statutory agencies stand alongside the statutory bodies as major
     providers of service in the field of substance and alcohol misuse.

2   The HAS has adopted the terms **use** and **misuse.** We acknowledge that
     clear distinctions between *use,* often styled as *experimental or recreational
     use,* and *misuse* are hard to draw. *Use* of most drugs is also illegal and some
     who experiment may experience problems consequent on intoxication.
     Experience indicates that, while the trend towards increasing use of drugs
     and alcohol by young people is undesirable because of their increased
     exposure to the potential dangers of social, psychological and physical
     problems, experimentation alone cannot be seen as indicative of personal
     disorder. In this report, *misuse* is defined as use that is harmful (see
     paragraph 25), dependent use, or use of substances as part of a wider
     spectrum of problematic or harmful behaviour. In these terms, young
     people who misuse substances may also have significant problems with
     their psycho-social development.

3   While research data about substance use and misuse by children and
     adolescents in the UK is limited, certain trends are apparent and give cause
     for concern. These include:

     •   the increased use of a wide range of drugs by the younger age group;

     •   increasing use among girls;

     •   the emergence of poly drug use as the norm;

     •   lowering of the age of initiation into substance use.

     Adolescents are also growing up in a culture in which drugs are much more
     easily available, acceptable and their consumption more readily perceived
     as 'normal' within peer groups.

4   The analysis of considerable background research that provides the
     grounding for this thematic review - including wide-ranging studies carried
     out overseas - makes it clear that young people's involvement in drug and
     alcohol misuse is often complicated by a range of other factors. Each
     individual's substance-using and/or misusing profile generally involves a
     complex array of cognitive, psychological, attitudinal, social, personality,
     pharmacological and developmental factors. In effect, there is no typical
     substance-using adolescent and no specific personality type. This inevitably
     makes the task of providing clear, co-ordinated and properly evaluated
     services more difficult. It also makes specific demands on the levels of
     awareness and competence required by staff, not only in specialist services
     but also throughout the spectrum of primary care and direct contact
     services.

5   The scope of this review covers alcohol, the use of illicit and prescribed
     drugs including steroids, and volatile substances. The main findings of this
     report are summarised below.

- There is a lack of leadership in the commissioning and provision of services for young people who misuse substances.

- With certain notable exceptions, there is virtually no provision in the contractual arrangements made by the statutory health agencies with providers stipulating services specifically for children and adolescents who misuse substances.

- The review recommends strongly that steps be taken by commissioners to ensure that suitable environments for assessment and treatment are provided separately from adult services as these are considered inappropriate to meet the needs of young people.

- The skills and experience of non-statutory agency staff and the work of these agencies with children and adolescents are not sufficiently recognised. At the same time, their resources are over-stretched by the annual contracting processes.

- Overall, there is an absence of individual or joint purchasing strategies for this age group.

- Responses are poorly planned and poorly co-ordinated with pockets of isolated excellence throughout the country.

- Generally, there is a lack of recognition by professionals in, and managers of health services of the particular and definable needs arising from substance use and misuse by children and adolescents.

- Specialised treatment for young people in England and Wales is extremely limited as a result of a range of factors including: lack of definition and understanding of the problem; lack of basic information about existing services; unclear and disputed funding responsibilities; and competitiveness and lack of trust between existing service sectors and service components.

- Some people in this age group are less likely to gain access to services than others. They include: those who are unaware of what services are available; young people in prisons; homeless young people or those who live in hostels; those living in rural areas; and young people with multiple problems.

- The fieldwork revealed that local responses to the problem are often *ad hoc*. Services and interventions, where they exist, have developed in an isolated, uneven, patchy and idiosyncratic manner.

- There is some evidence of a slow growth in local initiatives to provide better direct-contact services for children and adolescents. In a number of instances, these have developed from the enthusiasm of local practitioners and are provided as offshoots from the community mental health services for adults and offer self referral, information and some limited counselling and support.

- Inpatient facilities for detoxification or assessment of psychiatric co-morbidity (either in specific units or attached to adult mental health services) do not usually admit those people who are under 17 years of age.

6   This gloomy picture of current service provision is compounded by other factors. For example, while the health services visited by the HAS review team showed various levels of concern about their own responses, there is

an apparent lack of clarity in most of these services about the nature and extent of the problem, the roles of the services already involved, and the balance to be struck between education, prevention and more direct intervention with young people who have problems. Staff are also concerned about the legal implications of working with young people. Generally, there is little proper knowledge or formal training concerning issues of confidentiality and consent. There is particular concern about the provision of needles and syringes to under 16 year-olds without parental consent.

7   The review team's analysis of programmes of education geared to children and young people indicates that it is easier to improve knowledge than to affect attitudes. Behaviour change is most difficult to accomplish through education programmes. Analysis indicates that the more effective programmes tend to be those based less on the teaching of facts, or on increasing fear, and more on those approaches that involve discussion of attitudes and social issues. Programmes involving peers in the education process are considered to have potential. The HAS also recommends the promotion of behavioural alternatives to substance use by young people so that they may be helped to develop preferences for more healthy lifestyles. All the analysis indicates that educational interventions in drug use and misuse should be carefully designed. Different programmes may be needed for young people at different stages of development and they should be targeted to meet the underlying as well as the overt needs of vulnerable young people.

8   Providing a focus on the need for developments in this broad field, the Government's White Paper, *Tackling Drugs Together* (1995), and the recent consultation document issued by the Welsh Office, *Forward Together,* make it incumbent upon service commissioners that they ensure that accessible and appropriate services are put in place. The White Paper warns of *"the prospect over the next few years of more drug misuse by younger people causing more damage to themselves and their communities."*

9   Empowered by *Tackling Drugs Together*, significant emphasis should be placed by health service commissioners, purchasers and providers on the development of strategy. A successful strategy should aim to achieve the following:

  • hold and convey a concept for the service overall;

  • clarify the intention, role and target client groups for the service;

  • recognise the multi-sectoral, multi-focal and multi-disciplinary nature of good services;

  • be capable of use by agencies acting together as a tool in joint commissioning and joint provision;

  • enable purchasers, including GP fundholders, to conduct their roles within a negotiated framework;

  • enable individual commissioners and providers to understand their own, single agency roles and responsibilities and use their powers to achieve these;

  • provide a basis for collaboration between agencies and co-ordination between service elements, components and staff.

10 Following on from this, three mechanisms of service development are proposed:

- creating completely new services;

- bringing together existing services, but in new ways;

- allocating lead responsibility to one existing service or agency, but with the requirement for collaboration with other services.

All three of these mechanisms should be used in different combinations to reflect the local circumstances.

11 While reviewing problems faced not only by health services but by related statutory and non-statutory agencies, this report identifies the challenges that need to be addressed now. These include the need to:

- gather information about the nature of substance misuse by adults and younger people in the area covered by each health authority. In this process, the most vulnerable groups should be identified and information should be sought about use in rural areas, for example among travellers;

- obtain information on the resources provided by services in the non-statutory sector;

- develop local needs assessments based upon a sound and comprehensive knowledge-base;

- create services in well publicised, user-friendly environments that are appropriate and appealing to girls and young women and boys and young men;

- provide accessible and appropriate information to young people and parents;

- provide more accessible primary and specialist mental health services for children and adolescents;

- develop preventive and harm-reducing outreach services;

- achieve formal and effective liaison between accident and emergency departments and agencies that work with vulnerable young people;

- ensure close operational links between mental health services, drug and alcohol advisory services and social, housing and education services and agencies in the non-statutory sector;

- provide services which accept self-referrals;

- provide training and support for staff on working with younger people who have problems arising from substance misuse;

- develop healthy alliances through multi-agency and multi-disciplinary work;

- develop mature relationships with non-statutory providers, including contractual partnerships that promote the continuity and stability of services;

- appoint lead officers in each sector to be responsible for co-ordinating work across agency boundaries.

12   Appropriate services for children and adolescents who are approaching
      the threshold of use, and for those who use or misuse substances have
      plural objectives. These are:

      •   prevention of drug use, including helping younger people to achieve
           and maintain drug-free lifestyles (primary prevention);

      •   minimising harm related to the use of substances (secondary
           prevention);

      •   care, treatment and rehabilitation of young people who have
           developed dependency on substances, harmful patterns of
           substance misuse or disorders in which substance misuse plays an
           aetiological role (secondary and tertiary prevention).

13   In *Together We Stand - The Commissioning, Role and Management of Child
      and Adolescent Mental Health Services* (1995), the HAS put forward a
      four-tier strategic approach designed to improve the planning, co-
      ordination and delivery of services for children and adolescents with mental
      health problems. As a strategic model, the four-tier structure is popular
      with the NHS locally, local authorities, criminal justice and non-statutory
      agencies as a basis of understanding the intent and roles of their services
      and as a tool in service review and re-design. Readers are referred to
      Together We Stand to learn the basic features of the four tiers. In this report,
      the HAS has adapted the model to apply it to the delivery of services for
      children and adolescents who misuse substances.

14   By way of an overview of the proposed structure:

      Tier 1

      Tier 1 services are those that are accessible directly by the general public.
      They are provided by primary care workers such as GPs, health visitors,
      staff of non-statutory organisations, social workers, police officers and
      school medical officers. These workers can have an influence on the young
      people with whom they come into contact but do not necessarily have the
      sole purpose of informing or intervening with children and adolescents
      who are at risk of substance use or misuse. At Tier 1, staff are important in
      recognising and identifying problem substance use and they require the
      competence to advise accordingly and make appropriate referrals to more
      specialist agencies in other tiers. Some staff who offer Tier 1 services may
      also continue to play significant roles in the shared care of children and
      adolescents after their referral to more specialised services.

      Tier 2

      Tier 2 services are those in which the staff have a more specialised
      understanding of child and adolescent development; knowledge of
      substance use and misuse by young people; and the ability to practice in
      circumstances that are appropriate to the culture of young people. Chief
      components of Tier 2 services are the capacity to: provide accurate
      information and advice; conduct assessment of needs; identify problems
      related to substance use and misuse and other problematic behaviours;
      offer advice and information to carers and families; and involve other
      appropriate agencies. Tier 2 staff include primary care workers with a
      special interest in drug and alcohol misuse problems; child and adolescent
      psychiatrists, educational psychologists, social workers with a specialised
      knowledge of substance use and misuse by children and adolescents, staff

in comprehensive centres/one-stop shops, staff of more specialised non-statutory agencies, health promotion workers and youth justice workers. Frequently, in Tier 2, individual specialist staff may work with young people or in supporting Tier 1 staff.

Tier 3

Tier 3 consists of components of service that are more specialised, usually because of the need to respond to the complexity of the problems presented to them. They include: youth-orientated specialist addictions services, either statutory or non-statutory; certain components of child and adolescent mental health services; and other specialist youth services. Frequently, in Tier 3, specialist staff may work in multi-disciplinary teams with individuals to bring the necessary skills to bear on their complex problems.

Tier 4

Tier 4 consists of very specialised services, such as those that offer: inpatient assessment, care and treatment; care and treatment for children and adolescents in secure provision; highly specialised clinics for young people who have significant problems arising from two or more co-morbid disorders; and a range of specialist rehabilitation services for children and adolescents who misuse substances.

15 The key to effective service provision within this structure is good communication both between those service components and staff within the same tier, particularly in Tier 1 (involving the broadest spread of services) and good communication between different tiers. This demands properly co-ordinated approaches to inter-agency referral and appropriately trained staff acting as gatekeepers between the different tiers of service.

16 The need for more appropriate training is clearly underpinned in this report. Training is the means by which services can ensure that quality standards are met and that interventions made with young people are appropriate to each individual's age and stage of development. Commissioners and purchasers themselves require training to discharge their responsibilities effectively, while key provider staff require training to be able to deliver their services effectively and to meet the standards required in purchasing specifications. In general, the development and maintenance of appropriate skills requires four levels of training:

- general training for all health, social work, education, youth work, criminal justice and non-statutory service sector staff;
- advanced training for selected staff of a wide range of agencies;
- specialist training for the staff of specialist services;
- specific training for staff of highly specialised, and, sometimes, low-volume services.

17 This requires that programmes of training are adequately resourced and co-ordinated at local levels to ensure multi-agency participation and, at the national level, to identify and promote good practice and to encourage national training bodies to ensure that education about substance misuse receives proper emphasis. These four levels of training have the advantage of corresponding with the four-tier strategic approach. Programmes of training at all these levels should be reinforced by appropriate systems of support and supervision for staff.

18 Given the fragmentary and, in some areas, non-existence of services for young people with problems arising from the use and misuse of drugs and alcohol, there are considerable challenges to overcome before there will be appropriate provision in England and Wales for this group. As in the HAS report on child and adolescent mental health services (*Together We Stand*, 1995), collaboration is the key to development. No proper or effective service can be implemented locally unless certain linchpins are in place:

- an accurate knowledge-base about the problems and issues;

- an overarching commissioning strategy that takes account of the local needs and generates an approach to purchasing in which service specifications seek specific standards of service from a mix of provider services. Contracts should be used to support, consolidate and confirm developments in services;

- appropriate training for key staff;

- adequate systems of supervision and support for staff;

- assessments of individual children and adolescents that determine the extent and method of their use and the problems resulting from intoxification and continued or excessive use of substances;

- interventions that are targeted in ways that recognise younger people who are at particular risk and the differing needs of children and adolescents at different points in their development;

- interventions that are able to cope with multiple individual problems when they exist;

- proper communication and effective co-ordination between agencies and individuals that enables pooling of expertise between the different agencies that provide the range of service components in the four-tier structure;

- mechanisms for creating integrated programmes of care for individuals that recognise the importance of care pathways and the role and patterns of shared care involving direct access and specialist services.

19 The development of more effective and appropriate substance misuse services for children and adolescents should become a major item on the agenda of all health authorities.

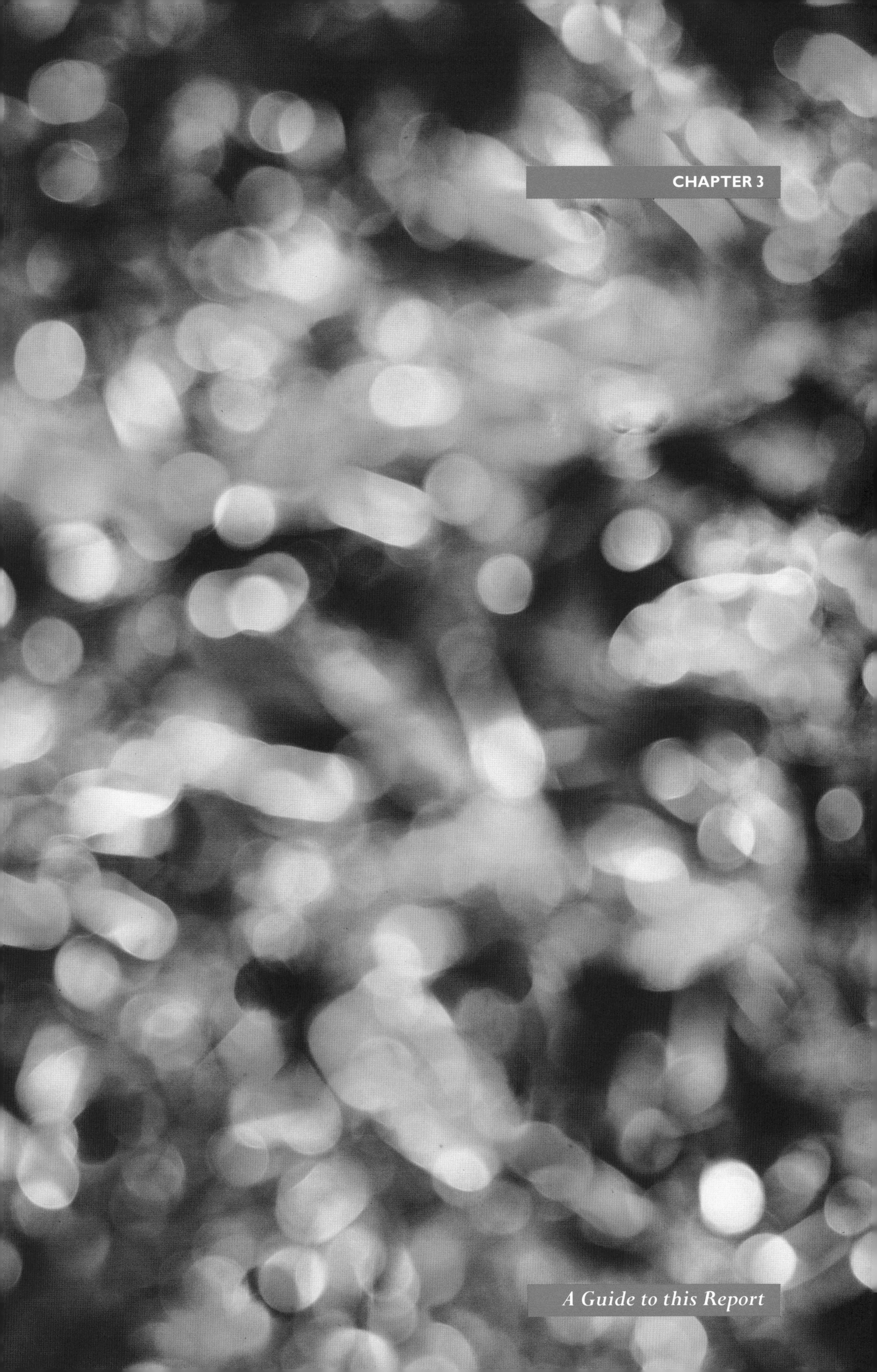

CHAPTER 3

A Guide to this Report

THE AIMS

1   This review aims to raise the awareness of commissioners, managers and workers in a broad range of sectors of care about the use and misuse of alcohol and other substances by children and adolescents. The age range of the services under consideration in this review is similar to that adopted in *Together We Stand*. The boundaries of childhood and adolescence are unclear and a flexible approach to the definition of age is needed. The HAS recommends that services should provide for children and young people up to the age of 21.

2   While recognising their importance, the authors of the review agreed that they would not specifically address the issues relating to the children of adults who use alcohol or substances.

USING THE CONTENTS OF THIS DOCUMENT

3   Part A contains the necessary background information on alcohol and substance use and misuse. Chapter four reviews the different definitions used by a range of organisations and professional bodies and offers the HAS' preferred working definitions. A brief discussion on adolescent health in general leads onto an examination of prevalence and trends, together with an identification of aetiological risk factors and associated problems. These provide a broad basis for policy and strategy development and their implementation. In particular, the possible relationships between substance misuse and crime are considered.

4   Chapter five reviews the current situation in the fields of education and prevention. Chapter six contains an overview of the current status of commissioning and provision of substance and alcohol misuse services for young people in the United Kingdom, America and Australia. This chapter begins the process of identifying the problems inherent in planning and delivering services to younger people.

5   In Part B, chapter seven offers a summary of the key concepts in, and challenges to service design if we are to meet the healthcare needs, associated influences and effects of substance use and misuse. These concepts and the challenges that they offer to commissioners, purchasers and providers are linked in a way that encourages appropriate responses to particular problems. These are taken up in chapter eight which provides a strategic overview of the way forward recommended by the HAS.

6   Part C is addressed primarily to those who are responsible for commissioning, either on a single agency basis or jointly. Chapter nine focuses on the specific issues relating to the commissioning of services for children and adolescents who misuse substances, within the framework first set out by Dr Brian Mawhinney and Mr Duncan Nichol in *Purchasing for Health (1993)*. Chapter ten follows with a Commissioning Action Plan, delineating the processes and key issues as they apply to young people.

7   Part D deals with the principles of effective service delivery. As such, it forms a bridge between those matters of prime concern to commissioning agencies and those mainly of concern to providers. Both types of organisation and their staffs have a common interest in the legal position of children and adolescents and the impact that this has on service design and delivery. This is set out in Chapter eleven. All parties share an interest in issues of good practice, as set out in Chapter twelve. Chapter thirteen stresses the crucial importance of training to both commissioners and providers.

8   Part E covers subjects which are of particular relevance to providers - both managers and clinicians. The route towards a comprehensive service is outlined in chapter fourteen. Chapter fifteen, recognising the diversity of settings in which services are provided, contains summaries of the advice and guidance to the different professions. Chapter sixteen highlights the importance of evaluation in ensuring that those services which are planned and provided are as effective as possible.

9   Every effort has been made to make the review accessible by using bullet points, tables and, in Part F, the tables which appear throughout the text are repeated as checklists for easy reference.

10   The background data is essential to anyone involved in any way in commissioning or providing services for younger people who misuse substances, and to a wide range of other professionals working with vulnerable children and adolescents. The legal dimensions are important in this field, and this is recognised in specific chapters in the text.

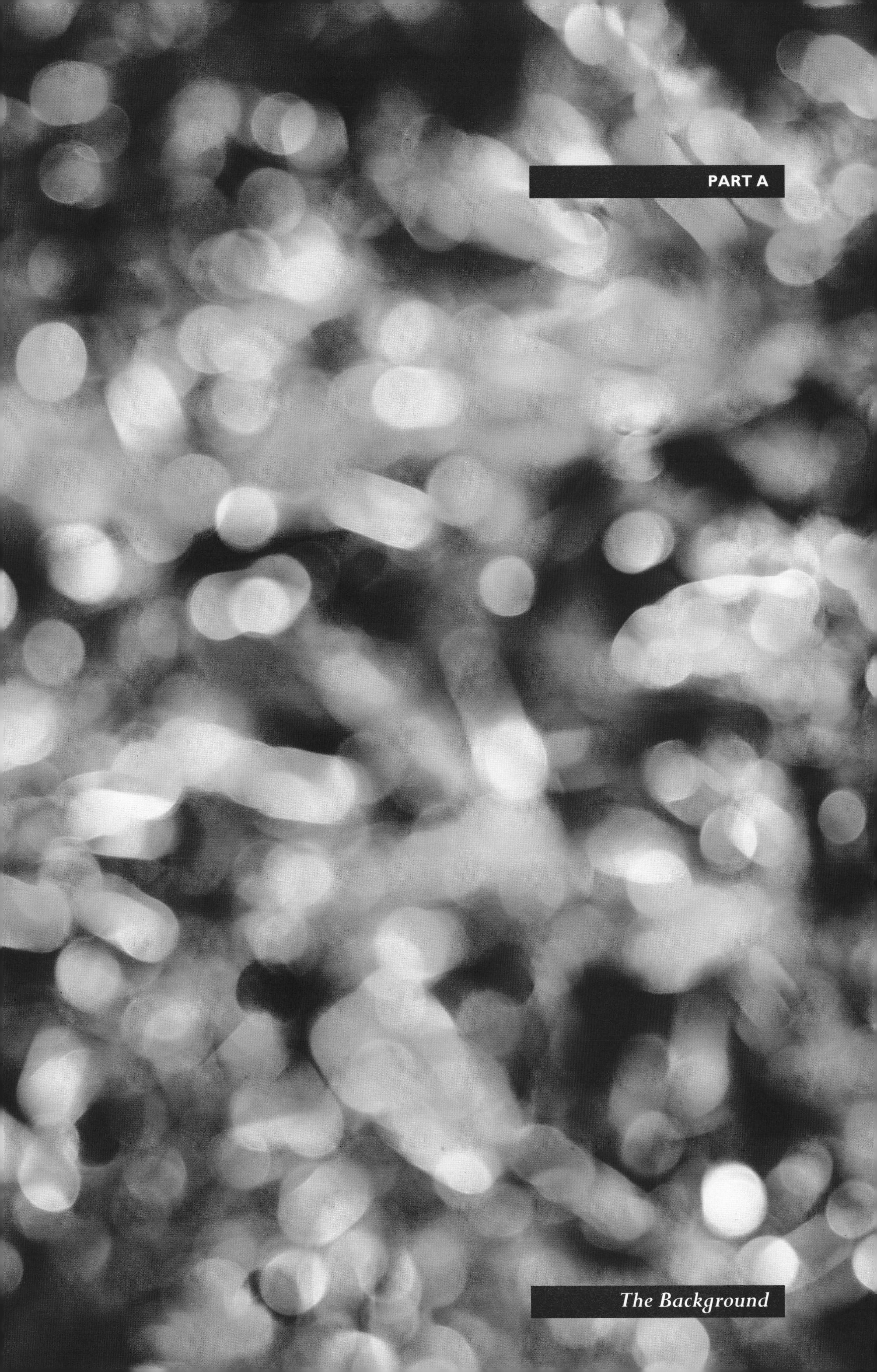

PART A

The Background

CHAPTER 4

*Influences, Definitions
and Associated Problems*

ADOLESCENT HEALTH

11   In the decade from 1982 to 1992, the total number of adolescents in England fell by 21.7% to less than six million, while the total population rose by 3.4% to just over 48 million. Thus, the proportion of adolescents fell from 16% of the total population in 1982 to only 12.1% in 1992. However, it is thought that this trend will reverse over the next 20 years with forecasts of an increase of over 10% in the adolescent population compared with a probable 7% increase in total population.

12   The major causes of mortality in young adolescents are injury and poisoning, followed by neoplasms and diseases of the nervous system. Between 1982 and 1992, there was a reduction in the total number of deaths of adolescents. The only notable exception was of those deaths in adolescence related to mental disorders. In *Health of our Children*, it was noted that British children are now less likely to die of infectious, genetic disorders or cancers, though 7% of three year-olds in inner cities have moderate to severe behaviour problems. Furthermore, there has been an increase overall in children's adverse health behaviour with high levels of alcohol, drug and volatile solvent abuse, early sexual activity, a decrease in physical activity and an increase in obesity.

13   Studies of adolescent morbidity are few, and routinely collected statistics do not provide specific adolescent disease profiles. Adolescents are usually regarded as being healthy, although this claim has been disputed (McFarlane, 1987). This survey of adolescent health in Doncaster showed that 37% of adolescents had visited their general practitioner in the previous three months, and three-quarters had taken some form of medication for minor illnesses in the previous month. In the USA, the Office of Technology Assessment noted that *"the conventional wisdom of American adolescents as a group are so healthy that they do not require health and related services, this is not justified."* Available data indicates that adolescents have a number of health problems which should be of significant concern. These include family problems, school problems, chronic illnesses, lack of recreational opportunities, nutrition and fitness problems, dental and oral health problems, acquired immunity deficiency syndrome and other sexually transmitted diseases, pregnancy and parenting, mental health problems, alcohol, tobacco and substance use, criminal behaviour and other delinquent behaviours and homelessness.

14   General practitioner consultations provide an indication of morbidity. UK data indicates that young people consult their general practitioners three to four times a year on average, with respiratory tract disease being the most common cause of consultation. These rates are broadly similar to those for adults aged 25 to 64. The attendances of adolescents reported by outpatient and accident and emergency departments have increased slightly.

15   At the end of 1993 in England, AIDS had been notified in 48 and HIV infection in 498 adolescent males, while there were 68 AIDS cases and 72 cases of HIV infection in adolescent females. Most sexually transmitted diseases become increasingly common in later adolescence, particularly in females. These figures show the continuing need for advice on sexuality and safer sex practices to be focused on young people.

16   The prevalence of mental health problems is considerable with some sources estimating that up to 40% of children and adolescents have at least mild problems. The overall prevalence of diagnosable mental disorder (DSMIV, ICD 10) is estimated as up to 25%, with 7-10% of adolescents having moderate to severe problems (Graham, 1986). Generally, problems are twice as common in those living in inner city areas as they are in adolescents who live in rural areas. The prevalence of depression rises during adolescence. Eating disorders peak during this time (17 years) and are much more common in females. Of major concern at present is the rise in suicide rates in young males. Risk factors include previous attempts and drug or alcohol misuse. Young offenders in prison are six times more likely to commit suicide than their peers. In England, the *Health of the Nation* strategic initiative addresses this rise in suicides as a major cause of concern and there is a parallel initiative in Wales. This is set out in the Welsh Health Planning Forum's *Protocol for Investment in Health Gain - Mental Health.*

DEFINITIONS OF SUBSTANCE USE AND MISUSE

17   It is important to be clear about the meaning of the terms which relate to substance use by children and adolescents. Lack of clarity leads to confusion and uncertainty about the presence or severity of problems, the need for and the availability of services, the effectiveness of interventions, the balance between prevention, education and direct intervention, and the need to allocate resources appropriately.

18   The World Health Organisation's definition of health is *"...complete physical, mental and social well-being"* (*Ottawa Charter for Health Promotion*, 1987). In reality, the health status of a population is often measured in terms of mortality and service utilisation, but many observers believe that adolescent health should be defined in broader terms emphasising mental and social, as well as physical aspects of health. The Office of Technology Assessment (USA Congress, 1991) suggested that a broad definition would include:

- aspects of the more traditional definitions (presence or absence of illness);

- absence of adolescent problem behaviours (drug use, delinquent behaviour);

- positive components of health (eg, social competence, health-enhancing behaviours);

- health and well-being from an adolescent perspective (eg, quality of life as perceived by young people);

- social influences on health (eg, schools, families, physical environment).

19   In *Together We Stand*, the HAS adopted the following definitions of mental health.

- The ability to develop psychologically, emotionally, intellectually, and spiritually.

- The ability to initiate, develop and sustain mutually satisfying personal relationships.

- The ability to become aware of others and to empathise with them.

> • The ability to use psychological distress as a developmental process, so that it does not hinder or impair further development.

20 Within this broad framework, and incorporating the developmental nature of both body and mind in childhood and adolescents, mental health in young people is indicated more specifically by:

> • a capacity to enter into and sustain mutually satisfying personal relationships;
>
> • continuing progression of psychological development;
>
> • an ability to play and to learn so that attainments are appropriate for age and intellectual level;
>
> • a developing moral sense of right and wrong;
>
> • the degree of psychological distress and maladaptive behaviour being within normal limits for the child's age and context (Hill, 1995).

21 Paragraphs 22 to 38 of *Together We Stand* also consider the definition of *mental health problems* and *mental health disorders*.

22 Many authors comment on the normality of drug use. Historically, virtually all societies have used drugs, although the type and purpose of their use has varied greatly. If drug use is set within the parameters of cultural and social life, it could be seen as normal rather than pathological. As young people grow up they become involved in experimentation and occasional use of alcohol and other substances, usually in specific culturally accepted situations. Definitions of use and misuse often depend on a society's acceptance and/or tolerance of the recreational use of drugs and of substance-related problems behaviours. The opinions of society are often expressed by the law, actions taken to enforce it and by the establishment of prevention and treatment services.

23 Many people have tried to develop terminology for children and young people who use substances and those who have problems related to this. The terms *experimenter* and *recreational user* have been commonly adopted and have typically referred to non-pathological or use styled by some as *normal*. However, the boundaries of these terms with regard to quantity, frequency and/or consequences are not clear. Also, the meaning of adjectives often used in describing substance use, such as heavy, extensive, chaotic etc, are unclear (Kaminer, 1991).

24 Some authors suggest that it is critical to draw a distinction between use and abuse of drugs (Newcomb & Bentler, 1989). They have noted that *"accepted definitions among professionals and citizens do not exist because abuse is clearly a multi-dimensional phenomenon."* Robins defined substance abuse as *"social, psychological or physiological symptoms resulting from the use of psycho-active substances"* and she differentiates it from substance use.

25 The World Health Organisation's *Documents on Nomenclature and Classification* (1981) distinguish between forms of substance-related problems.

Unsanctioned use

Use of a drug that is not approved by society, or by a group within that society.

Hazardous use

Use of a drug that will probably lead to harmful consequences for the user - either dysfunction or harm.

Dysfunctional use

Use of a drug that leads to impaired psychological or social functioning (eg, loss of a job or marital problems).

Harmful use

Use of a drug that is known to have caused tissue damage or mental illness in a person. One type of dysfunctional and harmful use is that which leads to dependence.

26   There is an absence of research establishing either the validity or reliability of diagnostic entitles applicable to children and adolescents. In DSM-4 (American Psychiatric Association, 1995) and ICD-10 (World Health Organisation, 1992) the terminology of *substance use disorders* has been developed for adults with little or no empirical evidence of its appropriateness for children and adolescents.

27   *DSM-4* (American Psychiatric Association, 1995) and *ICD-10* (World Health Organisation, 1992) have adopted a broad approach, making a distinction between consumption, dependence symptoms and adverse consequences. DSM-4 defines abuse as maladaptive pattern of substance use, manifested by recurrent and adverse consequences related to the repeated use of substances.

28   ICD-10 contains a wide variety of disorders related to the use of substances from *"uncomplicated intoxication and harmful use to obvious psychotic disorders and dementia but all are attributable to the use of one or more psycho-active substances"*. Harmful use is defined as a pattern of *"psycho-active substance use that is causing damage to health... either physical or mental"*.

29   *Drug misuse* is defined as the non-medical use of drugs that are only intended for use in medical treatment, and the use of drugs that have no accepted medical purpose. Such drugs are controlled under the Misuse of Drugs Act 1971. But, it should be noted that this Act does not cover the misuse of solvents or other volatile substances.

30   In 1987, The Royal College of Psychiatrists adopted the term drug misuse as *"any taking of a drug which harms or threatens to harm the physical or mental health or social well-being of an individual, of other individuals, or of society at large, or which is illegal"*. In 1982, The Advisory Council on Misuse of Drugs (ACMD) used the term *problem drug taker* defined as *"any person who experiences social, psychological, physical or legal problems related to intoxication and/or regular excessive consumption and/or are dependent as a consequence of its own use of drugs or other chemical substances"*. However, in *Drug Education in Schools: The Need for New Impetus*, (ACMD, 1993) the term drug misuse was used throughout. This was considered more appropriate *"given from a point of view of parents in schools, any form of drug use other than proper use of prescribed medicines is quite clearly a serious problem"*.

The Definitions Adopted by the HAS

31   In this report, the HAS uses the terms **use** and **misuse.** The services required by people who use and misuse substance overlap and can be seen as a continuum from education through to the most specialised of treatments and rehabilitation. The increasing and widespread use of substances is of concern to society as a whole while prevention and treatment of their misuse by individuals are matters which should directly involve health services and local authority social and education services.

Use

The HAS acknowledges that clear distinctions between *use*, often styled *experimental or recreational use*, and *misuse* are hard to draw. *Use* of most drugs is also illegal and some who experiment may experience problems consequent on intoxication. Experience indicates that, while the trend towards increasing use of drugs and alcohol by young people is undesirable because of their increased exposure to the potential dangers of social, psychological and physical problems, experimentation alone cannot be seen as indicative of personal disorders and is not styled as misuse.

Misuse

Misuse is the broad encompassing term favoured in *Tackling Drugs Together,* the reports from the ACMD and the Misuse of Drugs Act 1971. In this report, *misuse* is defined as use that is harmful (see paragraph 25), dependent use or the use of substances as part of a wider spectrum of problematic or harmful behaviour. In these terms, young people who misuse substances may also have significant problems with their psycho-social development.

THE PREVALENCE AND TRENDS IN SUBSTANCE USE AND MISUSE AMONG YOUNG PEOPLE

The United Kingdom

Alcohol Use

32   Ascertaining the extent of alcohol use and misuse by young people is a formidable problem because consumption is unequally distributed across a heterogeneous population. Differences relate to gender, ethnicity, and region (Gilvarry et al, 1995). Many of the studies have relied solely on self-report questionnaires which may under- or over-estimate prevalence rates and others have used unrepresentative or atypical groups. However, the findings in most of the literature of relatively stable alcohol consumption in the last two decades contrasts sharply with the popular idea of young people's drinking reaching epidemic proportions. However, while research data emphasises the normality of alcohol consumption among young people, there is also a significant minority of young people who are at risk of chaotic intoxication and/or continued alcohol misuse.

33   Recent research (Newcombe et al, 1994) has suggested that the pattern of consumption is changing with young people drinking considerably higher quantities of alcohol per drinking session. This may be related to regional variations or change in types of drinks. Today, a wide range of high strength drinks are promoted to young people for example, designer cocktails, high strength ciders and wines (such as 20/20, Thunderbird).

34   Data from the 1980's concluded that few teenagers had never tasted alcohol and the proportion who currently drink increased with age. At all ages, most reported only modest consumption, though a minority reported drinking heavily (Marsh et al, 1985). In 1989, the Health Education Authority reported similar results in its commissioned studies.

35   Data from the British Marketing Research Bureau Target Group Index has noted that the number of female daily drinkers (aged 15-29 years) has remained stable at about 3% since 1979, as has the number of those who drink two to three times a week (2%), and those who do not drink at all (between 5 and 10%).

36   Nine to 15 year-old children and adolescents who were regular drinkers were more likely than others to be regular smokers and to have used illicit drugs (Health Education Authority, 1989). A survey of 16 to 19 year-olds indicated that a substantial proportion of the sample, particularly those from high socio-economic backgrounds, had elected to have a low alcohol drink, but also indicated that many young drinkers had experienced adverse consequences from alcohol, such as hangovers. Furthermore, the knowledge of safe limits and the unit content of specific drinks was poor (Health Education Authority, 1990). These studies, along with other evidence, lend support to the opinions that, while most teenagers drink on a regular basis, many may suffer, at least minor, adverse consequences and that their knowledge of health aspects of alcohol use is poor (Davies and Stacey, 1972; Hawker, 1978).

37   A substantial minority of young people do drink heavily and this proportion appears to grow in the older teenage years and in early adulthood. One survey noted that 7% of young male drinkers had consumed more than 51 units in the week prior to the survey, while 4% of young females had consumed more than 31 units (Plant et al, 1985). Another showed that 2% of males were drinking more than 50 units, and 1% of females were consuming more than 36 units a week (Goddard and Iken, 1988); while yet another found that 3% of males and 2% of females in the same age range were drinking at this level (Foster, 1990).

Drug Use

38   There is limited statistical and research data available in the UK on the extent and nature of drug use and misuse by young people. Different surveys produce different results depending on the way the studies are carried out, the size of the samples, the geographical areas, and the age ranges. Many have been small-scale and the results distorted by exaggeration, under-reporting and non-contact. Findings from school samples may not be representative as young people with problems often fail to attend school and more frequently experience suspension and exhibit other problematic behaviours. The range of data available often best describes the older opiate user known to treatment agencies. However, notwithstanding the methodological difficulties, many self-report surveys have been conducted in the UK with similar trends being noted.

39   These trends include the increased use of a wide range of drugs in the younger age group, the narrowing of the gender gap, the emergence of poly drug use as the norm and a decrease in age of initiation. Adolescents are growing up in a culture in which drugs are much more easily available, acceptable and their use seen as normal within their culture. Many commentators have written about the post-heroin generation, the

availability of a wide range and assortment of drugs, and the new 'pick-n-mix' scene. They have also noted the rapid narrowing of the gender gap, the poly drug use pattern, the ready availability and the integration of illicit drugs in youth culture, obvious in youth magazines, language and fashion. Poly drug use occurs in all socio-economic groups. The convergence of alcohol and poly substance use is particularly important in the consideration of educational programmes and treatment services which are geared to the 'new youth'.

40 Cannabis use was reported by 3-5% of children aged 11 to 16 in two large-scale surveys in the UK (Health Education Authority, 1992; Gilvarry et al, 1995). In the case of older teenagers, the prevalence rises to 17% (Mott, 1985).

41 Estimates of the misuse of volatile substances range from 3-11% in children at secondary school (Swadi, 1988; Edeh, 1989). In a 1992 Health Education Authority study, 2% of young people reported using solvents at the age of 15, though 9% reported using them in the past.

42 A recent survey of young people aged 9 to 15 years found that, by 15 years of age, 16% of males and 14% of females had tried cannabis; 5% and 2% had used LSD; 4% and 2% amphetamines and solvents; 3% and 1% tranquillisers and ecstasy. Heroin and cocaine had been tried by 1% of both males and females (Health Education Authority, 1992).

43 The changes in youth culture have been paralleled by a change in the pattern and types of drugs used. This is well documented by the media and the specialist press. The emergence of the dance scene, with all night parties and raves, has brought an upsurge in use of hallucinogenic and stimulant drugs such as ecstasy, amphetamines and LSD. The increased availability and acceptability of these drugs has been reported among young people in a recent survey conducted in the North West of England. Fifty-nine per cent of young people (14 to 15 year-olds) had been offered at least one drug, with females more likely to be offered them than males. Over one-third of those offered drugs had tried them. In some areas, protective factors included ethnicity (especially the Asian Muslim culture) and affluence (Measham, 1993). It is important to be cautious when construing substance use in different ethnic communities as patterns of use vary and some of the problems are clouded by poor relationships with the statutory agencies and, possibly, by institutional racism.

44 Other sources of information on the trends in prevalence rates are obtained from the Home Office Notifications and the drug misuse databases.

45 Since 1990, the proportion of notified drug addicts aged under 25 has increased by 20%. There has also been a substantial increase in young people under 25 who have been found guilty of drug-related offences (Home Office Statistical Bulletin Issues, 1994).

46 Surveys show consistently that males are more likely to use illicit drugs than females, though this gender difference is not always substantial. Drug use occurs in all socio-economic groups, although use of opioids appear to be more frequent in young people who live in more deprived backgrounds (Parker et al, 1988). There are relatively high levels of exposure to illicit drugs and of experimental use. Levels of experimental use are more common in older teenagers. These upward trends can be inferred from the statistics published annually, relating to drug seizures and drug offenders. While survey evidence is patchy, most evidence demonstrates a substantial increase in the use of illicit drugs by UK youth.

International Trends

The United States of America

47   Extensive data on illicit drug use in the United States suggests a different pattern to that of the UK: one of falling prevalence for the use of most substances, especially marijuana. The trends towards a decrease in drug use has been accompanied by increasing perceptions of risk associated with use.

48   There is also a significant increase in disapproval of use of every illicit drug and support for criminalisation and legal prohibition of drugs. However, the trend for smoking cigarettes has been one of no change over the last decade. While the downward trend in use of alcohol by adolescents has continued, occasional or binge use by young people has remained stable over the last decade.

49   However, as in the UK, the available prevalence data may under-represent the magnitude of the problem as most surveys do not include high school drop-outs who tend to be at high risk for substance use. Despite the downward trend for the use of nearly all types of drugs on nearly all measures of use, the use of drugs remains strikingly high in the USA. There are areas in which problem use is of high density and is associated with a wide range of health and social problems, particularly in poor inner cities.

Continental Europe

50   Existing research data is not directly comparable between countries because of the many different methodological procedures adopted. In general, higher rates of illicit use are observed in northern and central Europe (except in Sweden, where illicit drug use reduced significantly in the early eighties). Heroin and cocaine use remains below the rate of 2% in almost all countries.

51   Other patterns have emerged: there is a growing tendency to experiment and use a wide variety of drugs; males have a higher prevalence rate than females; there are no apparent differences in prevalence rates at different socio-economic levels and the prevalence difference between urban and less urbanised areas is decreasing. Stimulants, particularly MDMA, MDA or MDEA and amphetemines are increasing in prevalence across Europe, chiefly, at raves or house parties.

52   There is evidence of increased targeting of the availability of drugs in western Europe by international drug traffickers. Furthermore, many central European countries, the former Soviet Union, South West Asia, and Africa are facing increasing problems with drug use and misuse by children and adolescents.

Australia

53   In Australia, high school surveys have shown a trend towards reduction in drug use. Nonetheless, an increase in experimental and regular use of cannabis, increases in inhalant use and in the use of hallucinogens and cigarettes have been reported in the last few years. High levels of regular

use of alcohol and illicit drugs (particularly opiates and amphetamines) have been observed in groups of young people who are considered to be vulnerable.

Summary

54   National and regional surveys of drug and alcohol use provide important sources of information about the prevalence and trends of poly drug use in young people. Despite the methodological difficulties, there are common trends. These consist of an increase in the range and assortment of drugs available, ready availability of drugs, increasing poly drug use by young people, the acceptance and integration of alcohol and illicit drugs into youth culture, decrease in the age of initiation and the association of illicit drug use with alcohol, smoking and early sexual activity. In such a circumstance, the experts consider that it is important that drug use, with its social, situational and environmental determinants is not pathologised. Policing of drug use on the streets, in communities and in schools should address the issue of use and the increase in experimentation. However, increasing vulnerability comes with increasing consumption. Treatment services need to be geared to the needs of young people, both in terms of the consequences of intoxication and the longer-term problems that may stem from substance use.

AETIOLOGICAL AND RISK FACTORS

55   There is no typical substance-using adolescent and no specific personality type, family situation, socio-economic group or stressful experience that has been found to predict categorically the development of substance misuse by adolescents. The literature indicates that the initiation and recreational use of substances are promoted by a complex array of cognitive, psychological, social, personality and developmental factors, as well as by knowledge and normative expectations.

56   The prevalence of alcohol and drug use in the UK indicates the changing cultural norms of society and of young people. So many young people use or experiment with alcohol and illicit drugs that this behaviour cannot be justifiably described as abnormal. There is evidence of the increasing availability of drugs and a wide range of choices in this 'post-heroin generation'. A convergence in the use of alcohol and illicit drugs, a decrease in the age of initiation and significant signs of an increase in the number of young people who use drugs have been shown. Nevertheless, a minority of children and young people suffer adverse consequences either as a result of intoxication, such as bad trips, overdoses, traffic accidents, or because of recurrent and/or excessive physical and mental health problems. Some may present with problems relating to drug or alcohol use which are a symptom of underlying difficulties such as mental health problems and disorders such as depression and anxiety. Others have problems related to their alcohol or drug use in addition to, and alongside their other behavioural, social or mental health problems or disorders.

57   There is little evidence available on the relative importance of the various risk factors in the aetiology of drug misuse, or about their interactions. It is also difficult to discern between specific precursors of problems emanating from the use of drugs and alcohol and those contributing to more general behavioural problems. Many of the risk factors for adolescent drug misuse also predict other adolescent problem behaviours (Hawkins et al, 1988). Moreover these factors have been shown to be stable over time, though

some are more important in different phases of development. They arise from several domains, for example, characteristics of the individual, family, peer groups and school. There is evidence that the greater the number of risk factors present, the greater the risk of drug misuse. Also, some studies have noted a multiplicative effect of risk factors on childhood psychopathology (Newcomb et al, 1986; Rutter, 1980).

58   These risk factors, causal and/or associated, can be categorised into two main groups: those broad aspects of society and culture that provide the normative expectations of behaviour; and aspects of the individual and the interpersonal environment.

59   Shifts in cultural norms and economic and legal changes have been linked with changes in the prevalence of drug use and of associated problems. Legal restrictions that affect the price of alcohol or influence the availability of alcohol and other drugs appear to limit consumption. The fiscal policy of increased taxation of alcohol has been shown to be particularly effective in limiting alcohol use and reducing alcohol-related problems. Other environmental controls include the limitation of licensed outlets, restrictions on hours and days of sale, responsible services, and server liability. The USA General Accounting Office concluded that there was clear evidence that increasing the minimum age for lawfully purchasing alcohol reduced alcohol-related traffic accidents and that the converse also held true. For further information on alcohol policies and their effects, readers are referred to: *Alcohol and the Public Good* (Edwards, 1994).

60   A large amount of published work has examined social and cultural factors, such as socio-economic status, poverty, delinquency and family backgrounds. Other environmental associations include ideology and religion, drug availability and price, educational opportunities and educational disturbance, anomie, and alienation. It has been concluded that the main environmental variables associated with substance misuse of all kinds are those of:

- neighbourhood crime;

- poverty and decay;

- drug availability;

- perceived low risk;

- acceptance of drug use;

- lack of community support structures (Brook and Brook, 1990).

61   Certain characteristics of the individual and the interpersonal environment are associated with increased risk of substance misuse. Individual characteristics include:

- physiological factors;

- genetic factors;

- psychological factors.

The pharmacological aspects of drug use have received much attention.

62   Studies have repeatedly emphasised the importance of peer pressure in encouraging and maintaining drug and alcohol use. However, it has been suggested that the term peer pressure is misleading and that the terms preference or assortment may be more appropriate (Coggans and

McKellar, 1994). It has been noted that, when a younger person chooses to associate with either negative or socially acceptable peers, this choice is influenced by both the school and family environments. Those in more deprived environments are more likely to associate with peers who may show a range of antisocial behaviours.

63   American school surveys have concentrated on the age of initiation of young people into drug use, the impact of drugs on school performance and factors that are potentially predictive of the outcome. A large-scale survey noted that beginning drug use before the age of 15 predicted an increased risk of drug-related disorders, particularly of a severe type (Robins and Przybeck, 1985). Early onset of drug use and continued use are strongly associated with other problem behaviours such as: delinquency, precocious sexual behaviour, antisocial attitudes and dropping-out of school. The level of conduct disorder in children is a powerful predictor of drug use in the future. Substance abuse in the absence of conduct problems is rare and these findings are similar for males and females (Robins and McEvoy, 1990). Hence, it appears likely that the early identification of young people with moderate or severe conduct problems could provide the basis for prevention of substance abuse. Longitudinal studies have also noted that substance abuse disorders (ie, substance use that seriously affects users' physical and mental health) is a common sequel of early hyperactivity disorder and is virtually always mediated by intervening antisocial behaviour disorders. In other words, it is unusual for harmful substance abuse to arise *de novo* in adolescence, solely as a result of peer influence without a pre-existing major vulnerability factor.

64   Other risk factors include failure at school, low commitment at school, early rejection by peers, alienation and rebelliousness, and attitudes favourable to drug use.

65   Family factors include the influence of parents on children, their drug use, and the conflicts that may exist within families. Parental use and, in particular, permissive attitudes toward drug use, may be of particular importance in determining a young person's use of drugs. Researchers have noted that parental tolerance of drug use and their approval of drinking were significant predictors of drug use and the amount of alcohol consumed by adolescents. Other factors include poor and inconsistent family management practices, poor monitoring of behaviour, unclear expectations for behaviour, few rewards and approval, and excessively harsh and inconsistent punishment for unwanted behaviour. Children raised in families with high levels of conflict were at greater risk of delinquency and drug use.

66   There is a growing interest in the role of protective factors, not simply as the opposite of risk factors, but as independent variables in their own right. Protective factors include a positive temperament, intellectual ability, a supportive family environment, a caring relationship with at least one adult, and an external support system that encourages positive values. It has been noted that resilient children have a repertoire of problem-solving skills and a belief in their own self-efficacy (Rutter, 1985).

67   Because risks may be present in many domains and have an additive effect, prevention strategies should address and focus on reducing multiple risks and enhancing protective factors. Prevention strategies might also target those young people who appear to be most vulnerable to drug and alcohol use and related problems as well as to the development of a wide range of associated behavioural problems.

68   Tables 1, 2 and 3 which follow, summarise these societal and individual risk factors as well as those factors which help to insulate against these risks.

Table 1

Societal and Cultural Risk Factors
• The law and societal norms
• Substance availability
• Extreme economic deprivation
• Neighbourhood disorganisation

Table 2

Individual and Interpersonal Risk Factors
• Physiological factors
• Family attitudes to substance use or misuse
• Use of substances by parents
• Poor and inconsistent family management practices
• Family conflict
• Early and persistent behaviour problems
• Academic problems
• Low commitment to school
• Early peer rejection
• Association with peers who use drugs
• Alienation
• Attitudes favourable to drug use
• Early onset of drug or alcohol use

Table 3

Protective Factors
• Positive temperament
• Intellectual ability
• A supportive family environment
• A social support system that encourages personal efforts
• A caring relationship with at least one adult

ASSOCIATED PROBLEMS

69   Many people experiment with drugs, but only a proportion of these use them on a regular basis. Some regular users of substances may develop patterns of misuse that are associated with psycho-social and physical problems.

70   Adolescent drug use and/or misuse can have serious consequences both for individuals and for society. Drug and alcohol misuse may interfere with adolescent developmental processes, affect physical and mental health, increase the risk of accidents and contribute to other social problems.

71   The adverse consequences directly related to the use of drugs and alcohol largely derive from intoxication. Short-term consequences can be many and can be tragic, for example, a fatal accident when intoxicated. The long-term consequences may also be serious, for example, lung cancer related to cigarette smoking. The main adverse consequences of drinking reported by young people in surveys are intoxication, alcohol-related accidents, physical problems (such as gastritis), arguments with parents and friends, problems at school and financial problems.

72   Drug and alcohol use or misuse may be but a symptom of a person's underlying distress or psycho-social disorder, or be another manifestation of conduct or behavioural problems. Vulnerable adolescents may emerge in a variety of guises: homeless; pregnant; those leaving local authority or foster care; young people who are engaged in prostitution; children truanting from school; abused children; and those in contact with police, criminal justice or forensic mental health services. These children and young people, with a multiplicity of vulnerability factors, have a greater risk of misusing drugs and alcohol. They may well associate with peers who use drugs in circumstances where the use of substances is more tolerated and they are readily available. Services which intervene with these young people must address the complexity of their needs and address the multiplicity of vulnerabilities. All too often, vulnerable young people are highly mobile, change their accommodation frequently, and are less likely to be in contact with statutory hospital and community services. They are also more likely to be unemployed, and find difficulty in sustaining themselves through job training schemes.

73   The cost to society of alcohol and drug use is substantial. Drug and alcohol use and misuse by adolescents can have a high cost in terms of educational difficulties and under-achievement, physical health problems, public disorder, and road traffic accidents. It also makes demands on mental health services, and the cost of the intervention of other public services. The social cost of drug misuse in families can be high, including for example, family distress and breakdown and premature death.

74   Drug and alcohol misuse is associated with a range of health and social consequences for individuals and society. These include death from:

- solvent misuse;
- alcohol poisoning;
- drug overdoses;
- physical injury;
- psychiatric disorders;
- accidents;
- infectious diseases.

75   The public health implications for the transmission of viruses from this high-risk group are important. Many drug and alcohol users and misusers place a high demand on primary care, hospitals and the general community.

76   There has been much debate and research into the impact of alcohol and drug use on crime. One of the aims the Government's strategy, *Tackling Drugs Together*, is the need to increase the safety of the community from drug-related crime. This White Paper has estimated that acquisitive crime by heroin misusers in England and Wales for 1992, could have cost as much as £864 million. This accounts for approximately 20% of all acquisitive crime.

The Relationship of Alcohol and Drug Use to Adolescent Suicide and Deliberate Self-harm

77   The rate of suicide among males of all ages, and in most countries, has shown a significant increase since the 1970's but the increase is most marked in the 15 to 24 year-old age group. The suicide rate for young males (aged 15 to 24) in England and Wales has shown a 60% increase, while the rate for females has not changed. Nonetheless, females who are substantially more likely to deliberately harm themselves are also more likely to kill themselves and repeated self-harm is a predictor of subsequent suicide.

78   Alcohol and drug use are significant risk factors for a wide range of health and social problems (Bukstein, 1995; Williams, 1995). They can affect all areas of functioning and may be a precipitant to both suicide and deliberate self-harm (Kerfoot and Huxley, 1995). Approximately one-third of adolescents who commit suicide are intoxicated at the time of death, and a further number are under the influence of drugs (Brent, 1987; Williams and Morgan, 1994). It has been found that the percentage change in alcohol consumption has the single highest correlation with changes in suicide rates (Diekstra, 1989).

79   A study conducted in New York (Shaffer et al, 1993) of 170 adolescent suicides noted that two-thirds met the criteria for having a psychiatric disorder and most of the remainder had some psychiatric symptoms. Approximately two-thirds of male suicides between 17 and 19 had a significant problem deriving from alcohol use.

80   Indeed, it has been suggested that alcohol misuse may be the determining factor in the recent rise in male suicides.

81   Many young people who deliberately harm themselves also misuse alcohol and drugs. The rates reported range from 13% to 42% depending on the sample and definition of abuse or misuse (Hawton et al, 1982; Spirito et al, 1989).

82   Substance misuse, is a known risk factor for suicide and non-fatal deliberate self-harm, as has been highlighted in recent years. This suggests the need for *"appropriate preventive strategies as well as effective, well co-ordinated secondary care services"* (Williams and Morgan—*Suicide Prevention*, 1994). This report also suggests that *"focusing on drug and alcohol abuse would have a greater impact on adolescent suicide rates than any other primary prevention programme."*

The Public Health Perspective

83   As the number of HIV carriers increases, the lifestyles of some adolescents may place them at increased risk. Rates of sexual intercourse among young people appear to be increasing as is the number of sexual partners. The prevalence of sexually transmitted diseases is highest among adolescents. It has been estimated that young people have relatively high levels of knowledge about HIV-related diseases and roots of HIV transmission but there is little evidence to suggest that this knowledge has had a significant impact on their behaviour (Williams and Ponton, 1992).

84   Some researchers have noted a possible connection between high risk sexual activity and the use of alcohol and other drugs. This has led to the concept of disinhibition being invoked to account for the connection, though this causal connection has been disputed. Nonetheless, policy·

makers and those who design and implement prevention programmes should pay attention to the potential role of alcohol and drugs. They should ensure that all members of the community have accurate information about HIV and other infectious diseases. This is particularly important for young people who may be experimenting with drugs and alcohol and whose knowledge of these substances may be limited.

85   The links between drug use and the sex industry are complex. Research findings indicate that there is an association between drug use, particularly dependent drug use, and prostitution. Prostitutes also tend to be heavy users of alcohol and drugs.

86   The Government's strategy includes a major objective of reducing drug-related health risks. It plans to achieve a reduction in health and social damage by discouraging use, and through providing information, education and support to families and communities, and improvement of access to treatment and rehabilitation.

Psychiatric Co-Morbidity

87   Many people suffering from severe psychiatric disorders also have serious problems stemming from substance use. Those with dual diagnoses have been reported as presenting more problems in terms of assessment, management, treatment and outcome than those people who have a single disorder. This is partly because of the complexity of having two or more problems simultaneously and partly arises from the relationship between substance use and other psychiatric disorders (Bukstein et al, 1989).

88   Epidemiological studies have shown that there is a high prevalence of co-morbidity, or co-existing psychopathology, in the general population and also among people who are receiving treatment for problems arising from the use of substances. The more severe the problems with substance use, the greater the likelihood of a co-existent psychiatric disorder. The most common are anxiety disorders, affective disorders and antisocial personality. This highlights the need for comprehensive assessments of those users of substances who present to services.

89   Co-existing problems have also been found in adolescents who use/misuse substances. Alcohol and drug use have been associated with major depression in college students (Deykin et al, 1987). A few studies have examined the co-morbidity of anxiety disorders although it has been noted that nearly 40% of high school seniors appear to use drugs to *"relax and relieve tension"*. A strong relationship between eating disorders and alcohol misuse has been noted (Lavik et al, 1991). A report on the psychiatric diagnosis of adolescents who have been detoxified recently and then referred to psychiatric inpatient services showed that: 42% had a conduct disorder; 35% major depression; and 21% a combination of attention deficit, hyperactivity, or impulsive disorder. Educational delays and personality difficulties were common, though the most frequent diagnostic cluster in the sample was attention deficit disorder with hyperactivity and conduct disorder (DeMilio, 1989).

90   Few studies have focused on the relationship between juvenile delinquency and drug and alcohol use though an association has been noted for many years. Findings support the aggregation of substance misuse, conduct disorder and attention deficit disorder with hyperactivity.

Substance Use by Young People and Crime

91   The Government's strategy includes an objective to target effective action on reducing the incidence of drug-related crime. Various estimates, in the absence of reliable research, suggest that acquisitive crime by heroin users could be equivalent to one-fifth of the total cost of acquisitive crime in England and Wales. Statistics show an increase in seizures of controlled drugs and of people found guilty, cautioned or dealt with by compounding for drug offences. However, the nature of the relationship between drug and alcohol use and misuse and crime is complex.

92   Undoubted links between alcohol use and crime have been proposed. Psychological and sociological approaches indicate that the effects of alcohol are dependent on the drinking environment. Risks of violence and other problems can be reduced by attention to this environment. This involves training staff, improving the management of public houses, and improving public transport surrounding drinking outlets. Other researchers suggest that personality characteristics are important. Murdoch (1990) noted a strong associated between violence, crime and alcohol intoxication. In a review of over 9,000 crimes in 11 countries, nearly two-thirds of the people studied were drinking at the time of commission of the crime and nearly half of the victims were intoxicated when they were assaulted.

93   A direct causal link between the use of drugs and commission of crime is unlikely though, anecdotally, there is substantial evidence of a relationship between the use of drugs and crime. However, this situation is complex and determined by the relationship between drug misuse, crime (and their psychological and social consequences) and the social environment. Drug use and illicit income are correlated, but drug use does not seem to determine illicit income directly.

94   Large-scale prospective studies have found that drug use and criminal behaviour develop together across the teenage years (Jessor & Jessor, 1977; Elliott, 1985). This research suggests that prior criminality tends to predict drug use while drug use also tends to predict criminality. Other research has suggested that drug use may be a component of a broader pattern of delinquent behaviour. Delinquent behaviours of all kinds appear to be increased by prior criminal experience, having delinquent friends and lack of social supports (including having spent some time in care). Some authors have suggested fairly extensive drug use, including that of alcohol and tobacco, is now an integral part of experimental delinquent behaviour. This is borne out by anecdotal clinical impressions which indicate that drug-related crime committed by young people is increasing in the UK. Many young people referred to adolescent forensic mental health services report that they are misusing drugs and drinking alcohol to excess. However, this group of young people also sees the use of alcohol and drugs within its own social framework as an ordinary peer group activity. They deny having a problem and display minimal motivation to alter their behaviour.

95   While a large minority of young people experiment with delinquent behaviours, only a minority of these become long-term or career criminals.

96   A minority of young people fails to contain its drug and alcohol use effectively, even within this social framework. The characteristics of this group, that separate them from others, appear to be:

    •   having a history of early onset severe conduct disorder;

- coming from a dysfunctional family situation (notably the absence of father);

- socio-economic deprivation;

- having a family in which conflict and criminality are already present.

97   In a longitudinal study of 1,000 families, a link was established between chronic adversity in childhood and subsequent criminality (Kolvin et al, 1981). It has been noted that oppositional behaviour in pre-adolescence predicted convictions in early adolescence and conviction in the past was the best predictor of subsequent crime (Farrington, 1991). At an earlier age, inadequate parental discipline and school failure, coupled with economic adversity and parental criminality, were predictors of juvenile crime. However, adult convictions were predicted by familial criminality and economic adversity, strengthened by the addition of the risk factors of low economic status and poor quality of marital relationships.

98   Clinically, minor offending or conduct disorder is frequently reported as preceding drug use. Drug misuse precedes offending much less frequently. However, it seems that, as containment of drug use or alcohol misuse begins to fail, the frequency of offences involving property increases, occasionally to a level at which multiple offences are committed each day. Disinhibited offending, while under the influence of alcohol or drugs, appears to be less common. More commonly, the reality is that financially dependent young people have few options for funding drug-taking other than to do so by unlawful means. The enormous profits in supplying drugs bring violence in their wake, particularly as competition for these profits intensify.

99   The longer-term consequences are that many young males who are incarcerated are found to have a substance misuse disorder of diagnosable degree. Recent research has shown that substance misuse is a significant factor in predicting relapse following intervention programmes for specific offences.

100   Experience indicates that too few young people who present to services with serious difficulties of drug or alcohol misuse (and an associated profile of high-risk behaviours) receive the assistance they require. Most appear to fall between the nets of provision offered by different services.

Accidents

101   Alcohol use is associated significantly with accidents at home, at work and in other situations. This is the most important general impact of alcohol on the lives of young people. Some research has suggested that up to 50% of head injuries are associated with intoxication, that one-third of deaths by drowning is related to alcohol, and that 12-67% of deaths from burns and 35-63% of fatal falls are related to alcohol use with lower figures for non-fatal accidents (Hingson and Howland, 1993). Young and middle-aged males constitute a higher risk group for trauma related to alcohol use.

102   The Road Traffic Act 1967 introduced a legal upper limit of 80mg/100ml in the blood of drivers. The initial result of this legislation was an 11% reduction in the national crash toll, but its impact subsequently appeared to decline. Driving under the influence of alcohol has diminished. Between 1979 and 1989, there was a marked decline in the proportion of young people who were killed in road accidents while over the legal limit. The proportion of drivers aged 16 to 19 killed while having high blood alcohol levels fell by over 50% between 1979 and 1989.

103 One-third of pedestrians of all ages killed in the UK have alcohol blood levels over the driving limit. In the UK, nearly 10% of fatal accidents to pedestrians are drink-drive related (Department of Transport, 1990).

104 Most studies in this area have reported on how blood alcohol levels relate to deaths or injuries, though few have reported on the use of other drugs. Research has found that psychoactive drugs were present in 43% of cases of accidental injury (Lindebaum, 1989), drugs and alcohol in 26% and alcohol alone in 9%.

105 The increase of the use of drugs by young people and its relationship with, fatal and non-fatal, traffic and domestic accidents needs to be addressed.

CHAPTER 5

Education and Prevention

INTRODUCTION

106 This chapter deals with the two topics of *education* and *prevention*. They are reviewed within one chapter in order to allow readers to better contrast their properties and roles in a broad approach to helping young people who may require information about or help with problems relating to substance use and misuse.

107 It is important to emphasise that these two terms do not describe the same approach. While education and prevention are quite different in the functions they perform in informing and advising children and adolescents about the use of substances, nonetheless, these activities are complementary. It is for this reason that they appear in a single chapter.

108 Services for children and adolescents who are approaching the threshold of use, and for those who use or misuse substances have plural objectives. These are:

- prevention of drug use, including helping younger people to achieve and maintain drug-free lifestyles (primary prevention);

- minimising harm related to the use of substances (secondary prevention);

- care, treatment and rehabilitation of young people who have developed dependency on substances, harmful patterns of substance misuse or disorders in which substance misuse plays an aetiological role (secondary and tertiary prevention).

DEFINITIONS

109 The term *education*, as used in this report, is to be distinguished from *training. Training refers to the education of the staff of services* whereas *this chapter deals specifically with the education of children and adolescents. Education about substances has the overall aim of preventing people from harming themselves by the use of substances.*

110 By contrast, the HAS takes the term *prevention to embrace the promotion of lower risk use or harm-minimisation. This includes prevention of dependent forms of substance misuse and prevention of physical and psychiatric disorders that may be related to substance use and misuse.*

EDUCATING CHILDREN AND ADOLESCENTS

111 The important role which schools play in the provision of education about substances has been underlined by elements of the Government's drug strategy over the last decade.

- Between 1986 and 1993, the then Department for Education Grants for Education Support and Training (GEST) supported the employment of drug and health education co-ordinators in most local education authority (LEA) areas. Some LEAs continued to fund these posts after central funding ended.

- Further GEST funding was available from April 1995, and a second year of funding will be available from April 1996, to train teachers and to support drug education and prevention projects.

- In 1989, the introduction of the National Curriculum brought statutory requirements for aspects of drug education to be included in core subjects. Many schools made use of guidance published by the

National Curriculum Council in 1990 - *Curriculum Guidance 5: Health Education*. This document identified nine strands of health education which should run throughout the curriculum for 5 to 16 year-olds, including sex education, education on mental health and substance use and misuse.

• The new National Curriculum, introduced into schools in September 1995, retains the requirement for drug education in all four key stages of the science curriculum.

• More recently, the White Paper, *Tackling Drugs Together*, asks schools to develop policies on managing drug-related incidents and drug education. The Department for Education published guidance in the form of a circular *Drug Prevention and Schools* (4/95) to assist with this. The Office for Standards in Education (OFSTED) is monitoring schools' policies and practice in drug education and the management of drug-related incidents as part of its regular programme of inspections. A specific study of the provision of drug education in grant maintained and independent schools is also being undertaken during the 1995-96 academic year.

• The Welsh Office consultation document *Forward Together* also seeks to *reduce the acceptability to young people and others of taking drugs and of excessive or inappropriate drinking.*

112 Specific aims and objectives for school-based drug education are suggested in *Drug Education in Schools: The Need for New Impetus* (ACMD 1993). The aim for drug education in schools in this document is that of enabling pupils to make healthy informed choices. The main objectives of the recommended approach are those of:

• increasing the knowledge of pupils, changing their attitudes towards substance use and themselves, and enhancing positive skills;

• influencing pupil behaviour, for example by minimising the number that ever engages in drug use, delaying onset of first use, minimising adoption of dangerous forms of use and misuse, and persuading users or misusers to stop and/or to seek help;

• focusing on citizenship, for example by enhancing young people's capacity to contribute to school policies on drug use and misuse and wider community matters, and improving decision-making skills using education about substances as a vehicle.

These aims and objectives are adopted by the DFEE circular 4/95.

113 There have been four broad approaches to education about substances, used individually or in various combinations, in the UK to date.

Factual approaches

These include providing information on substances and their undesired side effects.

Affective education

This is intended to increase awareness, personal autonomy, coping and decision-making skills.

Situational education

This is an approach that takes note of the social factors that influence the choices made by individuals in particular situations.

Cultural approaches

These include teaching education-for-life skills because they approach understanding substance use from within a stance that starts with the wider context of people's social and working lives.

The Effectiveness of Education Programmes on Substances

114 Can education about substances deliver the full breadth of what is asked or expected of it? Available research would suggest that it cannot as education programmes aimed at prevention have been characterised by only a limited degree of success. However, methods that are tuned to what is known about the factors influencing effectiveness, and for which there are more limited expectations, have a significant role.

115 Reviews and evaluations of drug education programmes have shown that, in general, it is easier to improve knowledge than to affect attitudes. Behaviour change is the most difficult to accomplish through education programmes. In this regard, there is consistency between these findings and some drawn from research on other areas of health promotion. Also, this is similar to findings about other arenas of intervention and education with adolescents (eg HIV and AIDS education and education about diabetes mellitus, Challen et al, 1988; Challen et al, 1992; and Williams and Ponton, 1992).

116 Put another way, factual approaches to drug education on their own have been shown to be of limited value. Although in most cases, pupil knowledge increases, these approaches have little impact on their attitudes. There is a risk that some of these approaches may even increase interest in, and use of alcohol and other substances if they are used injudiciously.

117 Likewise, there is little empirical evidence to support the efficacy of affective approaches.

118 During the 1980s, most alcohol and drug education programmes used a social influences (situational education) approach. This was the base from which drug education programmes, that were used in the late 1980s and beyond, evolved. They used interactive educational processes and were directed towards enhancement of life-skills. Evaluations of these more recent approaches are more encouraging.

119 In schools, education about drugs and alcohol may take place in science, personal, social and health education programmes (PSHE) or be delivered through the pastoral system. The impact of the setting in which the students are taught is not clear cut, but research indicates that teaching the subject in the context of science leads to a factual approach, whereas teaching in the PSHE curriculum is more likely to facilitate discussion of attitudes and is likely to have greater impact.

120 Generally, programmes for education about alcohol based on a social influences approach have been shown not to be an effective means of reducing adolescent drinking. This is because the social acceptability of alcohol may be a stronger factor which cannot be overcome easily. By contrast, research has suggested that it is possible to influence attitudes and behaviour regarding tobacco and cannabis.

121 Another issue that requires consideration is that of how different students respond to similar programmes. Students who have different characteristics may react differently to the same programme. Gender, drinking behaviour, the presence of peer and parental models of alcohol use all have an influence.

122 In 1993, the ACMD report on drug education in schools stated that drug education should be part of a broader preventive health programme which takes *"account of the wider community and the influences on the life of a child outside the school."*

123 Shelder and Block (1990) concluded that efforts at prevention were misguided because they focused on symptoms rather than on the psychological syndrome underlying drug use. Education programmes such as *Just Say No* were seen as trivialising the factors involved in drug use. Their evaluation also concluded that the perception of drug use as a result of a lack of education diverted attention away from the real psychological and sociological causes of drug use.

124 Others have commented on the normality, the benefits and the universality of drug use among young people. They believe that programmes such as *Just Say No* did not address potent environmental factors including poverty, decay, inadequate housing and unemployment that are associated with drug use and problems that may stem from it.

125 Further research could usefully study:

  • the effectiveness of new developments in education about drugs and alcohol;

  • the use of peer leaders;

  • parental involvement in education;

  • the work of theatre groups in education.

The Lessons

126 In general, it is possible to conclude that education about substances:

  • has over-emphasised the role of peer pressure and self-esteem as causes of drug use;

  • has not taken account of the age range and the diversity of social spectrum of the targets of drug education;

  • has tended to view substance misuse in a vacuum, rather than as one aspect of problem behaviour.

127 In the later 1980s, the Scottish Education Department commissioned the development of educational material, and carried out a thorough evaluation of its effectiveness. The evaluation considered the relative impact of: standardised packages used as a whole; partial use of packages; the older *ad hoc* approach; and no drug education. The outcome was that those drug education programmes that had emphasised social and resistance skills and self-esteem deficits were shown to have made little or no impact. Where there were discernable and measurable outcomes, they were in terms of drug-related knowledge. But the small increases in drug-related knowledge found in the intervention groups were only statistically significant by virtue of the large sample size.

128 Over time, there have been one or two changes in the curricula for education about substances but mainly of an updating nature. Fundamentally, the approaches continue to address the same issues of peer pressure, as the cause of drug misuse, and inadequacy of personal self-image (in particular self-esteem) as being a key risk factor. Modern views are that peer influence, other peer factors and self-esteem play a role in the genesis of drug use, but that these factors are not satisfactory sole explanations for most drug use.

129 There are a variety of ways in which peer relationship factors could operate. The common interpretation of peer pressure is that it works as a form of coercion, (sometimes the vaguer term *peer influences* is used). However, relationships with peers are also supportive and relationships between similar aged children and adolescents result from choice as much as, if not more than, from coercion. This has not been taken into account in many of the drug education intervention programmes.

130 The HAS has come to the view that another reason for the poor results from interventions based on education is ineffective targeting. Attempts have been made to change the behaviour of all young people - in effect treating drug use as a homogeneous phenomenon. But research shows that there are young people who engage in what is essentially normative behaviour, in which they experiment with a cross-section of activities in the course of growing up. The vast majority of them do not go on to develop destructive, harmful, or offending lifestyles. Nonetheless, some young people do develop problematic drug misusing lifestyles. In this latter group, drug misuse may be part of a wider set of delinquent behaviours. Thus, it is important to identify different target groups for education about substances and apply approaches to meet their specific needs.

131 In contrast to the large body of research literature that shows that education about drugs has had little impact so far, there is a similarly large body of literature which shows that there are key factors in young people's development that are associated with the development of problem behaviours. Often, substance use or misuse is part of a set of delinquent behaviours which include aggressiveness, offending, stealing and fighting. Some of the predisposing factors identified in the literature are associated with family and developmental factors. Families that do not ensure that appropriate forms of support are available to their children are likely to experience problems in managing their offspring. Drug use and/or alcohol use by other members of the family may be associated with delinquency in the children of the family but the effects may not arise directly from the use of substances. The association may be mediated by the behaviours that are frequently associated with alcohol or drug misuse and particularly by the lack of the three key factors - support, control and cohesion. Thus it is the lifestyles of family members that can predispose young people to develop delinquent and offending lifestyles.

132 All of this analysis and re-examination of the research evidence indicates that interventions in substance use and misuse based on education should be carefully designed. Different programmes may be needed for different young people at different stages of development and they should be geared to meet the underlying as well as overt needs of vulnerable young people.

Recommended Approaches

Interventions based on realistic expectations of education about substances.

133 It is essential to have realistic expectations of what education about substances can and cannot achieve. For example, information-based approaches will have little effect in primary prevention but, they are a useful strand in harm-reduction strategies. In a range of schools in Scotland and England a whole-school approach, based on personal and social education and social development, provides a productive basis for inputs on alcohol and drug-related knowledge. Where schools have an integrated, highly developed form of personal and social education and use a wide range of materials, they do improve young people's knowledge of the perils of substance use in the wider sense.

Timely delivery of personal and social education

134 There is no point in bolting education about substances on to other curricula for adolescents at times when the information may be too late. Experience shows that there is a temptation for school staff to provide education in the second half of adolescence, at a time when many young people say that they have already passed the point when they make decisions about whether they are prepared to consider using drugs. Additionally, where vulnerable adolescents and children are concerned, novel forms of intervention may be necessary. An example of this could be a situation where parents come to schools to discuss with educational psychologists their own alcohol and drug-related problems, that may be associated with family disorder. Consideration should be given to interventions which draw in the wider family to a greater extent than applies at present.

Provision of behavioural alternatives for younger people to help them to develop preferences for activities that promote healthy lifestyles

135 For example a group of schools - a secondary school and the associated primary schools in its cluster - might introduce a programme of high quality daily physical education as a catalyst for other inputs on health education. In such a circumstance, the physical education programme could be tailored individually so that children who are reluctant to engage in competitive sports could still measure achievement in terms of their own physical progress. The important element is the individual focus. Additionally, giving young people concrete alternatives may help them to develop a preference for physical and other activities in the longer term, that could be more effective than would techniques based solely on discussion of their behaviour. Experience shows that the development of healthy behaviour is seldom achieved by tackling knowledge and attitudes alone.

The important role of peer education

136 It is recognised that in some circumstances removing expert adults from directly teaching adolescents across generational boundaries in educational settings can have beneficial impacts on the willingness of some young people to engage with new ideas and learn from and reflect on their own experiences in social learning. Within peer-led educational approaches, the role of the expert could be adopted by peers who lead the sessions. Elder peers, who have sufficient knowledge and positive attitudes, may be effective role models who are able to convey health promotion messages. It is important that the peers involved should be of high status with young people they are trying to influence, and socially close to them. In this

circumstance, the staff take an the indirect role through supporting and directing the work of the senior school students. Clearly, there are limitations in this approach but peer education has been shown to increase the prospect of younger people listening to information that conveys difficult and challenging messages that they might reject if delivered by adults.

Targeted interventions

137 Blanket interventions for all young people who may not need them or who are engaged in essentially normative behaviour may be ineffective. Targeted drug education is needed for young people who are at risk and/or engaging in behaviours that are potentially or actually highly destructive. It is necessary to provide support and education earlier for families whose ways of relating predispose young people to develop problems in later life. This approach links with considerations discussed later in this chapter on prevention.

Effective education programmes share certain features

138 These include:

  • effective training of the teachers;

  • use of peer tutors;

  • use of active learning methods.

Educational approaches should exploit and build on this knowledge and use an adequate range of high quality resources and materials. New approaches should be tried and tested, for example, those involving parents and people in the wider community.

National standards for evaluating education programmes relating to substances

139 Agreement and use of national standards for evaluating education programmes would enable comparisons to be made between studies and ensure that research findings cannot be called into question on the grounds of the methodology used. Future educational programmes could then build on the knowledge of what works that emerges from this approach. At present, we know that education about substances can educate, but we are not sure that it can prevent drug use. Further work is needed on this important topic.

Access for parents and guardians to services that provide accurate information about alcohol and all other substances

140 Parents, those who hold parental responsibility, and other adults may require advice and support when approaching a young person about the use of drugs and alcohol and about how to discuss these matters. Unfortunately, the HAS has found that some services for younger people discourage the involvement of parents. It seems that this approach has been adopted by some primarily to promote the belief of young people in the confidentiality of the service. However, many services now appreciate the needs of parents. Some services have developed helplines, parent clinics or surgeries which offer support, advice and counselling to parents. Given the diversity of roles, it is essential that each service is clear about the range of information and interventions that it offers (eg, information and education, support, family assessments). These community-based approaches are to be encouraged. All such programmes should be evaluated.

PREVENTION - PROMOTION OF LOWER RISK SUBSTANCE USE

141 Paragraph 108 summarised the plural objectives of services for children and adolescents who are approaching the threshold of use and for those who use or misuse drugs and alcohol. These are:

- prevention of drug use, including helping younger people to achieve and maintain drug-free lifestyles (primary prevention);

- minimising harm related to the use of substances (secondary prevention);

- care, treatment and rehabilitation of young people who have developed dependency on substances, harmful patterns of substance misuse or disorders in which substance misuse plays an aetiological role (secondary and tertiary prevention).

142 Already, this report has indicated that these activities have their own sets of practices built upon theory, practical experience and combinations of the two.

143 As a general point, messages that advocate avoidance of substance use are difficult to deliver in a society in which some forms of it are lawful and some are not. Young people receive inconsistent messages when current prevention programmes warn of the dangers of substance use while society continues to model and support the social and recreational use of some substances.

144 In the paragraphs that follow, this report focuses on prevention - the promotion of lower risk substance use and harm-minimisation in those young people who are already using substances.

The Lessons From Research

The Gateway Theory

145 Research evidence shows that most people who use alcohol and prescribed drugs do not misuse these substances and most young people do not habitually use illicit drugs. Many of those who do experiment with illegal drugs do not become regular users and use of the substances which have been termed *gateway drugs* (eg, alcohol, tobacco and cannabis) does not generally lead to dependence on harder drugs.

146 Nonetheless, it is true that children and adolescents who eventually use illicit drugs often begin with alcohol and cigarettes. Thus, prevention planning is sometimes promoted on the basis of delaying the onset of use of these gateway drugs in the hope that this may either delay or circumvent the use of illicit drugs by a proportion of those exposed to these initiatives. It seems that those who ascribe to the *gateway theory* base their thinking on there being a linear progression towards problematic use, though this conclusion has not been borne out by longitudinal research studies. The majority of people who use cannabis do not progress to using harder drugs and, in those people who do make this progression, the likely stepping stones have been found to be social and behavioural rather than pharmacological.

The Law and Societal Norms

147 The laws and norms of society that relate to the use of substances are important prevention measures. The availability of alcohol has been curtailed by a variety of measures:

- increased taxation;

- age restrictions and laws regulating:
  - the sale of alcohol;
  - to whom alcohol is sold;
  - how alcohol is sold.

The consequences of these measures include a reduction in consumption and problem use, reduction in the prevalence of liver cirrhosis and reduction in traffic fatalities. But strategies that reduce the supply cannot beexpected to eliminate drug use by themselves although they are important in communicating societal norms of disapproval. Table 4 shows some new measures proposed by the Royal College of Physicians and the British Paediatric Association in their report *Alcohol and the Young* (1995).

Table 4

Royal College of Physicians and British Paediatric Association Recommendations for National Policy Measures Promoting Safe Drinking Among Young People	
Annual Consumption	In the light of the fact that the alcohol consumption of young people is a reflection of the consumption of the total population, steps should be taken to ensure that this should not rise above the present level of 9.1 litres of alcohol per person in the population aged over 15 years (equivalent to 2.5 units per day). Further, Government should act to reduce annual consumption to about five litres (or 1.5 units a day) per head over the next 10 years.
Pricing/Taxation	The real price of alcohol and alcohol products should be regularly increased by taxation in order to achieve a strong price disincentive on alcohol for young people.
Advertising and Promotion	All forms of alcohol sales promotion directed towards the young (including arts and sports sponsorship by alcohol companies) should be subject to tighter regulation.
Marketing Codes of Practice	The code of practice for marketing alcohol products to young people should be reviewed in the light of an increasing tendency for alcohol companies to target their products towards the young. In particular, marketing methods which blur the distinction between alcohol and illicit drugs should be banned.
Labelling	Legislation should be introduced that requires alcoholic drinks to be prominently labelled with their alcohol content by units. Alcoholic drinks should also be labelled with recommended limits to assist consumer choice and self-monitoring.
A Review of Legislation	There should be a Government review of existing licensing legislation concerning the young with the aim of introducing legislation that is consistent, reduces the risk of alcohol-related harm to children and young people, and is enforceable.
Minimum Legal Age for Sales of Alcohol	Current legislation prohibiting sales of alcohol to young people under 18 years should be fully and firmly enforced.
Public Houses and Children's Certificates	The use of children's certificates should be properly regulated, and their effects monitored.
Licensees	All licensees should be required to possess the British Institute of InnKeeping Licensee Certificate. In addition, children's licensing certificates should only be issued where trained service/bartenders are present at all times. The age of alcohol servers should not be less than 18 years.
Drunken Driving Deterrence	The existing limit of 80mg% should be reviewed.
Learner Drivers	The legal limit of blood alcohol should be reduced to 20mg% for learner drivers and those who have passed their driving test in the previous two years. This is the lowest limit that can be reliably measured, and inexperienced young drivers should be advised not to drink at all before they drive.

Community-based Initiatives

148 In the USA, community-based initiatives have been promoted as a significant prevention strategy and prevention programmes have shifted to include endeavours to enhance the social competencies and life skills of those who attend. *Resistance Skills Training* is probably the most widely used programme in the USA and has also been used in the UK. These programmes focus on social influences and seek to reinforce positive group norms.

149 There have been some promising results shown by some studies, such as reductions in classroom behaviour problems, and improved social skills and self-esteem. However, programmes such as *Project SMART* and *Project ALERT* produced modest changes in the age of initial use of cannabis, and less change in alcohol consumption with the effects being eroded within one year. The programmes showed more success with drugs that are socially disapproved of and this suggests that the social milieu is an important influence. The main conclusion is that the majority of these programmes have little influence on the participants and their effectiveness in preventing alcohol use has not been validated by research.

150 Research indicates that multi-modal programmes are more effective than programmes with a single approach. Newer, comprehensive programmes, for example, those based on enhancing lifeskills and social competencies, have shown more promising results than the older ones, though the changes tend to be short-term only and small in degree. Few evaluations of comprehensive prevention programmes have demonstrated positive effects that are statistically significant and the impacts are small in the case of those programmes that do show some statistically significant effects.

151 Some organisers have tried to engage the target community in the design of programmes and to attend to community processes in their content. Gorman (1992) noted that interventions that attempt to reduce substance use by individuals are limited in impact and that they do not seem to lead to long-term change. He noted that, in the past, little attention had been given to the participation of subjects in the design of programmes and that they were standardised and did not sufficiently address the diversity of cultural, political, and economic settings in which people live. Three more recent community projects have attempted to address these issues and the results should be helpful in increasing our understanding of the processes involved.

Alternative Prevention Programmes

152 Alternative prevention programmes are based on the premise that real-life experiences can be as appealing as substance use. These programmes are intended to prevent or reduce substance use by encouraging young people to engage in alternative experiences of life. Alternative prevention programmes generally take on one of two forms: those activities that provide an alternative to the effect that the individual might seek in drug use, for example, mountain climbing, or other risk-taking activities and those activities that create opportunities for young people to develop skills and which promote their involvement in community projects rather than sensation-seeking activities.

153 In 1983, the National Institute on Drug Abuse (a United States agency) targeted a number of arenas in which to promote comprehensive

prevention programmes. These were: the community; parents and families; schools; and workplaces. The techniques used included:

- involving young people in community projects;

- health promotion;

- early intervention and treatment;

- use of local media;

- development of consistent and accurate information about drug use;

- networking with other organisations (both drug specific and non-drug specific).

In 1986, the National Institute on Drug Abuse published guidelines on preventing drug use in ethnic minority communities which include:

- identifying community leaders;

- promoting awareness of the problem;

- use of existing structures;

- identifying funding sources;

- the need to have small meaningful goals.

It also emphasised the importance of employment in preventing despair and drug misuse.

154 Other examples of alternative approaches include: the Chicago Youth Development project, which mobilises peer groups into constructive activity; the use of The Street as a site of outreach, for distribution of educational materials and for changing drug patterns; the Fast Forward approach, that emphasises peer education and a personal approach by youth workers; and ACTION, in the USA, which gives young people opportunities to participate in solving community problems.

155 Casual alternatives may improve self-esteem and encourage involvement in the local community but they have shown little effectiveness in reducing drug use if they are the only means of intervention. In 1987, the US Department of Education and US Department of Health and Human Services concluded that involvement in substance-free activities may have an effect on use, though those at less risk were more likely to participate. Some researchers have concluded that, while programme effectiveness in reducing drug use may not have been demonstrated in many projects, some observers look to greater community participation, less harmful drug use and better quality of life as useful aims and outcomes in themselves. Furthermore, the choice of programme should *"rest on a clear statement of aims and a realistic assessment of available human and other resources in the local area"* (Dorn and Murji, 1992).

The Effect of the Media

156 It has been recognised that the media can be a powerful influence in changing people's knowledge, attitudes and beliefs. Various mass-media campaigns concerning health promotion and drug-use prevention have been implemented. Generally, they have relied on factual education and fear-arousal strategies. The evaluations have provided very mixed results - from small positive effects through no change to negative effects (eg, increased drug use, negative portrayals and prejudice against high-risk

groups). Power (1989) concluded that the *"traditional preventive goal of reduction of alcohol and drug use has not been and probably cannot be achieved by information style media campaigns."* Nonetheless, despite the paucity of research, media campaigns are a potentially strong preventive approach. Experience indicates that the messages must be simple, must reach the target audience, and should not use fear-arousal techniques. High quality research is needed to refine campaigns and evaluate their outcomes.

157 It has been noted that the *"cost-effectiveness studies of drug-prevention programmes are almost non-existent"* (Hu, 1981) and research has *"uncovered no benefit-cost analyses of drug use prevention program"* (Plotnick, 1994). According to a 1987 US Department of Education report on the nature and effectiveness of drug use prevention programmes, the problems noted were: inadequate use of theory; failure to reach the high-risk groups; weak interventions and implementations; narrowly focused programmes; and poor evaluation. Nevertheless, some have argued that, with limited resources, preventive strategies should focus on drug misuse and problem use rather than on the general use of drugs (Newcomb, 1989).

Targeting Risk-factors

158 The pursuit of different goals (eg, no use of cigarettes as compared to responsible use of alcohol) may each require a specific type of intervention rather than a strategy based on the same underlying principles and techniques. Gorman (1992) and others have suggested that research on primary prevention should move away from the application of a single model across more and more disparate settings and instead evaluate techniques designed for, and targeted at specific populations.

159 The disappointing results of early education and prevention approaches argue for greater emphasis to be placed on prevention aimed at reducing the impact of risk factors. A risk-focused approach seeks to prevent drug use either by eliminating or mitigating the known risk factors. There is evidence to suggest that comprehensive, risk-focused interventions may also prevent or mitigate other problem behaviours.

160 Several programmes have targeted the risk factors that are implicated in a range of disorders, including drug misuse, delinquency and conduct disorders. Additionally, some of these interventions seem to increase the influence of protective factors in populations that are considered to be at high risk. Therefore, it is important to test those preventive approaches that have successfully addressed risk factors found in childhood.

161 Successful intervention with children and young people who have conduct problems and disorders is acknowledged to be difficult as they tend to drop out of conventional forms of therapy, their families may be disorganised and, by its nature, the problem may be persistent and entrenched. However, brief group work in school with children who, in the main, had mild or moderate conduct disorders has been shown to be effective when compared to no intervention. Furthermore, one research study showed that this difference accumulated over a three-year period.

162 Early childhood and family support programmes that may reduce drug use include:

- social supports for mothers;

- education and career planning;

- family planning;

- early childhood education.

They appear to mitigate other risk factors, childhood behaviour problems, family management problems and academic failure. Evaluations of interventions delivered in educational and family settings suggest that they can reduce the risk factors of academic failure, peer rejection and inconsistent parenting with long-term benefits for individuals and society . However, there are difficulties in recruiting and retaining high-risk families to interventions of this kind while, conversely, well-motivated families tend to select themselves, yielding better results for the programme overall.

163 Studies have demonstrated the benefits of improving parents' skills in reducing family and child behaviour problems. Little experimental research has been conducted on the effectiveness of parent-training specifically for preventing substance misuse. Nonetheless, evidence does suggest promising results for training parents in helping to prevent adolescent drug misuse. Kazdin (1987) reported on the benefits from a structured intervention known as *problem-solving skills training*, a form of child-oriented psychological intervention, especially when combined with *parent management training*. However, his work focused exclusively on children and young people in a residential setting. More recently, so-called *multi-modal intervention*, a combination of individual counselling, focused help for parents, group work, and specialist teaching, has shown promise. Furthermore, it can be used with children who live in their own homes.

164 Other preventive techniques that have shown positive effects on risk factors, and which might thereby reduce or prevent substance use, include early childhood education, alterations in teacher practices and academic tutoring for low achievers. But further study is required of the effects of these approaches on the initial use of substances, on continued substance use, and misuse after their adoption in different settings and with a range of different target groups.

LESSONS FROM OTHER WORK ON HEALTH PROMOTION WITH ADOLESCENTS

165 Throughout this report, we emphasise the importance of bringing together: practical experience of working with children and adolescents; knowledge of their developmental processes; and knowledge and expertise in working with people who have problems resulting from misusing substances. The importance of this triad is supported by the commentary in this chapter.

166 In this concluding section, we draw attention to the work of Hurrelman (1990) who has written about the design of health promotion programmes for adolescents. His approach takes into account the psycho-social functions of behaviours that put health at greater risk and the developmental significance of problem behaviours.

167 Hurrelman quotes Botvin and Dusenbury, *"According to problem behaviour theory, vulnerability to peer pressure and the risk of substance abuse would be greater for adolescents who have fewer effective coping strategies in their repertoire, fewer social skills for handling social situations, and greater anxiety about social situations. For these adolescents, the range of options for achieving*

personal goals would be restricted at the same time that discomfort in interpersonal situations was high, motivating them to take whatever actions they thought might be reasonable coping responses."

168   In very summarised terms, the major adolescent developmental tasks are:

- developing a range of personal competencies, skills and attitudes to oneself and others that enable the expression of greater autonomy;

- handling changing relationships. This involves reducing dependence on parents, guardians and other authoritative adults together with developing the capacity to choose, cope effectively with, and enjoy relationships based on elected mutual dependency;

- dealing with rapid changes in body size and capability and enjoying the potential for new relationships and new responsibilities that come with bodily maturation.

For the most part, these tasks are negotiated by:

- observing others;

- introspection;

- exploration;

- experimentation.

within the arenas of:

- the individual - one's own feelings and inner experiences and thoughts;

- the family;

- the peer group.

169   Strain and stress may develop in these same arenas of experience for a variety of reasons - the risk factors have been considered in an earlier chapter. As a consequence, some adolescents may progress to less satisfactory forms of behaviour including rebellion, disordered conduct and greater risk-taking in endeavouring to create for themselves illusions of needing adults less and success in growing up. Theories of this kind fit with the views of a number of adolescent psychologists who consider that the problem behaviours of some adolescents could be viewed as signals of strain *"resulting from a variety of stressful developmental tasks"* (Coleman, 1989).

170   If this were so, then these considerations could have significant theoretical implications for the design of educational and preventative programmes for young people. At least some adolescents may be at risk of using and misusing substances or be already engaged in these activities as a means of handling stress in growing-up. For them, these theories would predict that fear-arousing messages delivered by adults seen as distant could have a paradoxical effect. By inducing greater strain, the possibility of some adolescents engaging in risk-taking behaviours might increase - in order that they sustain a frail illusion of autonomy by rejecting adult messages. Developed further, thinking of this kind can contribute to understanding why it is that evaluation suggests that programmes that offer information are effective in improving knowledge but less successful in changing risky behaviours - these risky behaviours can have a range of undisclosed and, often, unrecognised functions.

171 Hurrelman advances theories of this kind in respect of a general approach to choosing strategies for intervention with adolescents in a broad range of health promotion endeavours. His analyses distinguish between different stages in the process by which problem behaviour emerges and separates education from prevention. Hurrelman reviews the limits and potentials of a range of different measures in health education. These include:

- A-type measures that train individual competency;

- B-type measures that modify behaviour;

- C-type measures that improve social living conditions;

- D-type measures that construct support networks.

172 He argues that each has its appropriate place in the overall ensemble of possible health promotion strategies and that they should be targeted by matching their application to the task and to knowledge of the developmental and therapeutic needs and circumstances of individuals and groups of adolescents.

CONCLUDING COMMENTS

173 Readers will contrast the theoretical finale in the section above with the evidence and advice on education and prevention offered in this chapter - advice that has been derived from reviewing the literature on effectiveness. Clearly there are overlaps. Both sources suggest that:

- there is no one pathway to risk-taking behaviours, including substance use and misuse, that applies to all adolescents;

- the developmental positions and needs of young people should be taken into account when considering intervention through education and prevention programmes;

- approaches that offer information are likely to increase knowledge but, on their own, less likely to change attitudes and problem behaviours;

- frequently, effective interventions should be multi-focal in:

  - encouraging individual responsibility;

  - involving young people in planning and implementing programmes;

  - encouraging peer support;

  - recruiting adult teachers and other workers who are open, supportive and non-judgemental;

- education and prevention are interdisciplinary concepts that include the fields of medicine, biology, epidemiology, psychology, psychiatry, and sociology as well as good educational theory and practice.

174 Perhaps, we can conclude that the design of both education and prevention programmes should continue to concentrate on the behaviours of groups of adolescents and on the behaviours of individuals but that the psycho-social functions of risk-taking and risky behaviours and their contextual circumstances should also be taken into account. In this way, programmes should have a tailored balance of measures directed at:

- training individual competence;

- improving social conditions;

- constructing social networks;

that mitigate against substance use and misuse. Table 5 summarises approaches that might be considered within the context of an educational setting.

Table 5

Measures for Consideration in Designing Targeted Health Promotion Programmes
Training Individual Competence
• Offer new skills;   • Develop self-esteem;   • Reduce anxiety;   • Promote understanding through providing high quality information with back-up support.
Improving Social Conditions

• Provide high quality interventions;
 • Ensure that student-teacher relationships are:
   - open;
   - supportive;
   - non-judgemental.

Constructing Social Networks

• Promote membership of positively orientated mature peer groups through mutual acquisition of:
   - new skills;
   - improved self-esteem;
   by group members together.

CHAPTER 6

THE BACKGROUND

175   The emphasis of the Government's strategy on young people and the formation of drug action teams, has been welcomed by many professionals who work with young people. Though a new emphasis on education and prevention is supported, many commentators have expressed the concern that the strategy refers only to illicit drug use and does not emphasise sufficiently enough intervention and treatment. However, it is noted that in 1996-1997, the Department of Health is committed to providing *"guidance to purchasers of drug services on the range of services required to meet the needs of young people. Its aim will be to ensure that young people have access to early intervention services in the light of the evaluation of the projects on early interventions, the recommendations of the Effectiveness Review, and the NHS Health Advisory Service's Thematic Review of Substance Misuse in Children and Adolescents".*

176   Other fora are beginning to address the needs of young people who misuse drugs and alcohol: the Department for Education and Employment has issued guidelines to schools; the Royal College of Physicians and the British Paediactric Association have published *Alcohol and the Young*; and working parties are addressing this issue and publishing guidelines for working with young people.

177   *Community Safety Strategies,* developed from the partnership of many agencies, parents, school governors and concerned individuals, have developed in the recent past. Their emphasis is threefold - enforcement, information, and education.

AN OUTLINE OF THE FINDINGS OF THIS REVIEW

178   The findings reported here are drawn from:

- reports of visits to local services in England and Wales made by the Drug Advisory Service in the previous three years (these visits have routinely and specifically examined the commissioning and provision of services for young people, enquiries which have been enhanced in the past three years in order to provide information for the work reported in this document);

- field visits to existing services in England and Wales conducted as part of the thematic review of child and adolescent mental health services (in most of the visits, additional enquiries relating to the subjects of this review were made by one of the authors);

- visits specific to the purpose to particular drug and alcohol services for adults;

- visits to mental health services for young people;

- visits to specialist drug and alcohol services specifically orientated to the needs of young people;

- opinion and experience collated at a conference of professionals with particular expertise in the field (see Annex F).

179   Though much interest has been generated, the overall impressions of the HAS, drawn from its fieldwork, are that much of the work that is being done locally remains poorly co-ordinated. Furthermore, problems in agreeing the definitions of use, abuse, misuse and the nature and extent of the problem appear to be placing hurdles in the path of development and progress.

180 The main findings were that there is a lack of recognition by professionals and the managers of health services of the particular and definable needs arising from substance use and misuse by children and adolescents.

181 Some young people are less likely to gain access to health and social care than others. These include:

- children and adolescents who are unaware of the existence of services;

- young people in prisons;

- homeless young people or those who live in hostels;

- children and adolescents who live in rural areas;

- children and adolescents with multiple problems.

182 There is no obvious single solution to the problems arising from drug and alcohol use and misuse. The fieldwork revealed that local responses to the problem have often been *ad hoc*. Services and interventions, where they exist at all, have developed in an isolated, uneven, patchy and idiosyncratic manner. Responses have been poorly planned and poorly co-ordinated with pockets of isolated excellence throughout the country.

183 Much of the service, where it does exist has been, and is provided by voluntary agencies in the non-statutory sector.

184 Despite the weight of the foregoing impressions, the HAS found, and is continuing to find evidence of a slowly growing number of local initiatives that are being developed in order to provide better direct contact services for children and adolescents. Some of these are being developed by non-statutory agencies and others by statutory agencies. In the statutory sector, this work is often being done by mental health trusts as an offshoot by their community mental health services for adults and community psychiatric nurses are frequently mentioned as being at the forefront. In a number of these cases, enquiry has indicated the presence of an enthusiastic consultant with a special interest in substance misuse who provides support to the front-line staff. Often services of this kind provide sources of contact for young people who want information and help, and some limited levels of counselling and support.

185 Much of the service that is being developed appears to be of good quality, though it is done by practitioners who are relatively less familiar with practice related to child and adolescent development theory.

186 Not withstanding these welcome and important initiatives, specialised treatment for young people with substance use and misuse problems in England and Wales is extremely limited in availability and scope and is characterised by:

- lack of definition and understanding of the problem;

- absence of clear commissioner, purchaser and provider leadership;

- lack of knowledge of the scale of the problem;

- lack of basic information on existing services - in respect of the available interventions, their competence etc;

- lack of systematic planning;

- poor co-ordination of services;

- uneven patchy provision;

- unclear and disputed funding responsibilities;

- lack of trust and competitiveness between service sectors;

- indications that many services are now addressing these issues, but with poor plans, poor training, and inadequate competence, though often in good faith.

187 The conference, that formed an important part of the review, debated the many issues that were, and are, common themes of concern around the country. These are:

- the lack of strategy;

- the definition of the nature and extent of the problems of substance use and misuse and those related to substance use;

- the broad spread of matters concerning use as distinct from misuse and abuse;

- the concept of vulnerable children and adolescents;

- the lack of information on existing services;

- the lack of information about the need for services;

- the lack of involvement of young people in planning services and developing strategy;

- the balance between public health strategies and approaches with a focus on interventions for individuals;

- the balance between efforts directed towards alcohol and drug use and to their misuse by children and adolescents;

- the balance between efforts directed towards alcohol use and misuse and to drug use and misuse;

- education for all versus targeting of interventions on vulnerable children and young people;

- the balance between approaches based on education and prevention and those services that offer intervention to young people with problems;

- the need for services to be accessible, appropriate and effective;

- the ability of staff to retain young people in contact with services.

These issues are seen as framing current challenges to statutory and non-statutory sector agencies and the responsible authorities.

Commissioning

188 The HAS reviewed the strategies, contracts and service specifications from the 90% of health authorities in England and Wales that contributed to the HAS' Library of Commissioning for 1993-94. The purpose was to ascertain whether there were specific contracts for services for children and adolescents who use and/or misuse substances. This search did not find *any* contracts that were targeted directly at this group of young people. However, two health authorities mentioned that they deliberately commission services for children under their arrangements for mainstream drug and alcohol services.

189 Other observations were made by the multi-disciplinary teams of peers that made visits to local services during the fieldwork conducted by the HAS. They found that few health authorities had strategic plans for developments to services for child and adolescents who have problems arising from substance use and misuse. Some local authority community care plans have identified young people with substance problems as a priority but few services had agreed the allocation of resources and little action was evident to the HAS visitors. Equally, many District Drug and Alcohol Advisory Committees had identified the issue. Some had set up working parties, but enquiries suggest that little had been achieved. A lack of clarity was evident in most of the services visited about the nature of substance use and misuse problems, the roles of the services already involved, and the balance to be achieved between education, prevention and more direct intervention with young people who have problems.

190 In summary, the problems experienced by children and adolescents who misuse substances are not addressed within the strategies of most health authorities, or within their plans for mental health services, drug and alcohol services or for child health services.

Service Provision

191 The availability of specific services for young people with problems arising from substance use and misuse has been commented on in earlier paragraphs. The paragraphs that follow offer more information on detailed issues raised during the HAS service visits.

192 Some services aimed predominantly at adults cover people over 16 years-old, while others make *ad hoc* local arrangements. There is evidence that drug and alcohol services that are geared to adults are beginning to see younger people (under 18 or 16 years of age). But the willingness of the majority of these services to see or accept referrals for all ages does not necessarily mean that they are fully competent to deal with the needs of young people, or that their staff are sufficiently aware of the ethical and legal issues. Guidelines for working with young people, particularly those under 16, are not widely available or agreed, though groups in various parts of the country have attempted to address this matter.

193 Community services are provided both by the statutory and non-statutory sectors. They range from volunteer helplines, advice and information and offer a range of interventions. In many areas, there are good links between provider units. However, links with child and adolescent mental health services and the wider child services are poorly developed.

194 Much work with younger clients occurs through informal contacts in community settings through, for example, outreach work, provision of information and advice, and needle and syringe exchange services. In many instances, the person receiving the services will choose to remain anonymous. Information from these sources is thus excluded from databases, though it may provide an important early indication of trends.

195 A small number of specialised community projects for people who use and misuse substances has been developed exclusively for young people. These rely more on the drive of interested personalities than on their inclusion within an overarching strategy. Some are led by child and adolescent mental health services practitioners who have links with drug services, and others are led by substance services for adults by workers who have specific training and a remit for young people. The latter tend to

operate in conjunction with child and adolescent mental health services and the non-statutory sector. There are great variations in the range of interventions offered, their confidentiality and their accessibility.

196 Inpatient facilities (either in specific units or attached to adult mental health services) for detoxification or assessment of psychiatric co-morbidity do not usually admit those under 17 years of age. Many psychiatric inpatient units for adolescents have drug or alcohol misuse as an exclusion criteria. This means that most young people who need admission are dealt with on an individual basis with much variation between areas and individual interventions. Often *ad hoc* arrangements have to be made and examples include the admission of intoxicated young people to adult wards or to locked secure units. Overall, the HAS visits revealed that there was little evidence of planning for the needs of this group for inpatient services.

197 Almost without exception, residential services (intensive services, other than inpatient units, that are provided by sectors of care other than the NHS) operate a lower age restriction though not all adhere rigidly to their advertised age limits. Commonly, the lower age limit is 18-20 years though a number accept referrals of people aged over 16. A small number have attempted to develop services specifically and exclusively for young people. Few have been the subject of systematic evaluation. Residential projects operate within a range of philosophies and approaches and some include short detoxification programmes. However, most have been developed from an ethos appropriate to adult clients or patients and the effectiveness of this with young people has not been evaluated. Our fieldwork reveals an almost total absence of residential provision for young people under 16 who have problems arising from substance use and misuse. This may, in part, be attributable to the complexity of funding arrangements.

198 A major area of concern to staff revealed by the visits to local services was that of the possible legal implications for those who work with young people, particularly children and adolescents under 16 years of age. This concern centres on the provision of needle and syringes to under 16 year-olds without parental consent. A wide range of contrasting and conflicting views is held - ranging from the promise of absolute confidentiality to heavy discouragement by awakening young people to the risks of legal action. It was evident to the HAS that many staff in local services are concerned about the meaning and use of the Children Act 1989 with respect to children and young people with alcohol and drug-related problems. Other areas of concern, to which the service visits draw attention, is the competence of staff, their needs for training, the use of contemporaneous recording by staff, the capacity of children and young people to consent to treatment, and the absence of involvement and guidelines from the Area Child Protection Committees with respect to substance use and misuse by younger people.

A COMMENTARY ON EXISTING SERVICES IN ENGLAND AND WALES

Introduction

199 Currently, the Government's arrangements for tackling problems arising from substance use and misuse involve five main areas of activity:

- improving international co-operation;
- increasing the effectiveness of the police and customs;
- maintaining effective deterrents;
- developing prevention publicity, education and community action;
- improving treatment and rehabilitation.

200 The reader is referred to Annex B of *Tackling Drugs Together* (1995) for a resumé of the current arrangements in England and *Forward Together* outlines a proposed stategy for the delivery of prevention, treatment and rehabilitation services in Wales.

201 Drug and alcohol services for adults have been developed within a broad framework which includes contributions from the statutory and non-statutory sectors. Traditionally, many have provided separate services for people with problems arising from drugs and alcohol, though some providers are now beginning to provide a range of services, regardless of the specific substance. This is particularly important for young people whose pattern is frequently one of poly substance use.

202 Specialist drug and alcohol services for adults provide a wide range of interventions:

- community services;
- information;
- advice;
- assessment and care planning;
- counselling;
- support services;
- needle and syringe provision and exchange;
- detoxification;
- a range of psychological and psychiatric interventions.

Most of these services have an adult ethos and are based on philosophies appropriate to adults.

203 Also, most drug and alcohol services attract a predominantly white clientele. This may be because black people perceive current services as inappropriate to their needs and inaccessible. Lack of information about services and concerns about confidentiality militate against their use. Some generic and specialist projects have been established to meet the needs of those with alcohol and drug problems from other cultural backgrounds, though in the main they have been developed for the adult population.

204 Many non-statutory sector providers have indicated to the HAS that they feel disadvantaged in the purchaser-provider system because of the drain on their resources caused by annual contracting. These agencies report that they are having to divert much staff time away from front-line work

with clients and into business planning and contract negotiation. Some also report that they feel inexperienced, and therefore doubly handicapped, in handling the business culture of the modern NHS and social services departments. In reality, the HAS has recurrently found the experience of senior managers in the non-statutory sectors with business matters to be greater than their equivalent in the health services. Nonetheless, this view continues to prevail in the non-statutory sector, which reflects the uncertainties that many agencies are experiencing.

205   The HAS recommends that commissioners should examine the prospects for working in a longer-term framework for contracting with non-statutory sector organisations. The aim would be to reduce the volatile forces at work within non-statutory agencies. Too much effort at present goes into negotiating pick-up funding with different arms of the statutory services, or on identifying alternative resources elsewhere, to the general detriment of the primary work of providing services. Experience has shown that a number of services for people who misuse substances, are brought into precarious existence through barely adequate pump-priming, and that many of these fail to survive beyond one or two years.

206   One of the answers is for service commissioners to recognise in their contracts the breadth of services they require and which may require co-ordinated provision by a number of agencies. Those organisations which offer training, professional supervision, information and support services should have this recognised in their contracts as these are important components of an overall service. The experience of the HAS is that there has, understandably, been a preoccupation with contracting for, and the performance management of services that are in direct contact with patients in the early years of the new system.

Child and Adolescent Mental Health Services

207   A number of child and adolescent mental health services (CAMHS) are now seeing patients who use alcohol and drugs. However, a significant level of alcohol or drug use is often an exclusion criterion for day or inpatient treatment. Generally, younger people who use CAMHS do not present with substance use as a primary problem but frequently use and problems associated with use emerge as a part of the spectrum of their behaviour. Children and adolescents may use drugs and/or alcohol at experimental or recreational levels or they may experience significant problems resulting from use of these substances.

208   In those CAMHS which are now taking a direct interest in substance misuse, a range of services is provided: information giving; advice on housing; help with conflict in families; financial and legal advice; and, occasionally, family-planning and sexual health advice. Some operate from mobile buses, others have drop-in facilities in city centre sites. The HAS is aware that one of these hosts a specialist alcohol and drug clinic. These centres have similarities to developments in school-linked, health or youth service centres in the USA. The existing one-stop comprehensive centres vary considerably in their range of provision of health-related services.

209   The advantages of these centres are that they are multi-focused, offer confidential services, and are accessible and appropriate to the needs of young people. However, there are a number of problems: the dearth of trained personnel; inadequate funding; community and parental resistance;

and a lack of systematic data on effectiveness. There is also lack of data on what these programmes hope to achieve and many have few links with existing local services, particularly primary care services.

210 Not outstanding examples of excellence, the experience of the HAS is that most CAMHS do not see young people who present with substance use or misuse as a primary problem. Frequently, young people with these problems are referred to drug and alcohol services for adults.

Forensic Mental Health Services for Children and Adolescents

211 Many young people who are subject to the criminal justice system or seen at adolescent forensic mental health services use alcohol and drugs. Some of them are reported as seeing their substance use as normal, admit to the use of drugs, deny they have a problem and display minimal motivation to alter their behaviour. Others have problems related to intoxication, and some are affected by the social, legal, psychological or physical consequences of their substance use. Often, the characteristics of this group include: a history of the early onset of significant conduct disorder; coming from a dysfunctional family; socio-economic deprivation; and familial conflict and criminality. Generally, young people who present with significant difficulties and an associated high-risk profile do not receive the assistance they require as they fall between the nets set by the services provided by various sectors.

A SUMMARY OF THE CURRENT SITUATION IN ENGLAND AND WALES

212 The needs of many young people with significant problems related to drug and alcohol use and misuse are not being met or not being recognised. This circumstance could be described as being one of hidden morbidity. Figure 1 and Table 6 summarise the opinions reported to the HAS with regard to the current circumstances in the UK.

Figure 1

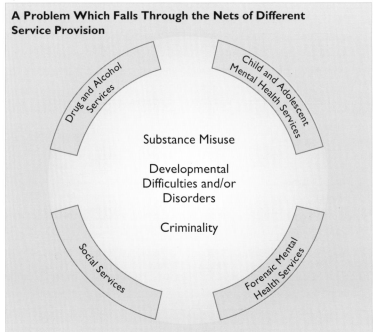

A Problem Which Falls Through the Nets of Different Service Provision

Drug and Alcohol Services

Child and Adolescent Mental Health Services

Substance Misuse

Developmental Difficulties and/or Disorders

Criminality

Social Services

Forensic Mental Health Services

Table 6

Factors Associated with the Difficulties Faced by Various Service Providers in Meeting the Needs of Children and Adolescents	
Services for People Who Misuse Substances	**Child and Adolescent Mental Health Services**
• patients are too young for the services provided for adults • the culture is inappropriate to children and adolescents • lower levels of dependent drug use to which adult services may not be orientated • fear of the impact of adult patients	• the problems of managing children and adolescents with substance misuse may be considered to be too difficult • problems of case-mix within those CAMHS that are more limited in scope and resources • fear of the impact of substance users on other children
Social Services	**Forensic Mental Health Services**
• the problems may be considered to be too difficult • staff may be inadequately trained • fear of entering a large arena of need for which services have not been planned or financed	• patients are too young for the services provided for adults • staff are unfamiliar with the client group • fear of the impact of adults with major problems on children and adolescents • pressures to provide services for other clients with major but different problems

213 The explorations of the HAS have produced a consensus of opinion as to other factors that are seen as hindering the development of services for younger people include:

Philosophy

- children continue to be perceived as innocent;

- a new orthodoxy in juvenile justice which suggests that responses to adolescent problems should be characterised by minimal intervention;

- lack of knowledge.

Commissioning and Purchasing

- absence of individual or joint commissioning strategies;

- lack of services currently, therefore a need for new money;

- services should be predominantly community-orientated and provided to outpatients while purchasing seems more easily linked to the provision of hospital-based specialist and inpatient services;

- low priority;

- low levels of awareness and understanding of the problems and issues;

- fear of the problems of this client group being the tip of an iceberg and potentially incurring high costs;

- difficulties in identifying funding for jointly planned services;

Treatment

- dearth of skilled staff;

- uncertain effectiveness;

- challenges in accurately targeting differing needs;

- challenges in linking different needs to appropriate service provision.

214 The paucity of services appropriate to children and adolescents cannot be attibuted to a single cause. The available evidence provided to the review team indicates a range of inter-connecting problems of general application and of specific relevance to services for children and adolescents. These are summarised in Table 7.

Table 7

A Summary of Problem Issues
● No clear leadership of the commissioning or provision of services
● Lack of systematic planning
● Lack of definition and understanding of the nature of the problem
● Lack of knowledge of the scale of the problem
● Funding responsibilities that are unclear or disputed
● Lack of basic information on existing services
● Poor co-ordination of services
● Lack of trust and the presence of competitiveness between different elements of present services

215 The funding for existing drug and alcohol services comes from many different sources. This diversity influences the way in which service contracts are placed and inevitably affects provision. Readers are referred to Annex B in this report, which carries details of current contractual and funding arrangements for these services, together with recommendations about promising or particularly appropriate approaches.

THE NEED FOR SERVICES

216 Against a background of a paucity of services dedicated to meeting the needs of children and adolescents who misuse substances, and *"the prospect over the next few years of more drug misuse by younger people causing more damage to themselves and their communities..." (Tackling Drugs Together, 1995)*, it is incumbent upon commissioners to ensure that accessible and appropriate services are in place. The trend towards increasing substance misuse is suggested by official statistics (see Tables 8 and 9) and research findings (see chapter 4).

Table 8

All Drug Addicts Notified to the Home Office During the Year by Age				
	1990	**1991**	**1992**	**1993**
Age under 21	1,501	1,500	1,870	2,231
All addicts	16,208	18,827	22,289	25,110

Table 9

Individuals Recorded by Regional Drug Misuse Databases (1.10.92 - 31.3.93)	
Total	17,822
Under 20	2,209

217 *Tackling Drugs Together* notes that *"it is important to ensure that different sections of the community have equality of opportunity to access drug services and that services are appropriate to those in differing circumstances...."* and that it is *"important to ensure that a range of drug services is available and accessible to young people across a spectrum of drug misuse from experimentation to dependency, including early intervention services, advice, counselling and treatment and local authority social services departments can support families and provide for the welfare of children, using their powers under the Children Act 1989."*

218 The Chief Medical Officer in his annual report for 1993, *On the State of the Public Health*, wrote of the *"need to provide a clinician to take responsibility ... during adolescence to provide the expertise...."* (Strasburger, 1991). Research has shown that adolescents see their GP more than any other health professional. It has also been demonstrated that general practice is an appropriate setting for adolescents to raise health concerns and receive advice on healthy lifestyles.

219 In practice, the upper age range of child and adolescent mental health services varies considerably from place to place and occasionally the mental health services for children and for adolescents are separate and distinct.

220 In *Together We Stand,* the HAS draws attention to the present state and status of child and adolescent mental health services. In doing so it deals with the age range of services and calls for a fresh look at this issue locally, and for the creation of *"youth mental health services."* The intention is the creation of services offering co-ordinated seamless care from childhood through to adult life. Much the same could be said and with equal force with regard to services for people who misuse substances.

221 Work from the USA has reported on the development of a specialty of adolescent medicine concerned (both in leadership and co-ordination) with adolescent health that focuses on primary care work in this age group. It has led to the development of specific programmes of care for groups of people, such as homeless young people, teenage prostitutes and adolescents who misuse substances. Another promising development which addresses the health and related needs of adolescents is that of the school link, health or youth service centres. The existing comprehensive one-stop shop centres vary considerably in their provision of health-related services for young people.

222 In the UK, the development of services has, necessarily, taken a different direction compared to the USA because of the substantial levels of primary care services that are already available in the UK. If further developments take place, they must do so within an overarching strategy for child health services and for drug and alcohol services. These services should augment existing services rather than compete with or duplicate them.

223 There are a number of distinct problems that require attention. Vulnerable young people with problems resulting from drug and alcohol use or misuse almost invariably have other behaviour or emotional problems and there is little or no effective co-ordination between the existing range of services for this group. The diverse range of their problems and behaviours, from truancy to child abuse, from criminality to homelessness, makes it possible for vulnerable young people to fall between services, or to be hidden from them. Add to this factors such as current attitudes of the statutory service to substance misuse in this age group, the dearth of skilled staff, the uncertainty of the effectiveness of interventions and the absence of specific commissioning and purchasing strategies, and the combined picture is a gloomy one. Nevertheless, a way forward must be identified and this should acknowledge and learn from existing difficulties. The emphasis must be on concerted action supported by an appreciation of the diversity of influences that give rise to substance misuse. This should be supported by an appreciation of the predominant factors that are hindering service development and a preparedness of staff at local levels to tackle them, though the agenda is a demanding one.

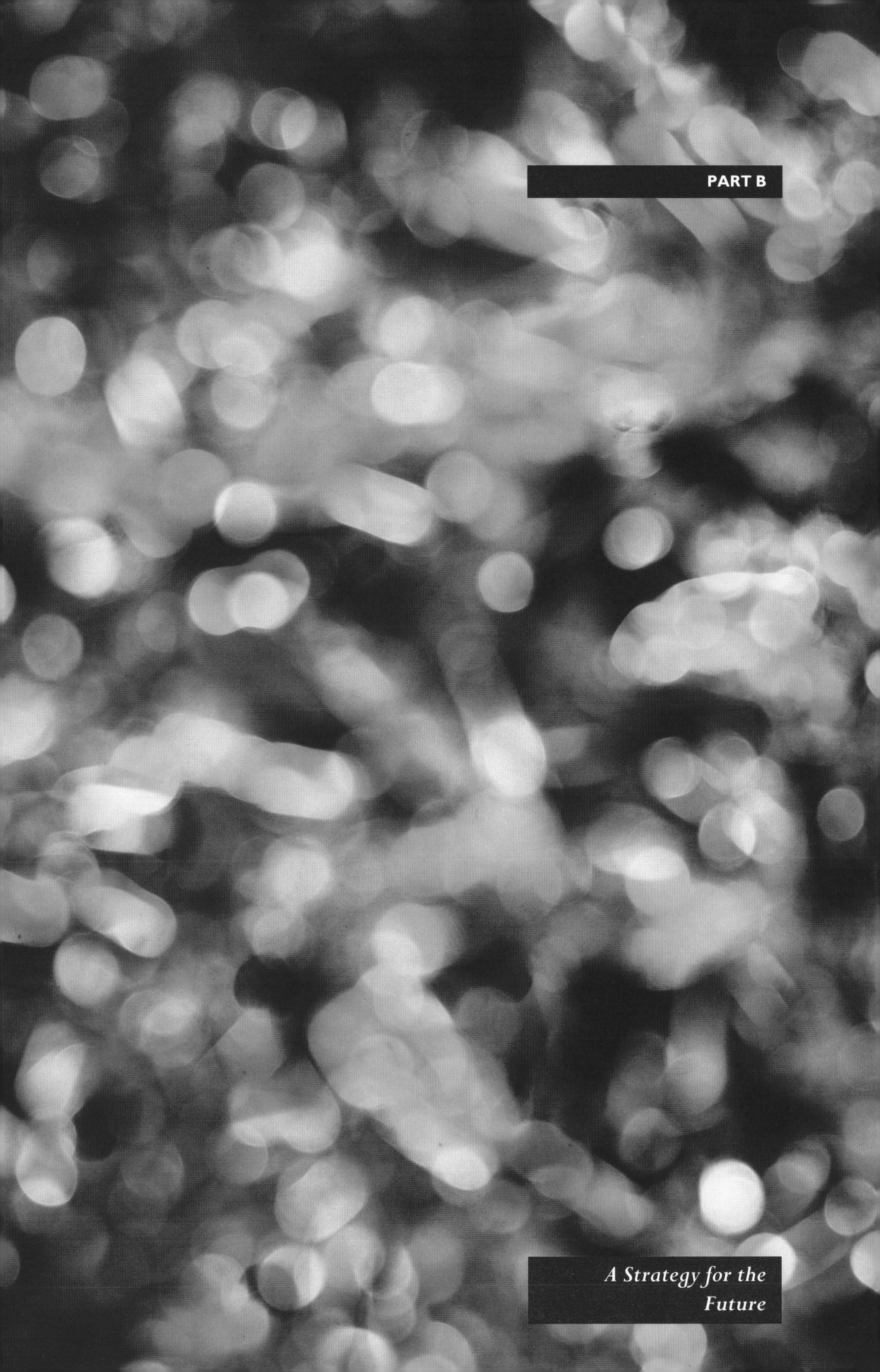

PART B

A Strategy for the Future

CHAPTER 7

A Summary of Key Concepts and Challenges

CONCEPTS

CHALLENGES

	CONCEPTS	CHALLENGES
1	Young people who use or misuse drugs or alcohol do not fall into a homogenous group.	To gain information on the nature of alcohol and substance misuse by adults and younger people who are in the area covered by each health authority, and to estimate the size of the populations involved and their locations.
	The number of female adolescents who use substances is increasing.	To identify the most vulnerable groups of children and adolescents in the local community.
	Needs assessment should identify the hidden population of younger people who do not currently present themselves or their problems to services.	
2	The problem of retaining substance users in attending services should also be appreciated and responses developed.	To provide services in user-friendly environments that are appropriate and appealing to girls and young women, and to boys and young men.
		To obtain information on the patterns of use and resources provided by services in the non-statutory sector.
3	Alcohol and substance misuse is not only an urban problem. Because of the smaller numbers of younger people involved, there is a risk of overlooking pockets of misuse in rural areas.	To gain information on patterns of use and misuse of substances by younger people in rural areas, including that by seasonal and migratory populations, such as travellers and those attending festivals and raves.
4	The rates of mental disorders in younger users and misusers of substances are higher than those of the general population matching age for age. The associated disorders may be severe. Mental disorders may be both a cause and a consequence of drug and alcohol misuse.	To undertake a needs assessment in which vulnerable groups of children and adolescents are identified. This needs assessment should be based upon a sound, comprehensive knowledge-base.
		To use this needs assessment in producing a comprehensive commissioning strategy for mental health services and other relevant health services.
5	Substance misuse is a significant problem for many homeless young people. They may have problems arising from substance misuse at the same time as a mental disorder.	To ensure that there are close operational links between mental health services, drug and alcohol advisory and misuse services and social, housing and education services.

CONCEPTS	CHALLENGES
6 Children and adolescents who misuse substances often have multiple and complex needs.	To organise services in ways which allow for full assessment of the needs of individuals.
These may arise from multiple health problems as well as from housing, social and financial difficulties.	To develop healthy alliances through multi-agency and multi-disciplinary work.
7 Young people who have problems arising from substance use or misuse do not always rank healthcare as their own top priority.	To undertake broad assessments of all young people who present to services, by whatever route, so that the different needs of vulnerable groups may be identified and responded to.
8 Younger people may need to recognise their needs for healthcare and are often resistant to messages from adults.	To provide services that actively and effectively promote healthy living and which target vulnerable groups in providing information.
9 The cultural and developmental needs of younger people differ markedly to those of adults and young children. The design and ethos of services must be appropriate to, and appreciated by younger people if they are to use them.	To provide healthcare in settings that are likely to be used by young people including one-stop shops, HIV clinics, and by employing outreach workers.
10 Many young people who misuse alcohol and drugs have contacts with the criminal justice system. Many who are looked after in some form of custodial setting also have mental health problems or disorders.	To consider, in any commissioning approach, mechanisms for diverting young people into services that provide alternatives to custody.
11 There is a strong association between substance misuse, and self-harm and suicide in younger people.	Commissioners should use the guidance provided in the HAS Report *Suicide Prevention - The Challenge Confronted* and in the *Health of the Nation Mental Illness Key Area Handbook* to decide how to actively target younger people in their endeavours to reduce suicide and deliberate self-harm.

CONCEPTS

CHALLENGES

12 Access to services is a major issue in providing all kinds of healthcare for younger people and especially for those who misuse substances. Difficulties in gaining access may be due to:
- lack of information about local health services;
- lack of a permanent address;
- inflexible appointment systems;
- the attitudes of the staff of agencies who work with people who misuse substances.

To provide some services which accept self-referrals.

To provide services which reflect the ethnic and cultural aspects of the local population.

To develop outreach services.

To provide services in settings used by young people, such as one-stop shops.

To provide training for staff on tackling the challenges of working with younger people who have problems arising from the use or misuse of substances.

13 Higher than average use is made of accident and emergency services by younger people who misuse substances. This is largely because of the problems they experience in gaining access to primary and specialist mental healthcare.

To provide, more accessible primary and specialist mental health services for children and adolescents.

To achieve formal and effective liaison between accident and emergency departments and agencies that work with vulnerable young people.

To agree guidelines that ensure that the staff of accident and emergency departments recognise and respond to the needs of vulnerable younger people, including those with problems arising from the use of misuse of substances.

To ensure that monitoring of the work of accident and emergency departments includes collecting information on younger people who attend, and who have problems arising from the use of alcohol and drugs. This should include all drug overdoses.

14 Non-statutory sector organisations are important providers of services for people who misuse substances. Often, they are an invaluable source of information about the needs of young people who use and misuse substances and about the networks of resources and agencies.

To develop healthy alliances with the non-statutory sector.

To develop mature relationships with non-statutory sector providers, and to enter into appropriate contractual partnerships that promote the continuity and stability of services.

CONCEPTS	CHALLENGES
15 Fragmentation of services impedes a holistic response to complex needs.	To organise assessment, therapy, social support and care in an integrated way, using inter-agency, multi-disciplinary approaches.
16 Collaboration between agencies, commissioning, purchasing and providing, at strategic and operational levels, will produce a more balanced and effective response to needs.	To ensure that there is maximum collaboration, at all levels, between health, social, education, housing and non-statutory sector services. To appoint lead officers in each sector who should be responsible for co-ordinating the work done across agency boundaries.
17 A shared vision is needed to ensure effective collaboration.	To gain the commitment to, and support of the members of health and local authorities, trust executive and non-executive directors and the chief officers and senior managers of these organisations for joint commissioning and joint working, where and when this is appropriate.

CHAPTER 8

A Strategic Approach to Services for Children and Adolescents Who Misuse Substances

THE KEY TO SERVICE DEVELOPMENT

224 Briefly, considerations in this report indicate that:

- at present, there is a lack of services and of service capacity;

- there is a need for the development of new services;

- the services that are developed should provide for a broad range of needs across a continuum of education, prevention, care and therapeutic interventions;

- the procurement and provision of services should be a multi-sector responsibility;

- future services should be based on harnessing together a range of components provided by a number of different host services and agencies;

- collaboration and co-ordination across agency boundaries should be key processes for commissioners, purchasers and providers.

Later chapters in this report explore these matters in greater detail.

225 These analyses also indicate how children and adolescents who are in need of services have fallen between the existing services. Chiefly, these are those services provided by the non-statutory sector and by the social services departments and by the NHS (child and adolescent mental health services, drug and alcohol services, forensic mental health services, paediatric and child health services, and community and hospital mental health services for adults).

226 These considerations also suggest that there are a range of alternatives open to commissioners and providers, now empowered by *Tackling Drugs Together,* and the Welsh Office consultation document *Forward Together* (1995) and the policy that will arise from this, in due course, who intend to improve provision for younger people. These include:

- creating completely new services;

- bringing together existing services, but in new ways;

- allocating lead responsibility to one existing service or agency, but with the requirement for collaboration with other services.

227 Current circumstances facing commissioners and providers suggest that all three mechanisms will be used in differing combinations that reflect the local circumstances.

228 Choice of service philosophy and design is the key to service development. These matters are important base-line considerations in avoiding unclear foundations for services and cannot be left solely to motivated, pioneering clinicians. There is an urgent need for ownership of these matters at commissioning agency level. Service development should be based on an overarching strategic concept which will serve to create a direction for local services, enable purchasers to contract within a clear framework, harness local effort and hold together the components of the service overall that are provided by different agencies and weld them into one enterprise.

229 This strategy should also act as a template that has validity, and can be used at a variety of levels by key people, including:

- chairs of local authority committees, health authorities and NHS trusts;

- chief executives of health commissions and NHS trusts;

- chief officers of local authority services and non-statutory sector agencies;

- members of boards and committees;

- drug action teams and drug and alcohol action teams;

- commissioning and purchasing managers;

- provider managers;

- front-line practitioners.

230 So a successful strategy will:

- hold and convey a concept for the service overall;

- clarify the intention, role and target client groups for the service;

- recognise the multi-sectoral, multi-focal and multi-disciplinary nature of good services;

- be capable of use by agencies acting together as a tool in joint commissioning and joint provision;

- enable purchasers, including GP fundholders, to conduct their roles within a negotiated framework;

- enable individual commissioners and providers to understand their own, single agency roles and responsibilities and use their powers to act to achieve these;

- provide a basis for collaboration between agencies and co-ordination between service elements, components and staff.

DEVELOPING A STRATEGIC APPROACH

231 Development of such a strategy locally demands the co-operation of a number of statutory agencies as key partners including commissioners, purchasers and the provider agencies. The creation of a strategy is a signal achievement in itself but success can only be judged in the improved delivery of services to the identified client group. Nonetheless, service delivery should be led by strategy and the execution of well-informed commissioning and purchasing processes that are described with reference to substance misuse services in Part C.

232 In *Together We Stand,* the HAS put forward a strategic, four-tier approach that satisfies many of the requirements listed above. This has proved to be very successful and popular with the NHS locally, as well as with local authorities, criminal justice and non-statutory sector agencies, where it is regarded as the basis for understanding the intent and roles of their services and as a tool in service review and re-design. Therefore, the HAS has developed this model further to encompass services for children and adolescents who use and misuse substances.

233 Adapted, extended and developed for substance use and misuse services, the four tiers of the CAMHS model remain appropriate and much that appears in chapter eight of *Together We Stand* can be applied to the services that are the subject of this report. The following paragraphs provide an outline of the nature and roles of the tiers as each applies to services for children and adolescents who use and/or misuse substances.

234 Readers are referred to Figure 10 on page 63 of *Together We Stand.* That schematic diagram summarises the four tier model proposed for child and adolescent mental health services.

235 Here, Figure two provides a schematic diagram that summarises the four-tiered service proposed for drug and alcohol services for young people. As with all schemata, it has its drawbacks. Many professionals, teams and different service agencies will overlap and interact within a concept of service organised in this strategic manner.

Figure 2

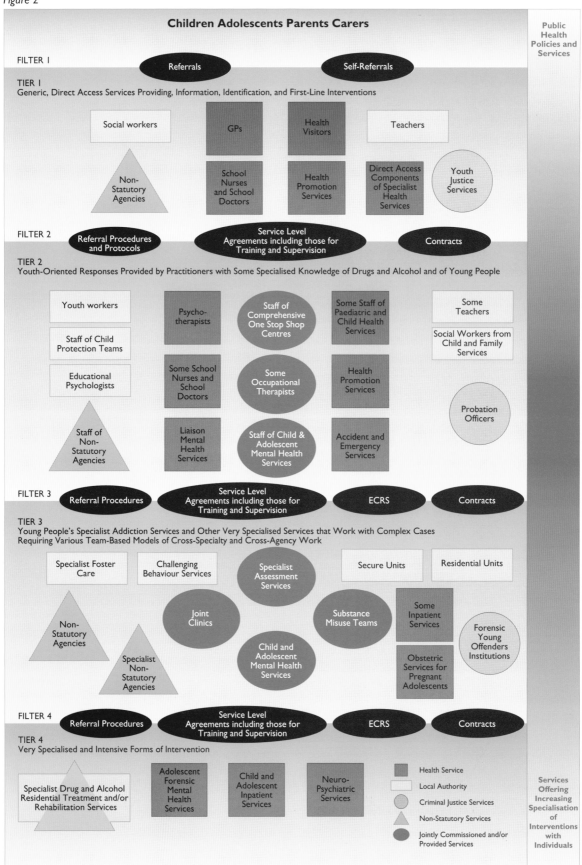

A FOUR TIER MODEL FOR SUBSTANCE USE AND MISUSE SERVICES FOR CHILDREN AND ADOLESCENTS

Tier 1 - Primary and Direct Access Services

236 Essentially, Tier 1 services are those which are accessible directly by the general public and which provide a first response to the needs of children and adolescents. They include education, preventive work and treatment. They comprise primary care workers such as general practitioners and health visitors, the staff of many non-statutory organisations, social workers, police officers and school medical officers. These services consist of professionals and other staff who are not necessarily employed for the sole purpose of informing or intervening with young people who are at risk of drug use or misuse or of promoting their mental health but who directly or indirectly influence these aspects of their lives.

237 The major contribution of Tier 1 service components includes the provision of information and advice in uncomplicated situations and the conduct of initial assessments of personal need. These service components are very important in the recognition and identification of drug or alcohol use and misuse which is causing problems, particularly in individuals who are not overtly seeking treatment. They are also important in providing advice and information to parents and schools. Staff at Tier 1 should consider the accessibility and appropriateness of their service to young people with problems related to drugs and alcohol. Direct access is an important principle as are issues of confidentiality and consent to treatment. Knowledge of the appropriate referral procedures and protocols and of the specialist agencies is very important. Some staff who offer Tier 1 services may also continue to play significant roles in the shared care of children and adolescents after their referral to more specialised service components in Tiers 2, 3 and 4. EL (95) 114 considers shared care arrangements for drug misusers and details the Department of Health's view of shared care and its relationship to the provision of General Medical Services.

Key tasks

- Promoting access to services

- Providing a range of accessible and approachable environments

- Providing information, advice and support

- Assessing levels of drug and alcohol use, including substance use in children and adolescents who are not presenting overtly for treatment

- Assessing associated or linked problems

- Assessing other vulnerabilities

- Assessing the urgency of problems and taking appropriate action

- Offering crisis management

- Giving appropriate initial counselling

- Making appropriate referrals

- Playing a continuing role, when appropriate, in the shared care of their patients after referring them to more specialised services.

**Tier 2 - Youth-Orientated Services Provided by Individual
Practitioners Who Have Some Specialist Knowledge of Drugs
and Alcohol**

238 The staff of this tier should have in common: an understanding of child and
adolescent development; knowledge of substances and of substance use
and misuse by young people; and the ability to practice in circumstances
that are appropriate to the culture of children and adolescents. Staff in Tier
2 will have had training to conduct their tasks. Chief components of the
services offered should be: the provision of accurate information and
advice; assessment of needs; identification of problems directly related to
substance use and misuse and of other problematic behaviours; provision
of advice and information to carers and families; and the capacity to work
alongside and with the involvement of other appropriate agencies.

239 Direct access to appropriate and acceptable services is essential. Many
young people who misuse alcohol and/or drugs may have other
problematic behaviour and be reluctant to seek help from conventional
services. Therefore, many Tier 2 and 3 services will need to provide a direct
access or Tier 1 component as a portal of entry. Imaginative outreach work
in settings used by such young people could help to identify their needs and
ensure that relevant information and advice on risk-taking and available
services is communicated effectively.

240 Professionals in this group include: primary care workers with a special
interest in drugs and alcohol; certain specially trained staff of adolescent
clinics and paediatric and child health services; the staff of youth services;
the staff of child and adolescent mental health services; educational
psychologists; the staff of comprehensive centres/one stop shops, health
promotion services; and professionals in the youth justice system.

Key tasks

- The ability to respond to the key tasks of Tier 1
  and

- The capacity to assess individuals for referral to more specialised
  services

- The capacity to offer co-working with specialist agencies

- The capacity to decide when Tier 3 and Tier 4 styles of intervention
  are required

- Provision of training and role support to staff in Tier 1

- Providing counselling about use and misuse

- Providing support to carers and parents

- The capacity to offer assertive outreach

**Tier 3 - Interventions Offered by Specialist Agencies in which
Staff Work Together in Teams**

241 Tier 3 consists of components of the overall service that are more
specialised, often by virtue of the complexity of problems presenting to
them. In this tier, staff, possibly from a range of agencies or occasionally
from within a single agency, work together and co-ordinate their work in
teams to fully assess and intervene with each child or adolescent. The

agencies involved will be generally youth-orientated specialist addictions services, either statutory or non-statutory, that have the capacity to work with child and adolescent mental health and other specialist youth services. Presently, cross-agency work of this kind is poorly developed for drug and alcohol problems in children and adolescents. There are a variety of models of cross-agency working but these models need to be evaluated.

242 One of the key properties of specialist agencies is that they have the capacity to assess both the drug and alcohol use and misuse of individuals alongside their other problematic behaviours. Because of the nature of the problems experienced by children and adolescents and the need to improve the accessibility and appropriateness of services overall, many agencies that offer Tier 3 interventions will also provide outreach services that offer Tier 1 facilities and direct access to those who need them. In this circumstance, some specialised agencies may offer services concurrently to differing populations of children and adolescents and work at Tiers 1, 2 and 3. Recognition of the important roles of each of these tiers is important as is the need for each agency to be critically aware of the services it provides in each Tier as a contribution to the planning of services overall.

243 A wide range of interventions including individual counselling and psychotherapy, infectious disease advice, substitute prescribing and detoxification, work alongside the education services, family assessment and therapy are all important at Tier 3. Services should work within the child protection guidelines. Effective leadership within provider agencies is necessary to ensure that appropriate services are provided and co-ordinated.

Key tasks

- The ability to respond to the key tasks of Tier 1
  and

- The ability to respond to the key tasks of Tier 2
  and

- Provision of specialised services based on multi-disciplinary team working

- Co-working across agency boundaries

- Provision of training and role support for practitioners in Tiers 2 and 1

- The capacity to assess individuals for inpatient or residential interventions and other Tier 4 services and refer, as appropriate

Tier 4 - Very Specialised Care and Interventions

244 This tier provides for intervention with individuals who have highly specific and complex problems that require considerable resources. These include services that offer: inpatient detoxification, withdrawal regimes for certain younger people who misuse substances and are in complex personal circumstances, and intensive treatments for specific substance use disorders; care and treatment of children and adolescents in secure provision; highly specialised clinics for young people who have significant problems arising from two or more co-morbid disorders; and a range of specialist rehabilitation services.

245 Services such as these are required occasionally by the population of a district and the call on them may not always be predictable, especially in smaller districts. However, they are essential and need considerable planning.

246 A typical complex case in which Tier 4 service components may be required is that of a 15 year-old adolescent with heroin dependence, who is pregnant, truanting from school, committing offences and who comes from a family in which there is significant dysfunction that is compounding her other difficulties.

247 Highly specialised, Tier 4 services present a challenge to individual commissioners and purchasers in maintaining the availability of supply in the face of uncertain variations in demands and need. Therefore, it is recommended that districts should work together to apply the full commissioning process to these services. In the future, mergers of districts into larger commissions may help to resolve some of these problems.

CHALLENGES TO EFFECTIVE FUNCTIONING

248 There are further challenges that must be understood if this four-tier strategic framework is to be helpful in developing comprehensive child and adolescent mental health services.

- Children, young people and families may not come to services in the way that the theoretical framework suggests. Examples of this may be:

  - becoming 'stuck' in primary care settings through inability to gain access to appropriate specialised services or failure by the staff of direct access services to recognise need;

  - making first contacts with social service departments;

  - making first contacts through the accident and emergency services;

  - making first contacts via the criminal justice system.

- Most commissioners are faced with an existing profile of services. If they wish to move towards a different composition of service, they may need to develop a strategy for disinvestment and reinvestment. This may be achieved by:

  - strategic use of bridging finance;

  - investment in training to develop the required skill mix;

  - estate management, if locations are to change;

  - facilitating the development of non-statutory services.

- In recent years, the Department of Health and the Welsh Office have stressed the importance of specialist mental health services adopting a focus on people with more severe disorders. At the same time, services are being encouraged towards becoming primary care-led. Consequently, there is an increasing accent on the provision of specialist services for people with serious disorders alongside primary care services in the community. Historically, the focus of child and adolescent mental health services has always been towards community services. Commissioners, purchasers and providers should consider similarly the balance of their allocation of resources to comprehensive services for children and adolescents who misuse substances in order to provide:

-   prevention;

-   recognition of, and intervention with children with more minor problems relating to alcohol and substance misuse;

-   recognition and management of children and adolescents who have more serious problems of misuse and addiction;

-   consultation and liaison services;

-   training and research.

A balanced service will include the capacity to respond to all these demands. In practice, the allocation of staff time and expertise to each of these endeavours should be monitored and actively managed to ensure that resource, where limited, is most effectively and appropriately used. This calls for local discussion and agreement between commissioners, purchasers and providers.

249 These challenges require a flexible framework developed through local networks. Co-ordination of the commissioners from the range of statutory agencies is essential if the contributions of the providers of the differing elements of the service and those from different agencies are to be understood and integrated within the overall framework.

PART C

Commissioning and Purchasing Services for Children and Adolescents

Commissioning Services
for Children and
Adolescents Who Misuse
Substances

COMMISSIONING, PURCHASING AND CONTRACTING

250 There is a tendency to use these words interchangeably. The guideline document, *Purchasing for Health,* (NHS Management Executive 1993) refers generically to the term purchasing. In this review, commissioning is the umbrella term, emphasising strategy. We take it to mean a strategically driven process by which purchasers (health authorities, GP fundholders, social services departments, schools and education departments and probation services) provide services for their local population. *Purchasing* refers to the various technical procedures carried out by purchasers to secure and monitor the services they are buying from providers. *Contracting,* a sub-division of purchasing, is the process by which services are purchased and the nature and level of services to be provided are formally agreed. In effect, commissioning encompasses purchasing and contracting and also implies a greater range of tasks because it is led by strategy and involves attempts to monitor, define and manage the market, thus creating a circular process.

251 Since the NHS and Community Care Act 1990, there has been a dynamic force in the system responsible for moving the *purchasing* of healthcare as close to the patients as possible. This has lead to organisations such as health authorities, family health service authorities (FHSAs) and GP fundholders experiencing shifts in the scope of their role as both *commissioners* and *purchasers.* EL(94)79 *Towards a Primary Care-Led NHS,* sets out an agenda that sees new health authorities, an amalgamation of the old health authorities and FHSAs, taking the responsibility for *commissioning* at a strategic level, informed by the public and the providers (including GPs), while increasing the direct responsibility of GP fundholders as *purchasers.* The change process attributable to this initiative means that in the future, health authorities will act primarily as the commissioners, while retaining some direct purchasing (increasingly of more specialised services), and GP fundholders will act as major direct purchasers while retaining the role of informing commissioning decisions. In order to accommodate this change process, the thematic review uses the terms commissioning and purchasing to describe the functions rather than to prescribe them to any one agency.

252 It is also important to recognise the differences of approach that are being taken, generally, by local and health authorities. The former, with conspicuous responsibilities for care management, are required to purchase packages of care for individuals, while health authorities buy sectors of care for populations. One result of this difference is that the assessment of individuals is, at least in part, a purchasing role in the case of local authorities, while it lies, almost entirely, within the provider province in the NHS.

253 Health authorities are being urged to move away from the extra-contractual referral (ECR) of individual or small numbers of cases. This involves a variety of techniques, including consortium and lead purchasing or the delegation of established ECR budgets to providers, with the intention of redistributing the financial risks. Despite these differences in approach, which must be surmounted through jointly agreed strategies and priorities and through the co-ordination of care for individuals, local authorities and, health purchasers are being encouraged towards joint commissioning. This chapter is concerned with elaborating an idealised cycle of events for commissioners and then interpreting these in relationship to the particular requirements of young people who misuse substances.

KEY PRINCIPLES OF EFFECTIVE COMMISSIONING

254 The work of the HAS on commissioning mental health services suggests an idealised approach. This has been applied to a range of services for different client groups by the HAS in its series of thematic reviews. Consequent testing of this idealised model has led to refinements and these are reflected in Figures 3 and 4.

255 The model begins with the formulation of outline strategic statements that indicate the client group and its size, the broad nature of its problems, and the general intention of the strategy and its outcomes. This triggers subsequent activity, including the stages of needs assessment and determination of priorities, that proceeds towards developing more detailed service specifications and consideration of the targets for monitoring and evaluation.

Figure 3

An Idealised Approach to Commissioning Mental Health Services

256 As Figure 3 indicates, this is a dynamic circular process that may take more than one year to complete satisfactorily. Thus, year on year, this strategic approach should build up and lead to the refinement of comprehensive commissioning plans.

257 It is important that everyone concerned operates to agreed criteria, and that definitions for recording data and providing services are complementary. One example could be for a range of agencies to agree to adopt the same definitions of substance use and misuse.

258 Ideally, the route from an outline to a more detailed strategy passes through a number of stages. Determining priorities is a key and demanding issue in this process. Health needs assessment should lead to consideration of the clinical realities, health gain issues, and user and carer opinions in coming to a balanced perspective on realistic goals for local services. This should enable the goals set for local services to reflect awareness of the existing capabilities and capacities of existing services, which have been clarified by mapping local resources. This background information should make priorities for current service purchasing and future developments easier to agree and better understood by commissioners, purchasers and providers resulting in a realistic and challenging strategy. This process is summarised by Figure 4.

Figure 4

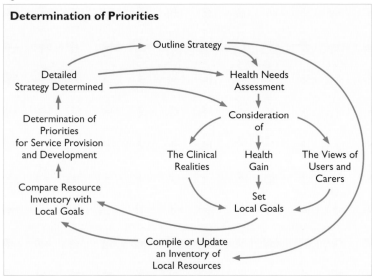

Determination of Priorities

259 A useful guide to the process of effective commissioning is set out in *Purchasing for Health* (NHSME, 1992). In relation to commissioning substance misuse services for children and adolescents, the fieldwork conducted by the HAS indicates that the following principles apply with particular force.

- It is essential that those agencies that are responsible for commissioning and purchasing services for children and adolescents who misuse substances should base their approaches on a jointly agreed strategy.

- In order to enable the development of an effective commissioning approach, commissioners and purchasers must have sound knowledge of the requirements of children and adolescents who misuse substances and of the effectiveness of potential interventions.

- Commissioners must be responsive to the needs of their local population if an effective climate for the strategic development of services for children and adolescents is to be achieved.

- The development of services for children and adolescents with problems arising from substance misuse, will be improved by mature relationships between commissioners, purchasers and service providers.

- Commissioners should collaborate with other commissioners and organisations to form healthy alliances. This will promote consistent policy, aimed at providing integrated prevention and treatment services for children and adolescents, particularly for vulnerable young people.

- In order to develop an effective commissioning approach to services for this group, the commissioning authorities must have the appropriate organisational capability.

- In order to achieve the defined strategic goals, purchasing agencies (increasingly GP, fundholders, SSDs, and local schools) must hold effective contracts with providers. These should specify proper monitoring procedures.

260 The Department of Health's *Practical Guidance on Joint Commissioning for Project Leaders 1995*, and the shorter accompanying *Introduction to Joint Commissioning 1995*, provide the strongest possible encouragement to this approach, describing it as *"both an overarching strategic activity and at the same time a problem-solving tool"*. It is an approach which also integrates the strategy processes of development and needs assessment, thereby providing a holistic picture of need that is unfettered by organisational boundaries. This will provide a more substantial basis for discussions between statutory and non-statutory agencies about services to be purchased and the co-ordination of efforts in developing networks of care.

261 Joint commissioning has considerable relevance to services for children and families generally. It can overcome organisational barriers between social, education, housing, and health services and other agencies, including the criminal justice system. The need for improved collaboration was one of the most important themes in *Together We Stand.*

262 Guidance about the joint commissioning of services for children and adolescents is provided in *Together We Stand* and chapter 18 in *Suicide Prevention,* considers the implications of deliberate self-harm for commissioners and contractual styles between statutory authorities and non-statutory providers of services.

COMMISSIONING SERVICES FOR CHILDREN AND ADOLESCENTS WHO MISUSE SUBSTANCES

263 The HAS recommends that readers should consider the Government's White Paper *Tackling Drugs Together,* and the Welsh Office consultation document *Forward Together* when seeking to turn the principles set out in *Purchasing for Health* into a commissioning action plan for services for children and adolescents who misuse substances.

264 Specific guidance to commissioners who function independently, or under the auspices of a Drug Action Team or, in Wales, a Drug and Alcohol Action Team, is provided in this section and draws on each of the principles outlined in the previous section.

265 Drug Action Teams and Drug and Alcohol Action Teams may wish to draw on the experience of both the NHS and local authorities since the implementation of the NHS and Community Care Act 1990, in considering their development of a strategic commissioning approach. Statutory authorities have had different but complementary experiences since this Act came into force, and the view of the HAS is that pooling this experience is of particular relevance to improving services for children and adolescents.

Strategy

266 It is essential that authorities that are responsible for commissioning substance misuse services for children and adolescents base their approach on a jointly agreed strategic framework. They should:

- build, wherever possible, on existing advisory machinery and previous strategy;

- align their strategic framework with their broader strategies for both child and adolescent mental health services and for substance misuse services for adults;

- include a balance of educational, preventive and treatment-orientated approaches in their strategic framework;

- ensure that the strategic framework is agreed and owned by all potential agencies that have commissioning and purchasing responsibilities, thereby recognising their interdependence in producing an effective system of care;

- identify and prioritise in the strategic framework the high risk groups (eg, intravenous drug users, pregnant drug users and users with a high risk of suicide).

Developing the Knowledge-Base

267 Commissioners and purchasers must have sound knowledge of the requirements of children and adolescents with problems arising from substance use and misuse, and the effectiveness of potential interventions.

268 The information required to develop such a sound knowledge-base falls into a number of different categories. These include: the definitions of use and misuse adopted by different agencies; the nature and extent of alcohol and substance misuse in the district; the nature, capabilities and capacities of the non-statutory service providers; and the effectiveness of local services.

269 A sound knowledge base may be gained through:

- consultation with non-statutory alcohol and drug agencies on the number of their clients, their patterns of use and misuse, and the nature of the services that they offer;

- information gathering from schools, social services departments, youth justice services, the probation service and the police;

- consultation with community organisations, including any that work within differing ethnic communities;

- understanding the various definitions of use and misuse among local agencies and estimating the way in which these definitions affect both the process of needs assessment and the perceptions of people requiring help;

- awareness of the clinical and social effectiveness of particular services and methods of education, prevention and intervention, that have been conducted locally as well as nationally;

- reviewing research literature from organisations such as the Institute of Substance and Drug Dependency (ISDD), Alcohol Concern, the Standing Conference on Drug Abuse (SCODA) and any academic institutions with an interest in addictions.

Responsiveness to the Local Population

270 Commissioners should be responsive to the needs of their local population in achieving an effective climate for developing there strategies and services. They should be aware of the following matters and respond appropriately.

- The baseline of public understanding and empathy may be low in this field. Commissioners may choose to invest in, or support the national public education initiatives to counter this.

- There may be a difference of views between users and carers in this field. Each voice needs to be recognised.

- Carers (usually parents) form a distinct constituency which requires services designed to meet its needs, in addition to those of their children.

- The role of the local media is significant in this field. Its contribution can be unhelpful, for example by stigmatising individuals, organisations, including schools, or whole localities, or it can be helpful, for example by aiding the public education process. Wherever possible, authorities should try to nuture this more positive approach by maintaining regular contact through briefings and press releases.

- Building contacts with different ethnic groups in the community may well be a slow and sensitive process. It is essential to work towards trusting relationships with the accepted leaders of the different cultural groups, and to be aware of the dangers of racial or cultural stereotyping.

- The user population may be transient, especially in inner city areas. For difficult and high-risk individuals, liaison across geographic boundaries may be essential if services are to be targeted effectively on very vulnerable younger people.

Partnerships with Providers

271 The development of services for children and adolescents with problems arising from substance misuse depend on the maturity of relationships between commissioners, purchasers and service providers.

272 The following issues are particularly significant in this field.

- There are a wide variety of providers in this field which may result in individual services having infrequent contacts with a small number of cases. Equally, there are many individual GP fundholders who are likely to have infrequent contact with younger people who misuse substances. Steps should be taken to ensure that this unfamiliarity does not jeopardise individual care or threaten monitoring of quality.

- There are three kinds of fundholding. GPs may be *total* fundholders; *standard* fundholders with year on year budgets, in line with the original concept; or the more minimal *community* fundholders, where groups of practices combine to form consortia. All of them have powers in buying elements of services for young people.

- A number of providers may be in the non-statutory sector. The organisational culture of these agencies may be different to that of the statutory sector. Purchasers should endeavour to understand these differences in order to maximise their contribution to the care of this group of young people.

- There may be different providers or trusts offering different elements of substance misuse services to children and adolescents. Commissioners should lead by creating a climate in which all providers operate together in the interests of young people through effective co-ordination of their contributions to an overarching service.

- Drug Reference Groups, as proposed in *Tackling Drugs Together,* or Local Advisory Teams, as suggested in *Forward Together*, may prove to be a valuable forum for promoting mature and responsible discussion on the commissioning and provision of services.

- Appropriate sharing of information is enabled by mature organisational relationships. In this setting, providers should not be burdened by requests for information for which they may not be able to see the relevance.

Healthy Alliances

273 Commissioning authorities should work together with other commissioners and organisations. Such alliances will promote consistent policies aimed at providing integrated prevention and treatment services for children and adolescents with problems arising from substance misuse.

274 This statement has the following matters among its implications.

- This field is particularly appropriate to joint commissioning. Key commissioners are: health authorities; social service departments; education departments; schools; GP fundholders; probation services and other criminal justice agencies.

- A prevention strategy will require effective healthy alliances. Health and social services will require good relationships with:

    - the youth services (for example, for alternative activities to substance use, and education, and counselling);

    - the leisure services (for example, for alternative activities to substance use);

    - housing departments (for example, for resolution of problems of homelessness and those of leaving care);

    - the prison service (for example, for education, and counselling).

Effectiveness through Contracting

275 Commissioning agencies and service purchasers should agree effective contracts with providers which include monitoring procedures. This means that:

- contracts with non-statutory providers should be based within a robust contracting framework to maximise the contribution of providers (that is, they should be longer-term, three-to five-year agreements which contain negotiated and realistic performance monitoring procedures);

- contracts should be based, wherever possible, on mainstream funding, thus recognising the need to convert short-term and pump-priming finance into robust financial arrangements;

- appropriate contract currencies that recognise the direct service needs of individuals, the needs of generic staff for role support and consultancy, and the importance of training, research and prevention;

- where necessary, commissioners should collaborate on purchasing highly specialised services for children and adolescents who misuse substances. This should offer an effective system of quality control and be capable of sustaining high-cost, low-volume, highly specialised services;

- within the context of the present very low baseline of dedicated specialised, particularly Tier 3 and Tier 4, services, it is important for purchasers to establish contracts that recognise the roles of services that are not specifically dedicated to meeting the needs of children and adolescents who misuse substances but which are used for this purpose.

Organisational Fitness

276 In order to develop an effective commissioning approach for services for children and adolescents who misuse substances, the commissioning authorities must have the appropriate organisational capability.

277 In this respect, commissioners may find it helpful to ask themselves a number of questions.

- Who in the authority has any knowledge of this field?

- Is the organisation aware of its responsibilities as set out in *Tackling Drugs Together* or *Forward Together*?

- How great is the organisational divide between alcohol and drug misuse services and between the statutory and the non-statutory sectors?

- How senior are the people who have commissioning and purchasing responsibilities for services in this field and what ownership do the authorities have for younger people in need?

- Is the authority showing, or responding to leadership in addressing the issue of substance use and misuse by children and adolescents?

- Are services for children and adolescents who use and misuse substances lost in the organisational structure, for example, between children's and mental health services?

- Is the authority clear as to whether this is a health promotion issue or one of service provision or both?

- Can the authority identify the resource, if any, it is investing currently in services for children and adolescents who misuse substances, either directly or indirectly?

CONTRACTING WITH NON-STATUTORY SECTOR PROVIDERS

278 This is an important issue. Many of the existing services for children and adolescents who use and misuse substances are found by the non-statutory agencies.

279 The HAS, in its earlier thematic review on *Suicide Prevention - The Challenge Confronted* - paid particular attention to the role of non-statutory provider agencies. The authors acknowledged that *"contractual relationships with these organisations are often ill-defined and open to the vagaries of the local financial situation."* They continue to say *"Commissioners should, however, recognise the effectiveness (and cost-effectiveness) of these services and should reflect this in their approach to contracting with them by seeking to secure more permanent and focused relationships with the non-statutory sector."*

280 Comments of this nature were reiterated in the HAS report, *A Place in Mind* (1995) on commissioning and providing mental health services for people who are homeless. They are seen as applying equally to the operation of agencies providing services for people who misuse substances.

281 The main reasons that statutory sector commissioners enter into contractual partnerships with non-statutory organisations include:

- broadening the range of services;

- offering greater cultural diversity of service provision;

- improving the access to services of hard-to-reach groups;

- creating a plural market within which a number of providers can contribute specific elements of care, but in a well co-ordinated way;

- developing and testing effective and cost-effective interventions;

- providing scope for evaluating the effectiveness of services that allow comparisons across a range of provider agencies.

282 Given the present marginal nature of services, there is now a particularly strong case for entering into discrete contracts for drug and alcohol services for children and adolescents, rather than allowing them to continue to be subsumed into general mental health services. This would also accelerate their identification and development. It is also recommended that there should be specific contracts which distinguish between the services for adults and those for younger people who use and misuse substances. Currently, there are no such specific contracts known to the HAS. Discrete contracts would have an advantage in making it easier to set relevant quality standards that reflect the different cultural position and needs of younger people. Excellent examples of standards appropriate to services for people who misuse substances can be found in *Quality in Alcohol Services; Minimum Standards for Good Practice and General Principles of Good Practice* (Alcohol Concern, 1992) and the paper *Standard Setting and Audit* (Standing Conference on Drug Abuse).

283 Problems are also posed by the need to commission and contract with services that are provided out of the district. They tend to deal with a small number of cases and to be of high cost, due to their degree of specialisation. Generally, places are purchased on the basis of ECRs. This renders these services subject to disputes between agencies over who should pay for places. Additionally, lack of long-term commitments in principle and/or by contract to the longer-term use of the services puts them into an unpredictable position and thereby makes the maintenance of these very specialised services vulnerable. A high risk is that loss of a service could well be accompanied by loss of skills through dissemination of key staff and failure to achieve a critical mass of expertise and experience. These out-of-district, high-cost services require the same rigorous commissioning, including monitoring and evaluation, as other more local high-volume services.

284 Again, issues of this kind are dealt with in *Together We Stand* and they support the need to create an overarching strategic framework within which services for children and adolescents who misuse substances are commissioned and purchased. This adds weight to the recommendations that a tiered approach to conceptualising service design be adopted.

A SUMMARY OF KEY ISSUES FOR THE COMMISSIONERS OF SERVICES

285 Commissioners should:

- monitor trends in the use of alcohol and substances by children and adolescents;

- agree and implement a district-wide strategy that is agreed with the commissioners from other sectors of care and the appropriate purchasers of services;

- devise and implement a strategy specifically orientated to the needs of young people who use drugs and/or alcohol or who have problems arising from their use;

- ensure that contracts for services for children and adolescents stipulate that an appropriate environment is provided;

- promote the development of services that are appropriate to the needs of all young people, including young women and young people from ethnic minority cultures and backgrounds;

- promote comprehensive and intensive early intervention projects eg. parents skills training, and *Help Starts Here,* and *Head Start programmes;*

- ensure that all services are evaluated.

CHAPTER 10

*A Commissioning Action
Plan*

INTRODUCTION

286 Increasingly commissioners are faced with the need to respond to a wide ranging set of priorities and demands. In 1996-97, health authorities in England are required by the *Planning and Priorities Guidance* from the NHS Executive to develop, in partnership with local authorities and fundholding GPs, a purchasing plan/strategy for child and adolescent mental health services. They are also charged with the responsibility to establish local Drug Action Teams which have a clear remit to develop local strategies designed to provide a range of local prevention and treatment options, including those which focus on young people. Local authorities are also charged to develop local *Children's Service Plans* which are likely to include reference to local authority services/resources targeted at young people who have drug and alcohol problems. The consequences of these requirements are as follows:

- there is now an obvious and timely opportunity to review local services and to apply the knowledge of effective practice (purchasing and providing) derived as a consequence of this review;

- there is a need to ensure that local initiatives are co-ordinated and that service users are presented with a single vision of local services leading to an effective and coherent profile of services;

- there will be a need to support commissioners in undertaking these tasks and in that regard a set of steps by which they can address these issues might be helpful.

287 Local commissioners might employ the five following action steps to respond to these requirements. These could serve to shape the local agenda for Drug Action Teams or Drug and Alcohol Action Teams (in Wales) and joint child and adolescent mental health service commissioning initiatives.

Table 10

Action Steps
1 Ensuring a co-ordinated multi-agency approach to services for children and adolescents who use and misuse substances
2 Service mapping and audit
3 Assessment of need
4 Service planning and development of a strategic approach
5 Consolidation and review by use of mature contracts (particularly for non-statutory providers)

1. ENSURING A CO-ORDINATED MULTI-AGENCY APPROACH TO SERVICES FOR CHILDREN AND ADOLESCENTS WHO MISUSE SUBSTANCES

Activity

This is designed to ensure that all the key agencies with a role in the commissioning of these services are linked to facilitate effective joint working and that separate planning initiatives and requirements are co-ordinated.

Key Questions

- Is there dialogue with all funding or commissioning agencies?

- Is this dialogue occurring at the right level of seniority in each organisation?

- Are the chief officers aware of and supportive of this dialogue?

- Has any joint resource for the benefit of the patients, clients or users of these services been identified and is it being deployed effectively on a basis of consultation with all commissioners?

- Is there a forum which includes all partner agencies in addition to any bilateral meetings?

- Is the Drug Action Team or Drug and Alcohol Action Team linked into health authority and local authority planning for child and adolescent mental health services?

- Are GPs and GP fundholders contributing to both of these planning frameworks?

- Has agreement been reached on who is leading or co-ordinating activity on substance misuse services for children and adolescents?

- Do the current relationships provide a strong enough base to facilitate joint approaches to service audit, planning, contracting and evaluation?

2. SERVICE MAPPING AND AUDIT

Activity

This is designed to create an inventory of the nature and extent of all services for children and adolescents who use and misuse substances within the district. This should include statutory and non-statutory providers and the provision purchased or funded by partner agencies.

Key Questions

- What do we currently purchase?

- What, if any, dedicated services for children and adolescents who misuse substances provision do we purchase?

- How much does it cost?

- What is purchased by others?

- Are there gaps and overlaps?

- Are these services financially and professionally secure?

- Do we have useful information from these services?

- How does the provision in total compare to estimates of service requirement based on our assessment of need and identified goals?

- What local initiatives aimed at preventing substance misuse problems are there?

3. ASSESSMENT OF NEED

Activity

This is designed to estimate the level of provision required to satisfy the needs of the population regarding problems arising for children and adolescents from their use or misuse of substances.

Key Questions

- Do we have a common language between agencies which facilitates the identification of need?

- Have agencies agreed a common definition of substance use and misuse?

- Is there local agreement on approaches to harm-reduction and risk-management?

- Can we identify problems on a scale that is relevant for commissioning purposes?

- What is our position on out-of-district services? Is this shared?

- Have clients, users and carers been fully involved in the assessment of need?

- What scope do we have for prevention of problems related to substance misuse?

4.   SERVICE PLANNING AND DEVELOPMENT OF A STRATEGIC APPROACH

Activity

This activity, which may be continuous, is designed to obtain agreement to the development of services within a strategic framework. This may not necessarily be explicit but must be understood by all purchasers.

Key Questions

- Do we have an agreed understanding of the short-term actions required by each agency and an agreed sense of the long-term direction?

- Do these include target groups and targets for identifying or increasing spend on services for children and adolescents who use or misuse substances?

- Are our plans capable of responding flexibly to changes?

- Do our investment plans enable us to respond flexibly to change?

- Can we evaluate and assess any progress made?

- Which parts of our strategic approach might usefully be published and shared with providers and other agencies (eg, the Courts of Law through Courts Users' Committees)?

- How does the strategic approach fit with the Children's Service Plans; CAMHS Purchasing Plans; the strategies of the Drug Action Team and the Code of Practice for the Education Act 1993?

5. CONSOLIDATION AND REVIEW BY USE OF MATURE CONTRACTS

Activity

This is designed to review the current contracting position for substance misuse services for children and adolescents and to produce a contracting framework to secure changes in the network of service provision negotiated through the wider commissioning process. In this approach, contracts are not the goal of commissioning, but are used as a confirmatory mechanism.

Key Questions

*   Do we have appropriate and discrete contracts for services for children and adolescents who use or misuse substances or any care packages for young people with problems arising from substance misuse?

*   Are the services we desire contractually and actually secure?

*   Do our contracts reflect and facilitate good practice in for example family work, consultation to primary care staff, self-referrals etc?

*   Do we have contracts with agencies that work on the prevention of problems relating to substance misuse?

*   Have we secured, through contacts, our desired level of out-of-district services, including day and inpatient provision and residential specialist rehabilitation services?

*   Are we contracting with the non-statutory providers in a manner which offers them financial stability and maximises their contributions?

*   Are we using the various budgets (the Single Regeneration Budget; GP funds; the Mental Illness Specific Grant; the Special Transitional Grant etc) in a co-ordinated way to increase value for money?

PART D

Key Issues Effecting the Design and Delivery of Services

Legal Issues

INTRODUCTION

288 This chapter outlines the legal principles upon which the operation and, therefore, the design of services for child and adolescents who misuse substances should be based. The key here is to consider the impact of offering services to people under the age of 18 years on service design and operational policies. Services for children and young people must be provided within the context of the Acts of Parliament which relate to the welfare of children and young people as well as to the criminal justice system.

289 Both commissioners and practitioners must recognise that, while harm-minimisation for young people is an important clinical principle, it must take place within practice that is lawful and to the overall benefit of the young people who are involved.

290 It is recommended that this chapter is read in conjunction with Annex A *Young People Mental Health and the Law* in *Together We Stand* and the second edition of *The Concise Guide to the Children Act 1989* (White and Williams, in press).

THE MISUSE OF DRUGS ACT 1971

291 The Misuse of Drugs Act 1971 regulates the production, distribution and use of drugs considered to be medically or socially harmful. This Act creates a number of offences, one of which is the unlawful production or supply of controlled drugs, their possession with intent to supply, and the unlawful possession of controlled drugs. Under the Act, controlled drugs are classified according to their relative harmfulness and it provides for penalties to be imposed by the courts according to this classification.

292 Recently, with the emergence of MDMA (Ecstasy) as a recreational or party drug, concern has been expressed again that there are some inconsistencies in the classification of drugs that are in common illicit use. In the regulations to the Act, drugs are divided into five schedules and each specifies the requirements governing such activities as import, export, production, prescription and record-keeping which apply to them. Buprenorphine (Temgesic) was rescheduled to Schedule 3 in 1989. Rescheduling in this way involves a prescriber in hand-writing prescriptions rather than their being computer-generated. Tighter controls on temazepan are being introduced as well.

THE NHS AND COMMUNITY CARE ACT 1990

293 While the NHS components of this Act apply equally to children as to adults, the community care components generated the Special Transitional Grant which applies primarily to people of 18 years and over. Therefore, the provisions of this Act cover the period of transition to adulthood and are relevant to certain groups of vulnerable young people. This includes those with learning disabilities, mental illness, and people leaving the care of the local authority. The Act charges social services departments with responsibility for:

* assessing the needs of the local population for which each is responsible;

* drawing up a community care plan, to include services for people who use or misuse drugs and alcohol;

- assessing the needs of individuals and arranging packages of care for them in response to the assessments made;

- commissioning, purchasing and providing care and other services.

294 The implementation of this legislation had an almost immediate effect on people over 18 years of age who needed residential drug and alcohol services. From April 1993, apart from those paying privately, admission to residential services became dependent upon a full individual assessment carried out by either the social services department or a specialist agency acting with delegated powers.

295 The NHS and Community Care Act 1990 requires social services departments and health authorities to work together to:

- identify the needs of each part of the population and these should be specified in the community care plan;

- determine eligibility criteria;

- determine what services each social services department should commission and what each health authority should commission. Each should develop a needs-based commissioning plan;

- determine what services should be jointly commissioned and then purchased.

THE CHILDREN AND YOUNG PERSONS ACT 1969

296 Supervision orders may be made concerning offenders aged between 10 and 17 years under the Children and Young Persons Act 1969 (as amended by the Criminal Justice Act 1991 and other legislation). Section 7(7) of the 1969 Act provides a power for the courts to make supervision orders in which a child or young person may be placed under the supervision of a social worker or of a probation officer for a period of up to three years. This is equivalent to a probation order, but for under 18 year-olds, and it can be made with or without conditions of residence or treatment.

THE CRIMINAL JUSTICE ACT 1991

297 The Criminal Justice Act 1991 contains a power relating to people who misuse substances. This gives courts the ability to make attendance at an appropriate treatment agency a condition of sentence. Social workers and probation officers may be required, under the provisions of the Criminal Justice Act 1991, to prepare pre-sentence reports to assist the courts in determining the most suitable methods of dealing with offenders before certain sentences are imposed. It is general experience that supporting specialist advice is necessary, offering an assessment of problems related to the use of drugs or alcohol by the subject. This is usually the case when a reporting officer wishes to recommend the provision of particular services delivered by the statutory or non-statutory sectors (eg, for mental disorder or drug or alcohol misuse) that would help to reduce offending behaviour.

THE CHILDREN ACT 1989

298 The Children Act 1989 repealed much previous legislation and replaced it with one legal instrument, concerned with the welfare of children from birth until the age of 18. The Act outlines the responsibilities of local authority social services departments including that for the provision of

accommodation for children who are defined as being in need. Within the definitions of the Act, a child is to be considered in need if he or she is unlikely to achieve or maintain a reasonable standard of health or development, or if his or her health or development is likely to be significantly impaired without the provision of such services.

299 Part 3 of the Act relates to the powers of local authorities in respect of children in need (Section 17(1)(a)) and the protection of children suffering or likely to suffer harm (Sections 31 and 44). The needs of children who misuse drugs and alcohol are not specifically referred to but can be regarded as being included within these definitions. However, substance use should not be given undue weighting when assessing the needs of the child.

300 The Children Act 1989 enables local authorities to continue to have some responsibilities with respect to young people up to the age of 21. These responsibilities may include payment for accommodation and clothing, and the provision of *"assistance, advice and befriending"*.

CONSENT

Parental Responsibility

301 The Children Act 1989 introduced the concept of parental responsibility. Section 3(1) states that parental responsibility means *"all the rights, duties, powers, responsibility and authority which by law a parent of a child has in relation to the child and his property."* The definition is intended to emphasise that the duty to care for and to raise a child to moral, physical and emotional health is the fundamental task of parenthood. Each married parent and unmarried mothers have parental responsibility for their children (Section 2). An unmarried father may acquire it (Section 4).

302 Where a care order is in force under section 31, the local authority may exercise parental responsibility. The parent(s) retain responsibility and, as a matter of good practice, should still be consulted. If a child is accommodated, the local authority does not automatically have parental responsibility, although the parent may have delegated responsibility to the authority on the child's entry to accommodation. In the absence of any responsibility, the local authority or the health authority could seek a court direction under Section 8 of the Children Act 1989 or through the High Court exercising its inherent jurisdiction.

303 Prior to the Act, case law had established that the older the child the less extensive parental responsibility may become. Lord Denning observed in Hewer v Bryant [1969] 3 All ER 578 at 582: *"the legal right of a parent ends at the 18th birthday, and even up till then, it is a dwindling right which the courts will hesitate to enforce against the wishes of the child, the older he is. It starts with a right of control and ends with little more than advice."*

304 The House of Lords, in Gillick v West Norfolk and Wisbech Area Health Authority [1986] AC 112, emphasised that the parental power to control a child exists not for the benefit of the parent but for the benefit of the child. Lord Scarman said: *"Parental rights clearly do exist, and they do not wholly disappear until the age of majority .... But the common law has never treated such rights as sovereign or beyond review and control. Nor has our law ever treated the child as other than a person with capacities and rights recognised by law. The principle of the law ... is that parental rights are derived from parental duty and exist only so long as they are needed for the protection of the person*

and property of the child ... parental rights yield to the child's right to make his own decisions when he reaches a sufficient understanding and intelligence to be capable of making up his own mind on the matter requiring decision."

305   Although in an emergency a doctor may undertake treatment if the well-being of the child could suffer by delay, it is normal practice to obtain the consent of a parent as an exercise of their parental responsibility. Section 3(1) provides for these situations but there may be circumstances in which children will make their own decisions.

Children of 16 or 17 Years

306   Section 8(1) of the Family Law Reform Act 1969, provides that a child of 16 or 17 years, may consent: *"to any surgical, medical or dental treatment which, in the absence of consent, would constitute a trespass to his person, [and the consent] shall be as effective as it would be if he were of full age; and where a minor has by virtue of this section given an effective consent to any treatment it shall not be necessary to obtain any consent for it from his parent or guardian."*

Children under 16 Years

307   In certain circumstances, a child of sufficient age and understanding, who is under the age of 16, can give valid consent. In the Gillick case, it was held that a doctor may lawfully prescribe contraception for a girl under 16 without the consent of her parents. She could have legal capacity to give a valid consent to contraceptive advice and treatment, including medical examination. Whether she gave a valid consent in any particular case would depend on the circumstances, including her intellectual capacity to understand advice. Thus, there is no absolute parental right requiring the parent's consent to be sought.

308   Speaking of medical treatment generally, Lord Scarman said: *"It will be a question of fact whether a child seeking advice has sufficient understanding of what is involved to give a consent valid in law. Until the child achieves the capacity to consent, the parental right to make the decision continues save only in exceptional circumstances. Emergency, parental neglect, abandonment of the child, or inability to find the parent are examples of exceptional situations justifying the doctor proceeding to treat the child without parental knowledge and consent, but there will arise, no doubt, other exceptional situations in which it will be reasonable for the doctor to proceed without the parent's consent."*

309   Applying this to contraceptive advice and treatment, he said: *"there is much that has to be understood by a girl under the age of 16 if she is to have legal capacity to consent to such treatment. It is not enough that she should understand the nature of the advice which is being given: she must also have a sufficient maturity to understand what is involved."*

310   Put into the language of parental responsibility rather than rights, these comments remain relevant after the Children Act 1989 when the question of a child giving consent to a course of action is in issue. The position may be different where the child is withholding consent to medical treatment, in view of the decisions by the Court of Appeal in Re W (A Minor) (Medical Treatment) [1993] Fam 64 and Re R (A Minor) (Wardship: Medical Treatment) [1992] Fam 11.

PROVIDING A HOME FOR A CHILD

311 A key aspect of parental responsibility is that of looking after and bringing up a child. Associated with providing a home is the necessary accompanying power *inter alia* physically to control the children. This does suggest that in most cases there is a practical need for the carer to be informed about an event in the child's life as important as the prescription of drugs. Even though a person with parental responsibility is not providing a home for the child, the Children Act 1989 assumes that that person should be involved in decisions about the child.

312 Nonetheless, it must be recognised that there is a significant minority of children, who come within the definitions of the Children Act 1989 (whether they are *'in need'*, as defined by Section 17, accommodated under Section 20 or *'suffering significant harm'* as defined by Section 31) where the exercise of parental responsibility is such as to require decisions to be taken without consultation with a parent. For their own reasons, mature children may not wish their parents to be involved in personal decisions about their future.

APPLYING THESE PRINCIPLES TO DRUG SERVICES FOR CHILDREN AND ADOLESCENTS WHO MISUSE SUBSTANCES

313 It is important to understand that, while the Gillick decision related to a specific set of circumstances, the House of Lords was considering the principles which, by the doctrine of precedent, could be applied to similar circumstances. How widely a future court might apply the principles cannot be said for certain.

314 Questions arise about the provision of drugs, or material in conjunction with the use of drugs, such as needles or syringes, which could come within the same principles. Careful thought will need to be given in each case as to how the provision and operation of, for example, a needle and syringe exchange can be justified as a medical treatment.

315 Five preconditions which emerge from the Gillick case, could be applied to the provision of services to young people below the age of 18 in respect of their use of substances:

a. that the young person (although under 16 years of age) will understand the advice;

b. that the young person cannot be persuaded to inform his or her parents or to allow them to be informed that the young person is seeking drug advice or treatment in respect of substance use and/or misuse;

c. that the young person is very likely to begin or to continue using substances with or without the advice or treatment;

d. that, unless the young person receives advice or treatment on the use of substances, his or her physical or mental health or both are likely to suffer; and

e. that the young person's best interests require the adviser to give advice and/or treatment without parental consent.

316 Valid consent would be ineffective if the prescription of a substance or the giving of advice or treatment in itself was a criminal offence. Therefore, it is important for any adviser to ensure that the actions involved in the treatment are not themselves capable of interpretation as a criminal offence, for example by becoming *de facto* a drug-pusher. If the adviser is to avoid possible prosecution for being an accessory to the unlawful use of drugs, there must be an honest intention to act in the best interests of the young person. This requires that their action is based on a proper assessment of the circumstances of the case.

317 The Gillick decision referred to proper assessment by a doctor and to clinical judgement. When dealing with the mental health of children, a competent assessment may be made by others. All professionals and staff, including volunteers, must have had training and experience in working with young people and with the issues relating to substance use and misuse. To provide evidence of this work, it is essential to maintain proper records of all such advice, the reasons for it and the considerations of the author.

318 Supervision of staff who work with young people, and their operation within a team, should benefit both the young person and the staff. Supervision should ensure that more detailed principles are developed from the basic considerations upon which future practice is based. This practice should also provide some legal protection to staff.

CONFIDENTIALITY

319 Staff working with vulnerable young people will be particularly concerned to provide them with a high degree of security against disclosure of confidential information received. There is a recognised public interest that encourages a duty of not disclosing confidential information without the consent of the client, but no absolute guarantee can be given.

320 Alternatively, there is no legal requirement to report a criminal offence to the police, except in Northern Ireland (Criminal Law Act 1967), although a failure to disclose information might, in certain circumstances, lead to an allegation of being an accessory to or aiding and abetting a crime. Local codes of conduct or practice, including those in schools, may impose a duty on an employee to report an alleged offence to the employer, but authorities should still give careful consideration to the effect on the welfare of the child and the school of reporting an offence to the police.

321 Doctors, solicitors and health visitors may have a professional duty in extreme cases to override their normal duty of confidence in the interests of their patient or client, or where a child may be harmed if the facts are not reported. Any person might feel obliged to disclose information for the safety of a young person or young people generally, for example, where there are allegations of sexual abuse, or where there staff of an agency are told about drug-pushers. In such cases, disclosure should be limited to the relevant authority responsible for safeguarding the public interest.

322 In certain circumstances, disclosure might be required by a court for the purpose of legal proceedings. Although information acquired in the course of a confidential, therapeutic relationship may be considered by a court to attract some measure of immunity from disclosure, the court still has the duty to consider whether that immunity should be overridden in the interests of justice or the welfare of a child.

CHAPTER 12

The Principles of Good
Practice in Service
Delivery

INTRODUCTION

323 The NHS and Community Care Act 1990 introduced the purchaser-provider system in which contractual arrangements for services place a high priority on quality and quality assurance. In this context, quality assurance means *"an efficient, integral approach to ensure that a service consistently provides what it is supposed to provide."* What a service is *"supposed to provide"* is determined by strategic choices that are best made through agreements negotiated between commissioners, purchasers and providers. The detailed interpretation of a chosen strategy, of the resulting service specifications, and of the definitions of operational performance, should be described in each providing agency's standards that define good practice.

324 Clarity of defined quality standards, together with the means to promote their achievement, is of particular importance in services for children and adolescents, because *a core task is to ensure that the welfare of children remains the paramount consideration at all times.*

325 The standards for local services should build upon core principles but they should be developed to reflect the individual circumstances of, and challenges faced by each district and localities within districts. This chapter describes those core principles of good practice in the delivery of services for children and adolescents who misuse substances which emerged from the work of the HAS. Table 11 groups these principles into key areas.

Table 11

The Principles of Good Practice in the Provision of Services for Children and Adolescents
Services should be:

• Accessible	• Collaborative
• Appropriate	• Co-ordinated
• Lawful	• Effective
• Competent	• Targeted
• Respecting and protecting of children and adolescents	• Evaluated

326 Underlying the tiered approach to a new strategy for services for children and adolescents who misuse substances, described in chapter eight, is the assumption that the providers which offer services within each of the tiers will have contact with children and adolescents who misuse substances. This reflects the current situation in which services of a more general nature, that are not directly orientated towards providing specialist services specifically for people who misuse substances, will be in contact with this client group. The number of young people with problems who are in contact with Tier 1 services is likely to be greater than the number in contact with more specialised services. However, the extent to which substance misuse by young people is recognised by the staff of these direct contact, non-specialist agencies is open to question.

327 The key principles for effective substance misuse services are equally relevant to Tier 1 non-specialist services as they are to the specialist services. Therefore, it is particularly important to provide training for the staff of non-specialist agencies so that they may be equipped with the necessary knowledge, skills and confidence to recognise substance misuse in young people. These attributes would also render staff better able to: make appropriate early interventions; make referrals to other services; and participate in multi-agency prevention or intervention initiatives.

328 Contracts for services should require providers to define their own standards and compliance with this can be used as part of a developmental approach to contract monitoring and quality assurance.

THE KEY PRINCIPLES OF SERVICES FOR CHILDREN AND ADOLESCENTS WHO MISUSE SUBSTANCES

329 The sections which follow examine each of the key areas into which the HAS has grouped the core service principles. In each instance, the principles are stated and each section finishes with some key questions for commissioners, purchasers and providers as a means of self-testing achievements in each area.

Accessibility

330 Currently, young substance users do not have access to the same range of services as their older counterparts. Even where substance misuse services do not exclude potential clients or patients on the grounds of age, these services may not be perceived by younger people as relevant to them or to their situations. Substance misuse services are often seen as catering for physically dependent, injecting heroin users, and this is not a situation in which many young people find themselves. Add to this the fact that many staff are perceived as being out of touch with youth culture and are seen as 'do-gooders', and it becomes clear how substance misuse services have a serious image problem among younger substance users.

331 This defines an important principle that significantly affects service design.

Principle
Agencies should promote their services as being available to young people by using language and images that are attractive to them. Services should be available in venues that younger people use.

332 Physical access is also important. Most young people do not own a car, many are engaged in education or training during ordinary office hours, or they may find a direct approach to a substance misuse service too daunting.

Principle
Agencies should be flexible in their opening times and the venues in which they provide services.

333 All services should be available to all potential clients or patients irrespective of their gender, their sex, their culture of origin or any disability.

334 In promoting accessibility to services where young people from black and ethnic communities are likely to be affected, the importance of employing staff from the same communities needs to be recognised. In any event, arrangements for trained interpreters and translating information materials should be put into effect.

Principle

Agencies should adopt non-discriminatory practices, and actively promote equality of access.

Table 12

Accessibility
• Where are services provided? Are they convenient to public transport routes?
• When are they open? Are they available out of ordinary office hours?
• Is a service well publicised? Where is it publicised?
• Is the publicity material written in straightforward language? Is it translated into relevant ethnic languages?
• Are there arrangements for providing interpreters?
• Is there access for wheelchairs, buggies and people with limited mobility?

Appropriateness

335 Substance misuse services for children and young people should be commissioned, designed, purchased and provided with the needs of this group in mind. It is not sufficient that drug services for adults should simply be made available to young people. The service should be provided in age-appropriate environments in which service users mix with their peers. Currently, this requirement is a particular challenge when hospital admission is required. An admission ward for adults who misuse drugs and alcohol and adult psychiatric admission wards for adults are clearly inappropriate. This is in line with the guidance from Action for Sick Children (Annex B). Equally, an admission to a paediatric or child and adolescent psychiatric ward may not be suitable for older adolescents who require detoxification. There is an argument for developing facilities specifically for adolescents, not only to provide treatments for drug and alcohol-related problems, but also to ensure that the broad range of health needs of adolescents are adequately and appropriately met.

Principle

Agencies should provide an environment which is orientated to the needs of young people, with access to age-appropriate activities and treatment should be conducted in the environment of a peer group.

336 The specific needs of each younger person and his or her family and/or other carers, will vary according to age, personal development and the severity and complexity of problems. Services should be commissioned to enable responses to a range of needs to be provided.

Principle

Agencies should offer a range of therapeutic and other interventions to meet the identified needs of younger people.

337 The needs of younger people may also be affected by other factors, for example their ethnic and cultural background, disability and gender. These issues will have an impact on the delivery of care.

Principle

The staff of all agencies should have access to a staff training programme, and links with community groups and other agencies that address matters of ethnicity, cultural background, disability, gender and any other issues that are relevant to the needs of younger people in the area served.

Table 13

Appropriateness
• Is the environment appropriate to younger people?
• Is the service designed to be sensitive to the specific needs of younger people?
• Is the service sensitive to the needs of younger people from an appropriate range of different ethnic and cultural backgrounds and communities?

The Operation of Services Within the Spirit and Intention of the Law

338 The provision of services for young people is undertaken in the context of several Acts of Parliament, including for example:

- the Education Act 1981;

- the Mental Health Act 1983;

- the Children Act 1989;

- the Education Act 1993 with its Code of Practice on the Identification and Assessment of Special Educational Needs (1994).

These address the needs of younger people and protect their rights in law.

339 Staff who work in services for younger people should understand the legal framework within which they are expected to operate (see chapter 11). There will be times when it will be difficult to achieve a balance between providing a service that is accessible and appropriate and one which operates within the required legal framework. Issues relating to confidentiality and consent to treatment are especially challenging (chapter 11).

340 Adolescence is the period of development during which there is an evolution from childhood to adulthood. As each young person achieves greater independence, they will engage in an increasing range of activities without parental consent or knowledge.

341 Staff who work with younger people should strike a balance between acknowledging each person's needs for nurture, protection, appropriate controls and guidance, and enabling each young person to make his or her own decisions in keeping with their age and maturity.

342 The competence of young people to give informed consent to most treatments is not unequivocally defined in law. (The complexities and dilemmas of this issue are explored in chapter 11.) Also, the degree of competence of the young to consent to treatment will vary according to the degree of complexity of the problem, the nature of the intervention, the time involved and the position of, and relationships with those who hold parental responsibility.

343 The needs and the wishes of each individual should be distinguished as should parental and societal attitudes and their wishes. There is potential for conflict in this balance. This is highlighted in the area of confidentiality and in the maintenance of professional standards. Chapter 11 identifies the duty of staff to seek to persuade each child or young person to discuss matters with their parents or guardian. This may not always be possible or serve the best interests of the young person. Chapter 11 offers guidance and tests that should be applied in determining whether it is lawful to treat a child under the age of 16 without parental knowledge or consent.

344 On the other hand, the importance of working jointly with other agencies or sharing information with other agencies or authorities limits the possibility of giving guarantees of confidentiality to young people. There may be other risks that require professionals to disclose aspects of what they know about an individual but each young person should be told when and for what reason a staff member intends to breach confidentiality. In many circumstances, the young person should be offered the opportunity to agree to the proposed course of action before the professional decides that it is his or her duty to breach a confidence.

345 Given the complexities involved, it is in everyone's interests that contemporaneous written records are maintained on all individuals. Again, chapter 11 offers guidance in this respect. Table 14 proposes a scheme for managing the collection, flow and dissemination of information about individuals.

Table 14

A Scheme for Recording the Management of Individual Cases
The following points should be included in the records of a young person who is receiving any intervention. This is in addition to the basic information collected ordinarily in the course of a clinical contact.
• The problem(s) being addressed should be stated. This may include problems other than those identified by the client/patient.
• The specific nature of the intervention planned should be stated, for example, counselling, referral to another agency, within agency and inter-agency discussion, prescription of drugs, admission.
• Consideration of the ability of the young person to give consent and the involvement of parents and guardians. This should include opinion on the matters listed in chapter 11.
• The explanation given to the young person.
• Depending on the severity of the problems identified, consideration of the need to involve the following agencies should be recorded: - social services, (eg for child protection issues); - a primary healthcare team; - specialist drug and alcohol services; - child and adolescent mental health services; - child health services; - the housing department; - the school welfare service; - the probation service; - non-statutory agencies; - others.
• The dates decided on for reviews and for updating plans of management, including treatment.
• A record of supervision and of discussions with line managers.

346 Also, general policies are needed to inform the management of individual cases and these should take the needs of both individuals and the staff of agencies into account.

Principle

Each agency should have a written policy on confidentiality which gives examples of occasions when confidentiality might be breached. This should be made available to all service users.

347 Each agency should have written policies and guidelines concerning their work with young people that provide guidance for staff about obtaining consent to treatment or other interventions.

348 Agencies have an obligation to ensure that they employ staff whose backgrounds do not render them inappropriate for work with young people.

Principle

Agencies should apply procedures for recruiting and selecting their staff that ensure that each applicant's identity and qualifications are verified, that references are taken up, and that a full history of previous employment is known.

Principle

Where and when appropriate, agencies should request a police check on the criminal background of prospective employees who meet the criteria defined in "Protection of Children : Disclosure of Criminal Background of those with Access to Children" HOC 47/1993.

Table 15

The Operation of Services within the Spirit and Intention of the Law
• Does the staff of the service have access to legal advice?

• Are there clear, written policies and guidelines on:
  - the recruitment of staff (including vetting procedures)?
  - obtaining consent to treatment or other interventions?
  - confidentiality?

• Is there a complaints procedure?
• Are adequate individual case records maintained?

Competence

349 Members of staff who work in substance misuse services are faced with particular challenges. They have to make decisions on complex matters about consent to treatment and other interventions, the degree of confidentiality to be afforded to each young person, and the nature of the treatment or other interventions to be offered in response to the assessed needs of each young person. These matters clearly indicate the requirement for each agency to construct guidelines and policies that promote and support best professional practice. These should aim to meet the needs of service users while also offering protection to staff who face situations in which they may be personally and professionally vulnerable.

350 Each member of staff should respond to the assessed needs of their clients and patients even if this conflicts with the child or young person's expressed wishes. This applies, for example, if a young person presents a problem that staff members may not consider to be the one to address as a priority.

351 Therefore, staff who work with children and adolescents who have problems arising from substance misuse should be competent in two areas: the skills and knowledge related to substance misuse; and assessing the needs of young people against a framework for understanding their development. However, it would be rare for any one member of staff to be competent to deal with all the problems that are commonly presented by young people and this makes it essential for each agency to have a clearly defined policy on staff supervision and a protocol for joint working that is agreed with the staff of other agencies.

352 Staff competence can be judged at a number of levels:

  • the level of competence of individuals augmented by specialist supervisory and consultation arrangements;

  • the aggregate competence of the agency or of the service;

  • the aggregate competence of the staff from a range of agencies who are engaged in working jointly or in providing shared care.

353 As noted earlier, the competence of each young person to consent to treatment or other interventions will vary according to the nature and magnitude of the problem presented and his or her individual circumstances. A similar analysis applies to the competence of staff. This is related to the magnitude of the problem, the nature of the problem and the potential technical nature and complexity of any intervention. This relationship is illustrated by Figure 5.

Figure 5

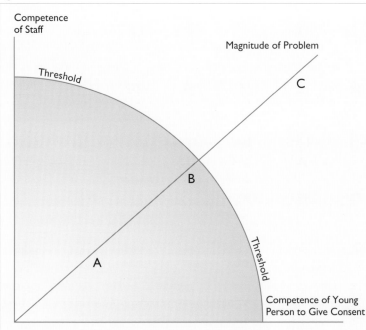

354 Figure 5 indicates the decisions that may have to be made by a member of staff who is dealing with a child or adolescent. The diagonal represents the level of complexity of the problem or the need of that young person. The horizontal axis represents the ability of the young person to give informed consent to the intervention needed and the vertical axis represents the competence of the staff member to manage the problem.

355 Three cases are outlined:

Case A   This represents a problem of low severity, for example where only factual information is needed. The importance of informed consent is limited as is the challenge to the member of staff.

Case B   The concept of treatment now becomes important and staff members must recognise that there may be complications or repercussions from intervening or not so doing or from the interventions or treatment itself. The level of expertise required could be greater than that possessed by a particular staff member. Here, either referral to a member of staff of the required competence or supervision is mandatory. The level of competence required of the young person to give informed consent is also higher, and, in some circumstances, the young person may not be able to give consent on their own account.

Case C   This represents a problem of a significant level of complexity. In the hypothetical circumstance envisaged here, neither can the young person give lawful consent, nor can a particular member of staff intervene by themselves with an appropriate level of skill. This illustrates those cases in which there is the need for multi-agency, multi-disciplinary involvement (often Tier 3 service provision) and includes cases in which the responsibilities and activities of the Area Child Protection Committee Guidelines may be invoked.

Principle
Agencies should have policies for staff development that are shared and ensure that all staff and volunteers receive induction and in-service training on substance misuse issues and with regard to the skills required when working with young people (as appropriate).

Principle
Agencies should have supervision policies that include detail on the availability and frequency of staff supervision and the qualifications and/or specialist expertise of the supervisors.

Principle
Agencies should have a written protocol that is agreed with other relevant external agencies that are involved in any joint work or shared care.

Principle
Agencies should undertake regularly a skills audit, to ascertain the competence of their staff to provide services for young people who misuse substances.

356 Figure 3 and 4 (in chapter nine) and the explanation that follows underline the need for a strategic approach to commissioning and delivering services in which a number of agencies are likely to have a complementary investment. At commissioning and purchasing levels, this enables the achievement of a balanced service overall, that brings together complementary service components provided by a range of competent statutory and non-statutory agencies.

357 At the provider level, the needs of individuals, the capacities of the components of service delivered by different agencies, and the levels of competence of staff in different agencies or departments, all require a predictable and clear approach within an overarching service framework.

358 For example, the type A case might be dealt with by Tier 1 services, while the type B case would illustrate the circumstance in which a staff member might work singly, but with supervision (ie, in Tier 2) and the type C case describes the circumstances that require a Tier 3 approach. Still more demanding cases may require highly specialised levels of skill, specific treatments or care settings that are best commissioned, purchased and provided as Tier 4 services.

359 These principles can be tested by the questions contained in Table 16.

Table 16

Staff Competence
• Does the staff, including volunteers, have training and experience in working with younger people and with the issues and problems generated by those younger people who use and/or misuse substances?
• Does the staff have access to expert advice and consultation? eg, from: - a consultant child and adolescent psychiatrist? - a consultant psychiatrist with special experience in substance misuse? - a paediatrician? - a social services child protection team? - a solicitor? - an educationalist?
• Does the staff have training in working with people from different ethnic and cultural backgrounds and communities?
• Does the staff have access to regular supervision from a suitably qualified person?

Assessment and Child Protection

360 The ability of staff to undertake a thorough and competent assessment is crucial to the delivery of a substance misuse service for young people which is appropriate, legal, competent and which respects and protects the interests of each child and young person.

361 Assessment is required by each agency that is involved in the service overall in three particular areas:

- assessment of the capacities, capabilities, competence and development of each child and young person referred;

- assessment of the problems, the needs and the requirements for intervention, treatment or care of each child and young person;

- assessment of staff competence to meet the needs of each child and young person lawfully and appropriately (see above).

362 There will be some circumstances in which it is difficult to undertake a comprehensive assessment of the needs and capabilities of young people. An important example is that of assessing the appropriateness or otherwise of supplying needles and syringes to individual adolescents on an outreach basis. Agencies should ensure that their staff are issued with guidance on handling these situations. They should consider whether it is preferable for some interventions and services of this kind to be available only from services which have the acknowledged specialist expertise.

363 Table 17 summarises issues which staff who are in direct contact with young people will need to be able to assess, in construing the information given to them.

Table 17

Assessing Children and Adolescents
• **Competence** The age, intellectual development and level of emotional maturity of the young person must be ascertained. These contribute to the assessor's judgement of: - the young person's understanding of the issues involved; - the competence of the young person to make a decision about the problem.
• **Truthfulness** The accuracy and veracity of the young person's information, including reasons for refusal of consent to inform the responsible parent, must be assessed. Assessment of both competence and truthfulness may need to be cross-referenced with information from other informants and contacts with other agencies.
• **The Needs and the Wishes of the Child or Young Person** Any difference of opinion among staff about the young person's needs as opposed to the wishes of that young person should be overtly stated and considered.

Table 18 lists the challenges that are commonly faced by staff in their assessments of children and adolescents.

Table 18

Typical Challenges Faced when Assessing the Needs of Children and Adolescents and the Interventions they Require
• Lack of knowledge is the simplest type of problem and can generally be overcome with accurate information.
• Many needs and problems require discussion at some length. This may involve formal counselling when there are choices that a young person can make.
• The assessment of some problems necessitates involving other agencies and disciplines because of their severity and complexity.
• Some of the more complex and severe problems may require the involvement of procedures provided for by one or more of the following: - the Children Act 1989; - the Mental Health Act 1983; - criminal justice procedures; - the Education Act 1981; - the Education Act 1993 and its Code of Practice.
• A young person may be a victim or perpetrator of physical, sexual or emotional abuse and others may be at risk.
• A judgement must be made about the potential damage that might be done by withholding or giving services requested by a young person. In some situations, the provision of services may accentuate existing problems or even create new ones and problems resolved in the short-term can lead to longer-term difficulties.
• Staff must invoke and operate within the guidelines and procedures set by the local Area Child Protection Committee, when these are appropriate.
• Staff must consider what action may need to be taken when dealing with illicit or illegal behaviours.

364 There may be occasions when a child or young person *"is unlikely to achieve or maintain a reasonable standard of health or development, or their health or development is likely to be significantly impaired without the provision of ... services."* Although the Children Act 1989 does not make specific reference to children or young people who misuse drugs and alcohol, by implication such children and young people may be deemed vulnerable and to be in need of protection. Care proceedings may be necessary if a child is suffering or likely to suffer significant harm, which is attributable to a lack of adequate care. If the experience of the HAS is repeated widely across England and Wales, few local authorities include hazardous or dependent use of drugs as a factor in their definitions of vulnerable children for whom the provision of services is considered to be a priority. Many of their staff who are engaged in work with children and families will not have received sufficient training on the issues related to substance misuse to be able to assess the vulnerability of a person with problems arising from substance use. Therefore, effective links between social services, child and adolescent mental health services, child protection teams and substance misuse services are essential.

Principle

Each agency should have written guidelines on the assessments to be conducted with respect to children and adolescents. Staff should receive training in assessing: children and young people; their needs; and the extent of their exposure to risk; in order to ensure that the guidelines are implemented.

Principle

Each agency should have written guidelines for the protection of children that have been approved by the Area Child Protection Committee.

Principle

Each agency should have effective working links with: local social services departments; other child and family services; and child protection teams. When appropriate, each should contribute to the training of the staff of those services.

Table 19

Assessment and Child Protection
• Are there clear, written guidelines, to assist staff in undertaking assessments of the degree of vulnerability of individuals, of the needs (as opposed to wishes) of younger people and of their maturity?
• Are there clear written procedures for child protection which apply to all staff and which are approved by the Area Child Protection Committee?
• Do local criteria for the assessment of risks faced by children and the identification of vulnerable younger people take account of the histories of substance use by the children themselves and by their parents?

Collaboration and Consultation

365 There are many agencies and individuals that have an active interest in the welfare of children and young people. Not the least of these is their parents and other carers. Parents are a key resource. Ordinarily, they wish to recognise and support young people with problems arising from substance use and misuse, but, in addition, they are an important client group which has its own needs for information, advice, support and, sometimes, integrated or collateral treatment.

366 Young people are likely to turn to their peers for advice and help, especially during the adolescent years. The contribution that these other young people have to make to services should not be ignored.

367 If services are to be attractive and accessible to young people and also to be relevant to the needs of their families and friends, active consultation with current or potential service user groups is essential. In particular, the views of young people should be canvassed.

368 No-one should work with young people in isolation. The need for joint work by the various agencies engaged in delivering services is referred to throughout this document. Joint work is particularly important in ensuring that the overall service meets the needs of all young people, including those with specific or special needs. However, developing alliances is a time-consuming process and may be difficult. Agencies have different philosophies, priorities and constraints that govern their work. Effective partnerships require a commitment of time and energy and a willingness for agencies to learn about each other so that it is possible to respect and value differences in style and approach. Without these differences, there would be little or no choice for service users.

Principle

Each agency should have a commitment, manifested in active operational policies, for consulting with and involving: young people; service users; carers; and the staff of other agencies; in appropriate aspects of service planning, delivery and evaluation.

Table 20

Collaboration and Consultation
• What arrangements are in place for service providers to consult with young people as service users, with their carers, and with other agencies on the services provided, and on the development of new services?
• Are there opportunities for younger people and their carers to become involved in planning the delivery of services?

Co-ordination

369 Collaboration and consultation are particularly important in delivering seamless services to users who are not usually interested in inter-agency tensions or the niceties of service roles and contracts. They are more concerned about receiving competent care. Experience shows that effective collaboration at the front-line of service provision depends on its being driven from the top of the organisations involved. This requires ownership of the agenda for collaboration at the policy, commissioning, planning and senior management levels. Staff on the ground can only play their part in carrying out joint arrangements if their commitment is supported managerially and organisationally. These issues are addressed in detail in chapters 14 and 15.

370 At the point of service delivery, the need for co-ordination will be most evident in the management of complex cases. When several agencies contribute to a package of care for a vulnerable child or young person, clear leadership is needed. The lead agency will vary depending upon the nature and relative priority of presenting problems. For example, when a child has pressing health needs, it is appropriate that a medical practitioner provides clinical leadership, while in child protection cases leadership may be provided more appropriately by a social work practitioner.

Principle

Each agency that is contributing to the service overall should be actively involved in local inter-agency working groups and, when appropriate, should contribute advice to the joint commissioning process.

Principle

Each relevant agency should participate in case conferences.

Principle

Each agency should agree a written protocol for its contribution to packages of care for individuals in circumstances when responsibility for that care is shared by a number of agencies. This should identify responsibility for leadership, case management and the responsibilities of the professional and/or volunteer staff.

Table 21

Co-ordination
• What arrangements are in place to ensure that there are good communications between components of an overall service and that joint work takes place?
• What is the mechanism for ensuring that there is both leadership and management of the shared care that is appropriate for complex cases?

Targeted Services

371 Necessarily, the services delivered to children and adolescents should vary depending on the specific and assessed needs of each young person.

372 This requires: knowledge of the specific problems faced by children and adolescents who use and/or misuse substances; good working knowledge of the psycho-social and physical aspects of childhood and adolescent developmental processes; and an understanding of the ways in which both these factors may interact in the lives of younger people and their families.

373 Much of the content of this report has considered substance misuse by younger people from this standpoint.

374 There are other ways of targeting services for younger people. Two are considered here. The first relates to the definition and delivery of services to certain higher risk or more vulnerable young people. The second method of targeting is that based on individual care programming.

Vulnerable Groups of Children and Adolescents

375 Specific groups of younger people considered as especially vulnerable include those who are:

- homeless;

- young offenders;

- school non-attenders;

- children with learning disabilities;

- children in care or leaving care;

- young single pregnant girls;

- young mentally ill people;

- younger people with physical disabilities.

376 Many of these vulnerable children and adolescents come from families in which they have lived with parents or carers who have their own serious problems which have been, and are very distressing to a developing person. They may well have been exposed to a parent or sibling who has been using or misusing substances. They may have experienced chronic family discord and tension and live in family environments in which they have experienced their carers coping with poverty, homelessness and migration. Often, these younger people come from a community in which there is a high level of turmoil and violence. They might well have experienced family loss through divorce and separation and may have experienced, directly or indirectly, physical, sexual or emotional abuse or a combination of these during their childhood.

377 Commissioners, purchasers and providers should recognise that members of these groups of younger people are not always readily identified as being at risk. Adults tend to be drawn to focus attention on younger people who are more conspicuously in trouble and who display themselves through disordered conduct. While this is an important group, it must be remembered that other younger people suffer in relative silence, although there are ways of detecting their plight. Many vulnerable young people attend school and are not known by agencies that deal with delinquent behaviour or physical and mental disorders. Nonetheless, these young people may have major problems associated with previous physical, or sexual abuse or with loss or separation.

378 Experience bears out the researched evidence that these groups of vulnerable young people are more at risk from substance misuse and have more problems associated with the use and misuse of substances than their more fortunate peers.

379 Additionally, they are less likely to come to services for help and are less likely to remain in contact with services or engaged in treatment programmes. Thus, they may become doubly disadvantaged.

380 Providers should be in a position to identify and assess the needs of these vulnerable young people and to provide services that can retain them within their framework. In this way, they can prevent more serious problems and treat existing disorders effectively.

381 At an early stage of their contact with services, vulnerable young people often require the physical resources of cash, clothing, a bed and shelter. Provision of these facilities enables young people to lock-on to programmes of care, support and active intervention.

382 Police officers, social workers, probation officers and officers in the prison service *(Briefing Paper HM Prison Service 28 April 1995. No 81)* should have a heightened awareness of the association of delinquency with substance misuse in young offenders. This applies whether a young person: is in

custody; is in prison; is in a young offenders institution; is in a secure unit; is in police cells; is in a non-custodial setting within the community; has been seen by a court diversion scheme; is under supervision; or is attending a specialist group in the community.

383 There are various styles of school non-attendance: disaffected young people who find the education system difficult to manage; young people who are excluded from school because of behavioural difficulties; and truants. All of these children and adolescents may have problems stemming from the use or misuse of substances. Delivering services to this higher risk group requires particular innovation by community-based services outside educational settings.

384 Young people who are in the care of a local authority and those in the process of leaving care are at high risk. Frequently, members of this group find themselves in a situation in which the services that they require are divided between a variety of providers - social services departments, probation services, child and adolescent mental health services, adult mental health services, education services and those in the environment of work.

385 Young people who have learning disabilities, mental disorders and physical disabilities require particular resources within the community. In particular, they require the provision of services that can follow them from one setting to another. But often, their experience is of services that cease when they move. (A small number will also require hospital settings.)

386 The assessment of vulnerable children and young people requires attention to the issues of the competence and truthfulness of the young person, and also to the critical issue of their needs as compared with their wishes (Gilvarry, Tayler and Murphy, 1994).

387 Particular groups of vulnerable young people require services offered in a range of venues. Their needs should be understood and targeted. This poses particular challenges in co-ordinating and delivering packages of care which, as explained below, should not relate to, or be limited by agency boundaries.

388 It is unlikely that any one agency can provide a general service, that is able to respond to all of the needs of all children and adolescents, and provide special services targeted on the needs of particularly vulnerable younger people at higher risk. Indeed, it is unlikely that any one agency will be able to provide for more than one high-risk group or for more than specific aspects of need.

389 This analysis reflects the current experience of younger people which is that the services they require come from a variety of statutory and non-statutory providers. This poses a challenge to commissioners, who have the ability to break out of traditional patterns of service delivery in deciding on the patterns of care in a district and calls for cross-sectoral approaches. Purchasers should ensure that they set contracts with an appropriate range of providers so that there are no large gaps in service provision. This situation also presents a challenge to the various service providers to agree mechanisms between them that underpin the collaboration and co-ordination required in designing packages of care tailored to the assessed needs of each young person.

390 This situation highlights the requirement for a strategic view of service concepts and practical organisation. It calls for a strategic lead from statutory commissioners to set a framework that enables effective

purchasing from a sufficiently wide range of providers. At present, purchasers are unlikely to achieve balanced services without making contractual arrangements with a number of providers. This requires a broad and clear conception of provision within which individual agencies deliver components of an overall service. The four-tier approach adopted in *Together We Stand* and developed in this review deals with these requirements. Figure 6 illustrates the vertical and horizontal strategic and operational co-ordination of services.

Figure 6

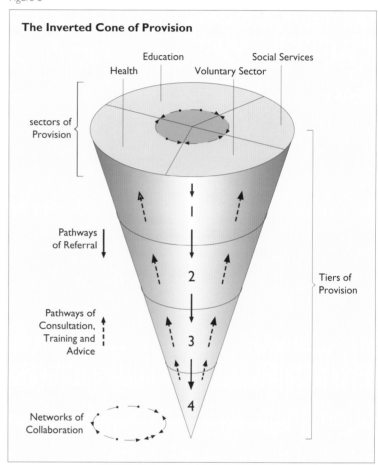

The Inverted Cone of Provision

Care Pathways and Individual Care Packages

391 Increasingly, the thinking of local authority purchasers is towards defining managed packages of care orientated to the assessed needs of children, adolescents and their families. In some areas, specialist CAMHS staff are beginning to focus on the development of care packages geared to each individual's particular problems and beginning to explore integrated care pathways (ICPs). Written care packages can provide: enhanced mechanisms for sharing information; a basis for informed debate; mechanisms for improved purchaser-provider communication; a platform for evaluation and audit; a means of stimulating good practice (Bailey, 1995). These clinically-driven approaches are likely to prove helpful in shaping specialist services. They could also help children, adolescents, their families and referring agencies to make better choices about the delivery of care.

392 The integration of provision for children and adolescents, requires each agency to be explicit about the kinds of service, interventions, treatments, and facilities that it provides so that the care of individual clients and patients can be programmed in ways which draw, if necessary, on the resources of a

variety of organisations. Each agency and service component should be able to provide a menu of the types of work that it is able to offer. This should enable key workers to focus their advice to children and families through the provision of well informed and co-ordinated care packages.

393 Figure 7 illustrates the pathway of a hypothetical adolescent through a programme of care provided by a number of agencies.

Figure 7

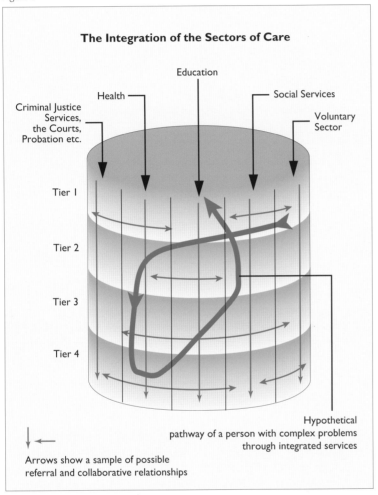

394 Services which do not act in concert risk further disruption to the sense of personal identity of the children who use them. Unwittingly, such services may, reflect and reinforce conflicts that already exist within families. Examples of the effects of a breakdown in relationships between services are well documented in reports from child abuse inquiries. All too easily, families may fall through loose and fragmented networks with calamitous consequences. Also, there may be unnecessary duplication of services resulting in inefficient distribution and delivery of scarce resources. Therefore, services for children and adolescents who misuse substances should have the notion of networking at their core, to ensure that all services are fully integrated across agencies and can offer a continuum of care, rather than handing on clients at key points in their lives.

Principle
Information, education, prevention, intervention and treatment services should be targeted on specific groups of vulnerable young people.

Principle
Services should be offered in accessible places through outreach work.

Principle

All agencies and their staff should be prepared to collaborate with relevant others in planning and co-ordinating packages of care designed to meet the assessed needs of individuals.

Principle

All agencies are encouraged to support the exploration, development and evaluation of Integrated Care Pathways.

Effectiveness and Evaluation

395 Good practice requires that the effectiveness of services is subject to review. The effectiveness of services can be judged in a number of ways, at different levels:

- *quality assurance and audit*
  Does the agency deliver what it sets out to deliver and to the required standard?
- *output monitoring*
  Does the agency achieve its objectives and targets by delivering specified interventions to a specified number of individuals or groups within a defined population?
- *consumer satisfaction surveys*
  Does the agency meet the identified wishes of the target population?
- *outcome evaluation*
  Does the agency achieve its aims in relation to stimulating lifestyle change, risk reduction, health gain etc?

396 All of these are important in building a complete picture of the effectiveness of services but all have their limitations and also resource implications. Arguably, from the perspective of achieving best practice in the delivery of substance misuse services for children and adolescents, audit and outcome evaluation are of particular significance.

397 Audit involves an examination of current practice. Without it, standards become merely statements of good intention, rather than the means of ensuring the achievement of an acceptable level of practice.

398 In the absence of an established pattern of services for children and adolescents who misuse substances, commissioners, purchasers and providers should be innovative in their efforts to develop a responsive service for young people. Outcome evaluation is particularly important in contributing to what we know about which responses are most effective and in ensuring that a body of knowledge is built up. Evaluation is discussed in greater detail in Chapter 16.

399 As a starting point, any review of effectiveness demands clear statements of the aims, objectives and targets of the service. Performance and development can then be managed from this base-line.

Principle

Each agency should have a written statement which defines its aims and objectives.

Principle

Each agency should agree with its commissioners a statement of the aims objectives and targets of the contribution it makes to the pattern of service provision overall.

Principle

Each agency should then develop standards that are capable of audit.

Principle

Each agency should have resources allocated within its contracts to enable it to undertake systematic internal audit and evaluation of its services.

CHAPTER 13

Training

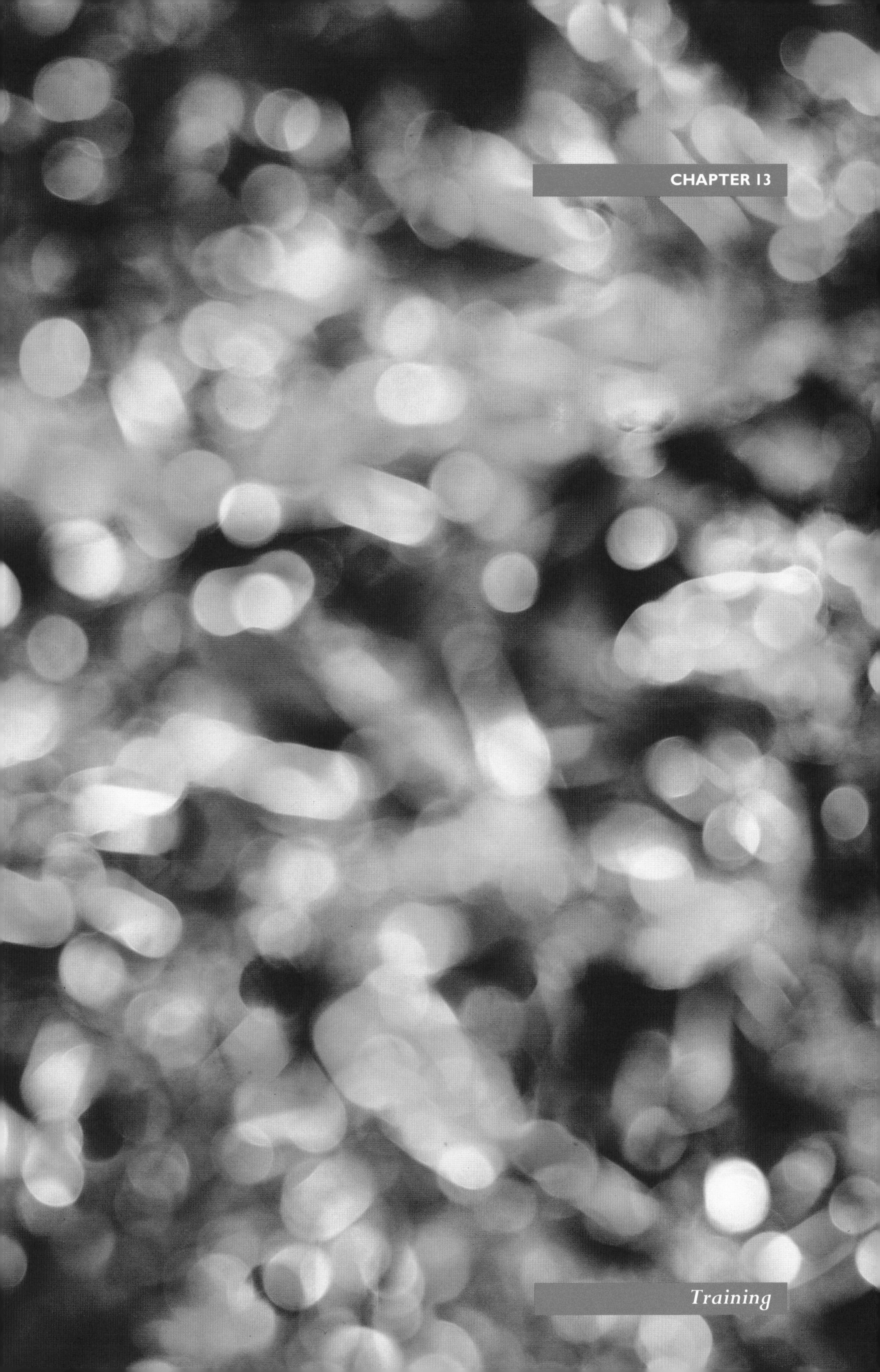

TRAINING

INTRODUCTION

400 The recommendations in this chapter are designed to deal with the concerns about services that were identified by the HAS and the priorities set by the White Paper. Thus, this chapter is intended to be complementary to the recommendations on training in *Tackling Drugs Together*. It outlines ways in which those recommendations might be interpreted and put into effect within local services.

401 Effective training for relevant staff is the key to achieving the recommendations of this report. Training is the means by which services can ensure that quality standards are met and that interventions made with young people are appropriate to each individual's age, stage of development and problems. The delivery of appropriate training programmes should also assure commissioners that they are moving towards the provision of balanced services.

402 Commissioners and purchasers require training in order to discharge their responsibilities effectively. This should be the subject of an organisational development programme within each authority.

403 Intervention with young people who misuse substances, who may have complex needs, requires particular skills and knowledge. The development and maintenance of knowledge and skills requires:

- a thorough initial training;
- specialist training for appropriate staff;
- training in leading and managing teams;
- training in designing and delivering integrated care programmes;
- continuing education;
- access to support and supervision.

404 *"It is .... important that all those involved with young people, both in formal and informal settings, should have accurate information about drugs and are helped to develop the confidence to develop effective and consistent drug prevention messages..." (Tackling Drugs Together,* 1995). It follows that those who are involved with young people in different settings have differing roles and responsibilities. The types of training provided should reflect this. The HAS has identified the requirement for four levels of training.

- General training for all health, social services, and education, youth justice, probation, police and non-statutory sector staff (Level 1).
- Advanced training for selected staff of a wide range of agencies (Level 2).
- Specialist training for the staff of specialist services (Level 3).
- Specific training for the staff of highly specialised low-volume services (Level 4).

405 In addition, there is a need for information and education on substance misuse to be readily available to parents, school governors and many others.

406 To achieve maximum impact, programmes of training should be adequately resourced and co-ordinated:

- at a local level, to ensure multi-agency participation in commissioning and delivering training;

- at a national level, to identify and promote good practice and to encourage national training bodies to ensure that education on substance use and misuse receives appropriate emphasis in the training courses of a wide range of professions and disciplines.

407 These four levels of training have the advantage of corresponding with the four-tier strategic approach. Nonetheless, it should be appreciated that the four tiers and levels of training do not match exactly. General training is required by all those staff who work in Tier 1 but, by virtue of their particular roles, some who elect or who are required to work more frequently with young people also require the more advanced level of training. Level three training is required by all staff who work in Tiers 2 and 3 and level four training is appropriate for all staff of Tier 4 services and to some staff of providers that offer Tier 2 and 3 services.

PROGRAMMES OF TRAINING

Level 1 - General Training

408 Basic knowledge about substance use and misuse and the skills to assess and manage children and adolescents should form part of professional training at qualifying level and in induction and training for all:

- doctors

- nurses

- social workers

- psychologists

- teachers

- youth workers

- workers in non-statutory sector projects who have a remit for work with young people

- probation officers

- police officers

- prison staff

- the support staff of the agencies that employ the staff listed above.

409 Managers of commissioning authorities and provider services should receive sufficient in-service training to ensure that they understand the nature of the interventions that may be provided by the professional staff of their services. Through training, these managers should become more aware of the need to promote the training and support of the staff of provider agencies.

410 The knowledge, attitudes and skills required at this basic level of training are summarised in Table 22.

Table 22

Level 1 - General Training - Core Knowledge, Attitudes and Skills
• A basic knowledge of the physical, psychological and social effects of mood-altering drugs and alcohol, including the impacts of substance misuse by parents on children and adolescents.
• Awareness of the professional's own attitudes towards, and experiences of substance use and misuse and how these may impact on their work with young people who use and/or misuse substances.
• The ability to recognise substance misuse by young people.
• Assessment skills, with particular reference to the ability to distinguish between substance use, for example of an experimental nature, and harmful substance use.
• Basic life support skills.
• The ability to deliver simple interventions, for example, information or advice about withdrawal from substance use and harm-minimisation, when appropriate.
• Information on local specialist substance misuse agencies and their specialist staff and about when and how to refer.

Level 2 - Advanced Training

411 After initial general training, specific training is required by some staff who have a specialised role, or who, by virtue of their particular job, may be more likely to encounter vulnerable young people at risk of developing problems arising from substance use. Additionally, when the circumstances do not suggest the need for more specialised training for their staff, agencies and organisations should consider designating a number of key staff to act as resources of information and skill for their colleagues. These designated staff should receive advanced training.

412 Those staff of non-specialist agencies who require advanced training may include:

- doctors, especially, hospital and community paediatricians, child and adolescent psychiatrists and general psychiatrists;

- social workers, especially these in child protection teams, child and family teams, hospital teams, youth justice teams and those who work in residential establishments for children and adolescents;

- school nurses and midwives;

- teachers who have a pastoral role;

- probation officers who work with young offenders;

- the staff of non-statutory sector drug, alcohol, or youth services which, although they do not provide a specialist Tier 3 or 4 substance misuse service, work with children and adolescents.

413 Staff of some disciplines, for example GPs, may require additional education and training in order to discharge their specific responsibilities.

414 Table 23 summarises the knowledge, attitudes and skills that should be the subject of advanced training programmes.

Table 23

Level 2 - Advanced Training - Knowledge, Attitudes and Skills
● The core basic knowledge, attitudes and skills summarised in Table 22.
● Skills in communicating with and counselling young people and/or their parents.
● Knowledge of, and skills in therapeutic interventions, including those that are brief and focused, and knowledge of the indications for longer-term and more specialised interventions.
● Skills in multi-disciplinary working in a range of different contexts.
● Skills of managing conflict in attitudes, opinions and beliefs.
● Knowledge of when to inform parents or the authorities and when to offer confidentiality.
● Knowledge of the law relating to purchasing and consuming drugs, alcohol and other substances with particular reference to young people.
● The ability to construe and manage the boundaries of staff members' expertise.
● Record-keeping skills - awareness of the needs for and methods of keeping detailed contemporaneous records.
● The skills of contributing to the development of services for managing people who misuse substances.

415 It is important that staff should be exposed to repeated in-service training of this kind and that it is supported by regular clinical supervision, if they are to maintain and develop their skills. The model of supervision provided most frequently by social services departments is one which offers regular, recorded sessions. This is considered to be appropriate for adaptation to substance misuse services as it combines supervision on substantive important professional issues with work on personal development.

Level 3 - Specialist Training for the Staff of Specialised Services

416 In this context, the adjective *specialised* refers to all staff whose roles are to provide: focused education on drugs, alcohol and other substances; specialised interventions and treatments for young people who misuse substances; or specialised services for young people who have mental health disorders. In practice, it is likely that these staff include:

- teachers with particular responsibilities for the personal, social and health education (PSHE) curriculum;

- staff in both statutory and non-statutory sector specialised services for children and adolescents who misuse substances;

- staff of child and adolescent mental health services.

In reality, the training needs of each of these groups is somewhat different.

417 Teachers who are responsible for personal, social and health education should understand the principles of educating young people about drugs, alcohol and other substances. They should have the skills and confidence to deliver this education effectively. The White Paper *Tackling Drugs Together* acknowledges their needs for appropriate training to support them in this task and *Drug Education in Schools: The Need for New Impetus* (ACMD 1993) provides detailed consideration.

Table 24

The ACMD Proposals on the Training Needs of Staff in Schools
• Knowledge of social, medical and legal issues relating to drugs
• Training on welfare issues
• Overt school policies on discipline
• Contact with parents
• Contact with outside agencies
• The abilities to handle issues of confidentiality appropriately

418 While the staff of substance misuse services and CAMHS have expertise in their respective specialties, experience indicates that the staff of each often lack specialist knowledge appropriate to the other. Specialist training should address this issue. Tables 25 and 26 outline the items of training at Level 3 required by the staff of each of these types of service.

Table 25

Level 3 - Specialist Training for the Staff of Substance Misuse Services
• The core knowledge, attitudes and skills outlined in Tables 22 and 23.
• A working knowledge of child and adolescent development.
• Understanding of the particular impact of major events on the lives of children and adolescents, for example, abuse, bereavement and major traumatic events.
• Skills in communicating with and counselling young people and their parents.

Table 26

Level 3 - Specialist Training for the Staff of CAMHS
• The core knowledge, attitudes and skills outlined in Tables 22 and 23.
• The ability to conduct therapeutic interventions (including brief focused practical work) with people who misuse substances, and knowledge of the indications for longer-term and more specialised interventions.

419 Additionally, both of these groups of staff require further specialist training with regard to the issues listed in Table 27.

Table 27

Level 3 - Additional Joint Specialist Training - for the Staff of Substance Misuse Services and CAMHS
• The skills of multi-disciplinary work and those of leading and managing shared care, including managing conflict in attitudes, opinions and beliefs.
• The knowledge and skills to handle issues of confidentiality and consent to treatment that involve the rights of young people, and the responsibilities of parents and professionals.
• Assessment skills, with particular reference to the ability to discern the severity and risks of substance misuse, the complexity of any planned intervention and the competence of a young person to consent to treatment or intervention.
• The law relating to drugs, alcohol and other substances, with particular reference to young people.
• The ability to manage and work with child protection issues including those that concern the relationship between substance misuse and the vulnerability of children and young people.

Level 4 - Training for the Staff of Very Specialised Services

420 The training requirements for staff in Tier 4 services are similar to those of Tier 3. In addition, they require intensive training and supervision with respect to the principles and practices of each of the intervention and treatment modalities they offer and on the implications of managing vulnerable young people in particular settings (for example, day and inpatient units and specialist rehabilitation units). Their very level of super-specialisation may render them remote from current practice and services in Tiers 1 and 2. Therefore, there are likely to be added requirements on national, regional and local training programmes for Tier 4 staff. All staff require training on issues relating to the impacts of ethnicity and culture.

EVALUATION

421 Evaluating the effects of training can be challenging. Nonetheless, it is reasonable to assume that the most important factor bearing on the effective performance of services is that they are staffed by knowledgeable, skilled and well trained people. Experience indicates that when things go wrong, the need for staff training is often identified. Since the training requirements identified in this chapter relate largely to the maintenance of standards of good practice, service audit mechanisms can be appropriate tools for evaluating the conduct and impact of training.

THE ROLE OF COMMISSIONERS AND PURCHASERS

422 While it is not the role of service commissioners and purchasers to provide training for providers, they may decide to use the commissioning and purchasing processes to ensure that appropriate training is provided as a part of their quality assurance and monitoring arrangements. For example, purchasers could:

- require providers to show evidence that they have defined the levels and types of expertise required or expected in service specifications;

- ensure that budgets include a suitable level of expenditure on training;

- use the contract monitoring process to work with providers to ensure that their staff have the necessary expertise by improving their access to training, professional support and supervision.

423 Commissioners and purchasers should be mindful of their own needs for training in order to keep their knowledge and maintain it. The organisational capacity of commissioning agencies should be such that the training needs of their staff are met appropriately by their individual programmes for continuing education and personal professional development.

CO-ORDINATION AND RESOURCES

424 The need for a local training strategy on substance misuse is well documented, most recently in the *Tackling Drugs Together* (1995) which requires that Drug Action Teams should submit plans which include *inter alia "arrangements for commissioning and co-ordinating services, training provision and other action to tackle drug misuse ..."* by 31 December 1995. That document recognises the need for training and education for a diverse range of professionals including:

- school staff, governors and parents

- police officers (including advanced training for officers who specialise in drugs work)

- probation staff who work with offenders who misuse substances

- prison staff

- the staff of social services who work with young people

- primary healthcare workers

- doctors

- nurses

425 Unfortunately, the Government's strategy for 1995-1998, contained in the White Paper, does not identify with the same thoroughness how this training is to be provided, by whom and with what resources. Training is an essential, but relatively expensive commodity. Without national leadership and co-ordination of training initiatives (as recommended by ACMD in 1990 and 1995), it is difficult to envisage how the training objectives suggested in the White Paper will be achieved.

The Implications for the
Providers of Services

CHAPTER 14

*Towards Comprehensive
Services for Young
People*

INTRODUCTION

426 The development of a comprehensive service for children and adolescents who use and misuse substances requires that commissioners understand that it is most unlikely that a single provider can deal with all of these needs. At one end of the continuum of need are young people who use drugs, alcohol or other substances *experimentally* or *recreationally,* while at the other end are smaller numbers of young people involved in *dependent* or *seriously harmful use* of substances.

427 The increasing use of drugs and alcohol by young people, undoubtedly, means that a greater number of them will suffer adverse consequences such as accidents and overdoses or develop longer-term problems of dependence. Knowledge of the increase in problems and of the dearth of services demonstrates the need for a range of services that offers balanced programmes of education, prevention, intervention and treatment adjusted and targeted by assessed need in each district.

428 In the future, Drug Action Teams or Drug and Alcohol Action Teams will be instrumental in making recommendations on the development of services and on their implementation. When developing services, it is important that a range of professional advice is available, directed specifically at the needs of young people.

429 By their very nature, *experimental* and *recreational* substance *use* remain relatively hidden and unlikely to come to the attention of professionals, service providers or commissioners, or to be quantifiable, unless specific techniques for early identification are adopted. All too often, experimental and recreational users of substances lack information about the substances they consume and of the possible consequences of their use. Therefore, many people underestimate the risks they run or lack caution in their use of substances. This emphasises the need to ensure that young people have easy access to appropriate information and education and opportunities to discuss substance misuse in a safe environment.

430 Equally, young people who are engaged in dependent or harmful substance use may present themselves to a wide range of agencies for information, advice and help. Often, young people request information and help from non-specialist, generic services and they should be encouraged to do so. Thus, agencies across the spectrum of social and health care already make a contribution to the provision of a service overall. In the future, they will continue to play important roles in the development of a comprehensive substance misuse service for young people in each district. The HAS service visits showed that the various elements of service that have been delivered have been provided outside any coherent concept of a whole service for children and adolescents. A joint approach to commissioning, purchasing and providing services could ensure that an integrated concept underlies future service delivery.

431 Assessment of need should take particular account of, and identify vulnerable children and adolescents who are at a higher risk or excessive risk of use and misuse of substances, and who may have other behaviour and mental health problems.

432 It is vital that the staff of services have:

- an understanding of the complexity of needs of young people;
- the competence and skills required to provide comprehensive assessments;
- effective professional and clinical leadership;

- sound management;

- good communication networks;

- effective arrangements for collaboration and care programming as care is often shared between staff members and between agencies;

- effective inter-agency communication at planning levels, as well as at the level of face-to-face contacts with clients and patients.

THE COMPONENTS OF A COMPREHENSIVE SERVICE

433 Table 28 lists the components of a fully comprehensive service that are required by children and adolescents who use and misuse substances.

Table 28

The Components of a Comprehensive Service
• Health promotion
• Education
• Prevention
• Information and advice for young people
• Education and support for parents and families
• Peer education
• Alternative activities that are enjoyable
• Direct access and self-referral services
• One-stop shops/comprehensive centres
• Outreach services
• Drop-in community centres
• Outpatient services
• Day care and treatment programmes
• Inpatient services
• Specialist rehabilitation services

434 Table 29 lists the range of settings in which these services should be available.

Table 29

Settings In Which Substance Misuse Services for Children and Adolescents Should be Provided
• The premises of primary healthcare services
• Social services premises
• Schools
• Premises provided by non-statutory agencies
• At the sites of community provision for homeless people, including soup kitchens, night shelters, hostels etc
• Drop-in centres
• Community mental health centres
• One-stop shops and comprehensive centres
• Outpatient clinics
• Accident and emergency departments
• Day centres
• Day hospitals
• Medical inpatient facilities and wards
• Psychiatric inpatient wards

435 Readers are also referred to the section in Chapter 15 in *Together We Stand* entitled *Key Leadership and Management Issues* as many of these apply in full measure to services for children and adolescents who misuse substances. Many of the principles of providing child and adolescent mental health services expounded in Chapter 12 of that report are also relevant. The following commentary on selected service components is offered as a guide in designing and delivering services for young people who use and misuse substances.

THE ACTIVITIES OF A COMPREHENSIVE SERVICE

Direct Contact Services

Health Promotion and Healthcare Advice

436 In recent years the primary focus of health promotion services has been on initiatives and campaigns designed to achieve the targets defined within the *Health of the Nation* White Paper (1992). Objectives and targets were set for each of the five key areas described in that document: mental illness; HIV and sexual health; accident prevention; coronary heart disease; and cancer.

437 Specific targets relating to alcohol consumption and drug use are included in the key areas of coronary heart disease, HIV and sexual health. Reduced consumption of alcohol and drugs may have an impact in achieving targets for the other key areas also. For example, *"focusing on drug and alcohol abuse would have a greater impact on adolescent suicide rates than any other primary prevention programme"*... *Suicide Prevention, The Challenge Confronted,* (Williams and Morgan, 1994).

438 A health promotion service should act as a focus and catalyst for individuals, agencies and communities involved in primary and secondary prevention initiatives related to drug and alcohol misuse. To fulfil this role, the health promotion service must maintain an overview of the population it serves by working closely with the Director of Public Health. Sensitivity to, and awareness of different cultures and ethnic groups is an important consideration.

439 Health promotion initiatives that target substance use by children and adolescents should involve a range of individuals and agencies, for example, parents, schools and the youth service. The co-ordinating role of the health promotion service is important. It should encourage joint working, provide support (eg, educational resources and materials, and guidance on setting-up projects), and encourage good health promotion practice (eg, by demonstrating how best to use educational resources) among practitioners and other components of the service. It must be able to define specific targets and monitor them.

440 The health promotion service should ensure that, in common with initiatives targeted at other groups, work with children and adolescents is orientated towards: building self-esteem and self-confidence; teaching skills such as assertiveness and decision-making; and providing positive images of alternative activities and lifestyles.

441 This range of activities and tasks for health promotion services has much in common with its work with other target groups and is unlikely to require specialist staff. Nevertheless, it is important to ensure that the staff has sufficient specialist knowledge about drugs and alcohol and their misuse and about the needs and psychological development of children and adolescents.

442 Healthcare advice must be up-to-date. Agencies and practitioners who offer advice must be aware of the current patterns of substance use and should be well informed about the risks arising from the use of substances, particularly those that are in common contemporary use. For example, as this report is published, paractitioners should be aware of the growing use of Ecstasy (MDMA) by young people and of its potential hazards. Many young people require not only accurate information about these matters but recreational users also need advice on harm reduction. In the case of Ecstasy, this includes providing specific warnings and stressing the importance of the availability of water and something to drink or eat that keeps the body's salt levels up at raves. Additionally the capacity to provide basic life support interventions to those who develop problems requiring them are important. The medical advice offered by the Department of Health on this issue is *"the same for someone who is dancing all night as it would be for someone who is running a marathon. People engaged in prolonged physical activity need to stop themselves dehydrating by drinking water and need to drink or eat something that keeps the salt levels in their body up. Salty snacks, fruit juice, fizzy drinks and sports drinks will all help to keep the body provided with the minerals it needs. Water is an antidote to dehydration, not Ecstasy."* Additionally, young people require accurate information and advice about the contemporary presentations of drugs, including the nature of the tablet and powder forms in which they may be supplied, and about the potency and side-effects of substances that are in circulation.

Education and Prevention

443 Education and prevention initiatives are valuable and important parts of a comprehensive service. Many will be delivered by primary direct access services at Tier I. It is important that these programmes are researched and evaluated, and adapted to the needs of the children in a particular area. Nonetheless, at any tier of the four-tier template, provision of appropriate education and preventive activities should form part of an integrated programme of care for each young person.

Alternative Activities That Are Enjoyable

444 Many prevention programmes are based on the notion that involving young people at risk in drug and alcohol-free activities may have an effect on their use of substances. The evidence suggests that those at less risk are more likely to participate. Youth workers have an important role in helping young people to find interesting and stimulating alternatives to drug use. For example, the Albany Plan in New York is a multi-faceted approach to prevention which includes providing summer jobs and recreation for young people alongside education programmes. The initiative mounted by the National Association for the Care and Resettlement of Offenders (NACRO) in the UK offers alternatives such as music sessions, dance classes, video projects, art and comic workshops. The success of projects of this kind has been found to be very variable.

Education and Support for Parents and Other Key Persons

445 Parents and guardians should have access to services that can provide accurate information about alcohol and all other substances. Unfortunately, the HAS service visits found that some services for younger people discourage the involvement of parents, often to promote the belief of young people in the confidentiality of the service. However, most now

appreciate the needs of parents, and some services have developed helplines, parent clinics or surgeries that offer support, advice and counselling to parents or guardians. Given the diversity of possible roles, it is essential that each service is clear about the range of information and intervention that it offers.

446 Parent support groups have been developed in the USA under the umbrella of the National Federation of Parents for Drug Free Use. However, they have found maintaining the interest and participation of parents difficult and virtually no research has been conducted to evaluate the effectiveness of these parent groups. Recently, more comprehensive, community-based prevention programmes that also involve parents have been developed in the USA.

447 In the UK, the Drugs Prevention Initiative has been instrumental in the development of community-based approaches; particularly the provision of information, advice and support and the organisation of educational seminars for parents, school governors and teachers. *Tackling Drugs Together* acknowledges the importance of support information and advice to parents. One of the Government's objectives is to *"raise awareness among school staff, governors and parents of the issues associated with drug misuse in young people"*.

448 The Drugs Prevention Initiative and the Community Safety Strategy are initiating and evaluating preventive techniques and programmes that involve parents, community groups and young people. These community-based approaches are to be encouraged but service design should take account of the research literature that exists on the effectiveness of these approaches. All programmes should be evaluated.

449 Ideally, preventive initiatives should not be separated from other interventions, including services that offer treatment because a continuum of care is required to meet the needs of young people. Services that provide education and support for parents and other key people in the community are an important part of that continuum.

Peer Education

450 Presently, there is much interest in peer education. Some prevention programmes have included peer leaders as either the primary agents in the work done, or as helpers. Peer leaders may have greater credibility than teachers and they have been recognised as effective in stimulating poorly motivated students. The selection of peer leaders is crucial - for instance those who are popular with teachers may have lower credibility with their own peers. It is unusual for peer leaders to have experience in teaching or classroom management, and there are some gender differences in response to peer-led programmes. A combination of teachers and peer leaders may offer the greatest advantage. The various forms of peer education programmes require evaluation.

Information and Advice

451 Children and young people require accurate information about substances and the problems that may be associated with their use and misuse. Many methods may be used to disseminate information: didactic lectures; discussion; audio-video presentations; posters and pamphlets; and group problem-solving exercises. A wide range of services can supply this information including: general practitioners and other members of primary health care teams; youth centres and youth workers; social services departments; drug prevention services; and school health services. Depending on their specialisation, these services correspond to Tiers 1 and 2 of the strategic template.

452 It is essential that the information given is accurate, appropriate and relevant to young people. It is important that the language is appropriate and that translation into the appropriate languages used in the area is organised. This information should be accessible at numerous outlets such as health centres, libraries, youth clubs, counselling agencies, family planning centres, schools, colleges, all-night garages, and other areas where young people congregate.

453 Experience has shown that some agencies that supply information can exploit appropriately their contacts with younger people to provide opportunities for them to discuss problems arising from substance use, to raise awareness of the problems of use, to encourage positive lifestyles, to educate young people on safer and responsible use of alcohol, and to offer individual counselling. The staff members involved are in a pivotal position to aid contact of individuals with more specialised services.

The Roles and Settings of Some Direct Contact Services

454 These services correspond to Tier 1 of the strategic template. They provide numerous and important gateways for identifying and assessing and for intervening with young people with drug or alcohol related problems. It is important that these services are culturally sensitive, appropriate to the needs of ethnic groups and have access to interpreters, when appropriate.

455 Table 30 summarises the potential roles of Tier 1 services.

Table 30

The Roles of Primary Level, Direct Contact Services (Tier 1)
• Providing interventions in a range of accessible and approachable environments
• Providing information, advice and support
• Assessing levels of drug and alcohol use by individuals
• Assessing associated or linked problems
• Assessing other indicators of vulnerability
• Assessing the urgency of problems experienced by individuals and taking appropriate action
• Offering help in the management of crises
• Providing initial counselling
• Making appropriate referrals to specialised services
• Providing support to parents and carers

Primary Healthcare Services

456   Primary healthcare services are in a particularly important position. They may be able to identify some younger people who are using substances, those who use them in problematic ways and those with other problems and disorders, such as conduct disorder, depression, or family problems. Assessment of consumption of drugs and alcohol should always include assessment of the presence or absence of the consequences of sustained use or misuse and of other possible related health or social problems. Information, advice and support, and interventions such as motivational interviewing and counselling on reducing of the use of alcohol and other substances, should also be available from primary healthcare teams. These brief interventions have been used successfully in primary care settings to help adults to stop smoking cigarettes and to help adults who are consuming alcohol at moderate to hazardous levels. They have not been evaluated for young people who use drugs and alcohol, but the HAS believes that they should be applied and then evaluated.

457   Some primary healthcare teams now provide well adolescent clinics, often run by nurses. They aim to:
- meet the young people who are registered with the practice;
- offer assurances of confidentiality;
- offer advice and information, when appropriate;
- provide opportunities to identify problems;
- provide opportunities for discussion of aspects of sexual health, contraception and the use of alcohol, cigarettes and drugs.

The impact of these screening clinics requires further evaluation.

458   An important principle of screening clinics is that they focus on several aspects of health, lifestyle and behaviour at the same time and have the capacity to offer advice and support on a broad range of adolescent health matters. In the future, an important target group should be male adolescents.

459   It has been argued that only well young people will attend these clinics and that this will invalidate their preventive and educative advantages. In relationship to depression, some enterprising service innovations have shown that this is not necessarily the case (Bernard and Garralda, 1995). Nonetheless, the development of these services should include their evaluation. Additionally, primary healthcare staff who conduct these clinics may require training that incorporates information on normal child and adolescent development and on specific issues relating to the health of adolescents.

School Health Services

460   These services should: be culturally appropriate; be sensitive to language; play an important part in the provision of health services for children and adolescents of school age; and provide advice to teachers. They are well placed to: identify vulnerable children; initiate early referrals; and advise parents, teachers and the staff of primary health care teams. Again, it is essential that all the staff are adequately and appropriately trained and supervised. Training on drug, alcohol and solvent use and on cigarette smoking is essential. Experience indicates that the staff of school health services require clear guidelines on concepts of confidentiality and consent as these matters are faced recurrently by health service staff who work in education settings.

Outreach Services

461 Assertive outreach activities are an essential component in the overall continuum of services for young people. Outreach can be delivered by many agencies including youth services, social services, primary healthcare teams and CAMHS. The task is to provide advice and information, and to assist adolescents to gain access to more specialised health and allied services. Outreach services are particularly valuable in making contact with those young people who are homeless or disadvantaged; and those who, generally, do not seek help, unless they are in a state of crisis.

462 Often, homeless young people use drugs and alcohol in problematic ways and are at high risk of substance misuse. Agencies that contribute to the service for children and adolescents who misuse substances should collaborate in developing a range of outreach approaches to avert crises and to attempt to retain young people in contact with the services they need. Approaches may include: street outreach workers going where 'street kids' congregate; leaving cards with access numbers and addresses; providing telephone hotlines; and putting young people in contact with drop-in shelters where clothes, food and bus tokens are distributed, and places where there is crisis counselling, as well as showers and storage space. Outreach organisations must be effectively structured and their staff need training. Youth workers who work with vulnerable young people in these ways require a range of back-up services that can provide short and longer-term shelter, medical and psycho-social care and specific interventions related to substance use.

463 It is important that outreach workers are sensitive to culture and race, operate in various communities, 'out of hours' when necessary, have good liaison with the police and are aware of matters impacting on their own personal safety.

464 Caution is advised in the provision of needles and syringes by outreach workers and others to young people, particularly those under 16, without an appropriate and comprehensive assessment. It may be that urgent referral to a specialist service is required before this facility is offered.

Drop-In Community Centres

465 Youth counselling and advice centres that are appropriate to the cultures and needs of young people should be available in all major centres of population. *Tackling Drugs Together* calls for *"activities which provide recreation and opportunities to develop a variety of skills... to resist drugs."* It acknowledges the importance of the statutory and voluntary youth services, education programmes and individual counselling. It notes the importance of targeting people who are most at risk through detached youth work, group work or special projects. Services should be provided in a range of environments through which contact is made with young people.

One-Stop Shops and Comprehensive Centres of Service

466 In the USA, there has been a lack of appropriate services for adolescents and/or lack of access to those that are available. Consequently, school-linked or community- based programmes have been established that offer comprehensive, accessible, appropriate and confidential services designed to meet the broad health needs of adolescents. Similar types of services are beginning to be developed in England. Often, the nature and expertise of the services that One-Stop Shops provide, means that they straddle the boundary between Tiers 1 and 2 in the stategic framework.

467 The accessibility of these services, particularly in respect of their location, their opening hours, and the range of services offered (for example, legal advice, contraceptive advice, recreational opportunities and counselling) and the commitment of staff to young people, make this option attractive. An important principle is that one-stop shops should be accessible to, and meet the needs of all groups, including disabled young people, adolescents from ethnic minority backgrounds, those from different cultures, and men and women. So far, the effectiveness of these services has not been well evaluated and this should be built in where they are developed.

468 The roles of these centres should be clearly defined so they do not duplicate primary healthcare and other existing direct contact services but do enhance access to more specialised services. One-stop shops should complement both primary care and specialist drug and alcohol services rather than substituting for them. They should be co-ordinated with other services.

469 The operational policies of these types of drop-in centre should contain guidance on staff training, confidentiality and supervision and procedures for handling a variety of incidents such as inoculation injuries. Although some services for young people guarantee absolute confidentiality to young people, all services should operate within the guidelines of the relevant Area Child Protection Committee. The staff of some organisations require specific guidance and help with drawing-up and implementing operational policies on these issues.

470 These centres, and the outreach components of any mental health service for children and adolescents, should attempt to be in contact with vulnerable young people, and children and adolescents who have a range of problems, including homelessness, drug or alcohol misuse, prostitution, family disruption, conduct disorders and mental disorders. A key feature of these services is their capacity to gain and then sustain contacts with young people. More specialised services for young people with problems arising from substance misuse (Tiers 2, 3 and 4) should be available to accept referrals from one-stop shops.

471 All of the agencies at Tier 1 discussed here should have staff identified within their agency who have the task of linking with agencies providing services in the other tiers. They should have specific knowledge of the services available for young people and the ability to refer to them.

Specialist Drug and Alcohol Services for Young People

Developing Specialist Services

472 Specialised services are predominantly represented by Tiers 2 and 3 of the strategic framework. The HAS service visits indicated that there are a few specialist services available specifically for young people who have problems as the result of their use of drugs, alcohol and other substances. As the age of initiation into drug and alcohol reduces, and the prevalence of use increases, the likelihood is that more young people will develop problems that will require services of this nature.

473 There are many issues to be addressed in designing and delivering a specialist service for children and adolescents:

- the accessibility of the service to young people;
- referral procedures for the service;
- the environment in which the service operates;
- its opening hours;
- policies on confidentiality;
- the competence of staff in respect of:
  - their commitment to younger people;
  - their ability to offer interventions and treatments to people who: use substances; have problems arising from substance use; or misuse substances;
  - their understanding of and abilities in applying child and adolescent developmental concepts;
- professional leadership;
- the involvement of other agencies including partnerships with other health and social services and other non-statutory sector agencies;
- the co-ordination and liaison that is needed with other services for children and adolescents in the area to maximise the accessibility and appropriateness of the service and to minimise duplication and gaps in service;
- assessment procedures;
- sources of funding.

474 One option for the future is that of exploiting the potential for expanding the scope of specialists services by invigorating collaboration between existing drug and alcohol services, child and adolescent mental health services, community child health services, social and education services and non-statutory sector services. Collaboration should also afford the capacity to establish and evaluate early intervention programmes and develop services orientated to those young people who have disorders that require this level of expertise.

475 It is essential that services for younger people who have needs arising from their use or misuse of substances are developed on the basis of a district strategy that is co-ordinated with and encompasses the overlapping strategies for child health and child and adolescent mental health services. Services should not focus on one substance alone, such as alcohol, but should take a broad view of substance use and misuse. Some services address the problems that arise from the use or misuse of one substance alone, either for financial reasons or for ideological reasons, but the emerging preferred view is that agencies should be capable of responding to the needs of young people that arise from use of any one or more of a range of substances, including alcohol, steroids, solvents, illicit and licit drugs. This may however have knock-on implications for adult services that focus on alcohol alone, or drugs alone (though presently, there is a move towards the integration of these services for adults). Presently, *Tackling Drugs Together* identifies the need for Drug Action Teams to establish strategies to address drugs, though the White Paper acknowledges that teams can also focus on alcohol misuse if they choose to do so.

476 Around the country, there are many examples of services that are beginning to be developed in this way. In one area, a counselling agency has been set up to cater for young people exclusively. It offers advice, information, intervention within a range of problems, hosts a drug and alcohol clinic specifically for young people and is provided by the local adult addiction service in which staff are supervised and assisted by CAMHS staff. Additionally, the staff of this addiction service are committed to receiving training on child health issues. This tripartite arrangement has produced an accessible service and brought a wide perspective to the problems experienced by young people. Experience indicates that the particular challenges that arise are those considered in earlier chapters, including confidentiality, consent to treatment, and the competence and training of the staff.

477 In others areas, staff identified from the local child and adolescent mental health service offer help. The experience of the HAS is that the impact of these initiatives is more limited as they depend on the interests and enthusiasm of particular members of staff.

478 Another option is to base the development of a new service on the existing specialist staff of drug and alcohol services for adults, provided by the non-statutory or statutory sectors or both, working alongside the local CAMHS staff. These two services can combine to provide joint assertive outreach and assessment services that are able to refer individuals in need to the appropriate agencies after assessment. A number of specialised services of this kind are now being developed or at a planning stage.

479 Whatever approach is adopted, it is essential that new specialist services are evaluated.

480 Conjointly provided services should develop explicit guidelines on good practice that recognise the developmental needs of children and adolescents and are agreed by all partners. All should work within the guidelines of the Area Child Protection Committee.

481 Social services have a vital part to play in achieving a continuum of care and a broad spectrum of services. *Tackling Drugs Together,* notes that local authority social services departments can support families and provide for the welfare of the children, using their powers under the Children Act 1989. Children who misuse drugs may be regarded as children in need within the meaning of the Act. Services offered by social services departments should be linked with all other services and particularly those in Tier 1 and 2 from other sectors such as: youth services; those that offer vocational training, other employment training opportunities, and alternative leisure pursuits; and addiction services. Social services may be located in many premises including one-stop shops, specific social services premises, youth clubs and primary healthcare facilities. Their availability in such places, maximises access and the co-ordination between services, eases referrals and makes for better contact with a wide range of other services in the same location (eg, financial, housing and legal advice, support and contraceptive advice). Social services departments may also purchase specific services for women, people from ethnic minorities and for people who have particular needs, including that for specialist residential rehabilitation.

482 In summary, specialised substance use and misuse services for children and adolescents should:

- be conveniently located and easy to find;

- be effectively publicised to potential users;

- be perceived as approachable, accepting of young people with problems and appropriate to their culture;

- be flexible so as to accommodate the varied needs of children, young persons and their families;

- be accessible to people with disability and to young mothers;

- not mix young people with adults who misuse substance;

- consider matters of race, sexuality, ethnicity and the availability of signing and interpreting services in their operational policies.

483 In addition, policies and guidelines should be developed (especially where there are to be partnerships across a range of agencies) to cover:

- management responsibilities and accountability;

- supervision;

- training of staff appropriate to their levels of specialisation;

- confidentiality;

- consent to treatment;

- child protection procedures;

- control of infectious disease, eg through procedures for responding to inoculation injuries.

The Interventions Provided by Specialist Services

Prevention

484 This section summarises the range of interventions that should be provided by specialist components of a comprehensive service. Earlier, this report identified the importance of early intervention (eg, advice, information, early identification, parent support and other preventive projects) through service components mainly in Tier 1 but also in Tier 2.

485 In the literature relating to adult services, there is evidence of the effectiveness of brief interventions for alcohol and smoking, particularly in the groups of people who did not overtly seek treatment. These brief interventions, which are often a mixture of cognitive behavioural techniques and motivational interviewing, might be very usefully adapted for young people and might be provided by staff in Tier 2 and some Tier 1 services.

486 Some early intervention programmes may also be considered that directly promote mental health with the intention of reducing future drug use.

487 Evidence suggests that pre-school education of children from poor communities has long-term beneficial effects. The data provided by Robins and McEvoy suggests that if identification of young people who are unlikely to use or misuse drugs and alcohol in the future is to be optimised, a focus upon those with the most severe extensive conduct problems is needed. Additionally, benefits have been established for multi-modal interventions that combine individual counselling, focused help for parents, group work and specialist teaching have been recorded. More research and evaluation should be conducted in the UK.

More Specialised Interventions and Treatments

488 Young people who attend the specialist levels of service provision proposed in this report are likely to have a complex array of problems. Careful assessment should be made of associated problems, of the consequences of alcohol and drug use and of any other behaviour or mental disorders and of the nature of the positive assets provided by the family or other social agencies. A comprehensive assessment will also cover the competences of the referred child or young person, his or her emotional maturity, and his or her wishes and opinions.

489 Essential Tier 1 and Tier 2 service components include the capability to assess individuals and the ability to provide access to services for common physical ailments. Urine screening, counselling on infectious disease (eg, hepatitis B and C and HIV) and testing for it, when appropriate and a prescribing service are other essential components of services at Tiers 2 and 3. As poly drug use, without dependence on a specific drug, is frequent in young people, caution is advised on prescribed substances, such as methadone, early in a relationship with a young person. Deaths of young people have occurred from ingestion of prescribed methadone or dependence has been established as a result of injudicious prescribing. It is also important that detoxification from alcohol, either through day care services or at home is available. Harm-reduction through, for example, discussion, counselling, promotion of the use of sterile needles through exchanges, and providing advice on managing overdosing is important. Much has been learned about good practice from experience with operating services directed primarily at adults.

490 Other interventions include cognitive-behavioural therapy, family assessment, and therapy, individual counselling and supportive psycho-therapy. Group work, particularly that based on cognitive-behavioural techniques, can also be useful.

491 A minority of young people who have problems arising from drug and alcohol misuse require admission to inpatient beds for more detailed assessment of their drug and alcohol use, other behaviour or mental disorders, for detoxification, or for specialist rehabilitation. Conversely, some young people, who have mental disorders that require their admission for assessment and treatment, may have concurrent problems arising from substance use and misuse.

492 While there is a small requirement for inpatient facilities, it is incumbent on commissioners to make suitable provision, but this may not necessarily be available in their local area. Commissioners should ensure that they purchase Tier 4 services that offer admission to facilities that are suitable for young people. It is not appropriate that this provision is within psychiatric wards for adults or secure forensic mental health units (unless other problems require secure accommodation). Usually, children and adolescents who require admission have multiple needs. They may include homeless adolescents who use substances and who have been referred to a secure unit for other reasons.

493 Access to these highly specialised Tier 4 services from specialist services within Tier 3 should be provided as a part of comprehensive individual care plans that are actively managed by a key worker who is assigned to each person in need and is employed by a specialist agency that offers Tier 2 and Tier 3 services. In very many circumstances in which Tier 3 and 4 services are appropriate, younger people will receive shared care. A practitioner from Tiers 1 or 2 may retain an inportant key co-ordinating role as well as the obligation to provide General Medical Services.

494 Commissioners should recognise and address the requirement for Tier 3 and 4 services that are able to deal with particularly challenging, though small volume, problems that arise in childhood and adolescence. These include services for those young people who have problems arising from the use of cocaine, those related to infectious diseases such as HIV, and services for adolescents who are pregnant and for those who have committed serious offences. It is important to establish close liaison with social services departments with regard to young people who require forensic mental health services. Also, it is important to establish close collaboration and co-ordination between the addiction services for those adolescents who may be dependent on methadone, and the full range of other services. Close co-operation and liaison is needed with paediatric departments concerning children and adolescents who have problems with their physical health either preceding substance use or physical disorders as a consequence of their drug or alcohol use.

495 Some rehabilitation units for adults with problems arising from drug and alcohol misuse also admit adolescents. The HAS was not made aware of any separate provision for under 16 year-olds. The experience of the HAS is that the ethos and philosophy of many of these units is not adapted to the needs of younger people. In some circumstances, it may be appropriate for local authorities to provide access to foster homes, or secure accommodation to meet the full range of needs of young people who require rehabilitation.

496 Small residential units may be useful for children and adolescents who would benefit from a change in their environment. They could help to meet the multiple needs of young people with complex problems. If residential units are used in this way, the registration and inspection units within social services departments should pay particular attention to the appropriateness of both the environment and the care practices as they reflect and effect the needs of young people.

497 Some specialised fostering may be useful for some young people who have complex needs.

498 It is essential that there are residential treatment programmes appropriate to adolescents who misuse substances available in secure units, local authority centres and prisons. Those who have committed serious criminal offences and been remanded or admitted to secure units may well have problems related to the use of drug or alcohol. Their identification, and the provision of a broad range of interventions should be incorporated in care planning. Every secure unit, remand facility and prison should have policies on inoculation injuries, confidentiality and consent to treatment.

499 Young people who misuse drugs and commit offences may present to a variety of agencies including the criminal justice services, health and social services and youth and community centres. The association between criminal offending and drug or alcohol misuse indicates the importance of links between forensic mental health services, community services and addiction services. Joint specialist outpatient clinics may be particularly helpful to some selected adolescents. Such joint clinics should have a multi-disciplinary staff and offer a range of focused therapeutic interventions. Partnerships of this kind, within a broad spectrum of specialist services that work together in a coherent and co-ordinated fashion, are an exciting prospect.

CHAPTER 15

A Summary of Advice for Specific Providers of Services

PRIMARY HEALTHCARE

500 GPs and other professionals employed in primary healthcare should:

- have knowledge of the use and misuse of substances by children and adolescents;

- be trained on all aspects of the development of children and adolescents;

- be aware of the constitution of services that are appropriate to younger people, of their availability locally, and of the mechanisms for referring vulnerable children and adolescents to them;

- promote the accessibility of services for young people;

- consider how they might review the needs of young people in their practice, by, for example, by establishing a well adolescent clinic;

- promote enquiry (eg, through screening) into the use of substances by young people;

- be able to give appropriate and accurate initial advice to young people;

- include information on substances when they provide information about other health issues and illnesses (eg, disease and accident prevention, sex education, mental health);

- consider using outreach techniques in their practice to promote accessibility and to detect vulnerable children and adolescents;

- be able and prepared to counsel and support the parents and families of children and adolescents who use/or misuse substances;

- consider the promotion of mental health as a key role;

- exercise caution in prescribing for adolescents - they should seek the advice of a specialist consultant, when necessary;

- continue to play a role, when appropriate, in the shared care of their patients after referring them to more specialised Tier 2, 3 or 4 services.

DIRECT-CONTACT SERVICES

501 These agencies should:

- consider their further development within comprehensive centres, but these should not duplicate the work of primary healthcare and social services, and evaluation of their work and impact should be included in their design;

- be able to demonstrate good accessibility, for example through: appropriate opening hours; drop-in arrangements; late night sessions; networking with other street workers; provision of helplines; and the range of services they offer;

- identify the range of services they offer and be able to demonstrate that their staff have competence in the interventions they provide;

- demonstrate formal links and co-ordination mechanisms with primary healthcare and social services; also that their staff are trained to work with young people from a variety of cultural settings and in multi-disciplinary teams;

- promote outreach, using own staff or volunteers and a variety of techniques;

- ensure that all staff who provide outreach services are provided with training on adolescent development, relevant health issues, and substance use and misuse by young people;

- encourage the participation of children and adolescents in designing services for them;

- give appropriate information about the range of treatment and other interventions that they offer to young people and their families;

- ensure that they are able to identify vulnerable young people who are at high risk of substance use and misuse.

RESIDENTIAL SERVICES

502   The staff of residential services that are not primarily providing services for children and adolescents who use or misuse substances should:

- be alert to the possibility of young people in their care having problems related to substance use or misuse;

- have clear policies and guidelines for providing for the needs of young people, when professional assessments of their needs conflict with their own wishes;

- work within the guidelines on child protection set by the local area Child Protection Committee;

- recognise that a multi-disciplinary approach is essential.

503   The staff of specialist residential services should develop:

- clear policies and guidelines for managing young people who misuse alcohol and other substances;

- procedures for endeavouring to prevent the admission of people who misuse substances to custodial services.

YOUTH SERVICES

504   *Tackling Drugs Together* stresses:

- the important role of youth services, both statutory and non-statutory, in reducing the acceptability and availability of drugs to young people;

- the complementary role of youth organisations in drug education in schools - they may be better placed to reach young people at higher than average risk of misusing substances and they may be in touch with more people from black and ethnic groups;

- the need for youth services to make full use of their eligibility to apply for funding for projects which meet the needs of young people at risk or in the early stages of drug taking under the Department of Health grants programme.

THE STAFF OF SCHOOLS AND SCHOOL GOVERNORS

505 Schools and school governors also have a pivotal role both in relation to individual and groups of young people and to their local communities in providing:

- guidance in helping young people to gain access to advice and counselling on substances;

- up-to-date information through telephone helplines and other services.

506 Teachers, school counsellors, and other school health workers need regular in-service training and up-to-date information to support their work with outside agencies, parents and young people who are at risk or who are already using substances.

507 School governors and head teachers have particular opportunities to create networks of parents within their local communities by organising meetings to raise awareness of substances and to disseminate information on preventing substance use and on the policies of their schools on substance-related matters.

SOCIAL SERVICES DEPARTMENTS

508 Local authorities should:

- formulate strategies for their services specifically for younger people that include reference to the use and misuse of drugs and alcohol by children and adolescents;

- formulate strategies for providing services for people who use and misuse substances that include particular references to the needs of young people;

- encourage creativity and flexibility in financing services;

- consider adapting current services or creating other residential services specifically for young people who have problems arising from their misuse of drugs and alcohol;

- consider setting up specialist fostering services for children and adolescents who misuse substances, ensuring adequate levels of trained supervisory staff for foster carers;

- ensure that residential and field social workers are trained in the skills required in identifying, assessing and managing emergencies involving young people who misuse drugs and alcohol;

- provide specialist support programmes for young people in secure accommodation who have problems arising from substance misuse;

- involve young people in planning and designing services;

- ensure that training for their staff on the preparation of pre-sentence reports for the courts stresses the importance of addressing the histories of substance use of the subjects and the need to offer recommendations for appropriate intervention;

- develop programmes that prepare vulnerable young people to leave care and, then, support them afterwards;

- provide services for young people who live at home and are considered to be at risk, in circumstances when good enough parenting may not be sufficient to address the prevention of potential problems.

PROBATION SERVICES

509 Probation services should:

- *Pre-Sentence*
  provide advice and standardised training for probation officers that covers the preparation of pre-sentence reports and stresses the importance of addressing the histories of drug and alcohol misuse of the subjects, the identification of specific problems related to substance misuse, and making recommendations about interventions.

- *Post-Sentence*
  be able to identify and assess young people who are using or misusing substances and make recommendations about their referral to agencies that are able to tackle problems arising from substance misuse, especially when young people are in youth custody or prison.

CRIMINAL JUSTICE SERVICES

510 Staff of the NHS and local authorities should:

- improve links between the criminal justice system and the courts and the health and social services;

- provide training for the staff of the criminial justice system to develop awareness about problems in young people that relate to substance use and misuse, and an understanding of what constitute reasonable grounds for recommending referral for a specialist opinion or treatment.

CHAPTER 16

*Service Evaluation and
Performance
Management*

INTRODUCTION

511 Effective evaluation of a service should assess whether it does what it says it does, meets the required standard of practice, achieves its intended objectives and is provided in a manner which accords with the expressed needs of the target population. Evaluation should also assess the effectiveness of the treatments offered and, in particular, the changes over time in the individuals that can be related to the treatment provided.

512 In Chapter 12, four ways of assessing the effectiveness of services, at different levels are identified. Namely:

- quality assurance and audit;

- output monitoring;

- consumer satisfaction surveys;

- outcome evaluation.

QUALITY ASSURANCE AND AUDIT

513 Audit is essential to a developmental approach to quality assurance. It is the means by which the reality of practice is compared to the standards which have been set, using explicit and measurable indicators. Service standards define what is considered to be good practice.

514 Given the broad scope of services outlined in this report, it will not be feasible to set standards for and audit all aspects of practice. It will be necessary to prioritise them.

515 Information on standard setting and audit has been published by the HAS (Williams, 1993). Particular guidance for drug and alcohol services has been published by the Standing Conference on Drug Abuse, Alcohol Concern and the Institute for the Study of Drug Dependence (Dufficy and Hager, 1993; Hager, 1993; *Quality in Alcohol Services: Minimum Standards for Good Practice* [Alcohol Concern, 1992]). These texts are seen as good starting points in developing a set of quality standards appropriate to services for children and adolescents.

OUTPUT MONITORING AND ROUTINE DATA COLLECTION

516 Routine input, process and output data may be collected consequent on a requirement specified within a service level agreement or contract, including the age, sex, ethnic group, services used, treatment received, waiting times and duration. Simple data of this kind may be used to determine whether or not a service is meeting its basic objectives. It can also be used to monitor the ability of the service to achieve certain standards, such as the length of time between referral and commencement of treatment or other features that could be proxy indicators of effectiveness..

517 In *Tackling Drugs Together*, key performance indicators are defined for each of the three areas covered by the Statement of Purpose (crime, young people and public health) which rely heavily on output and/or routine data.

518 For example in the section on *Helping Young People to Resist Drugs*, the White Paper states:

"Progress will be evaluated at a national level by the following performance indicators:

- *the reported level of the misuse of drugs among young people up to the age of 25 years by means of opinion polls and surveys;*

- *the number of young people recorded on the Regional Misuse Database (in age groups 9-15, 16-20, and 21-25 years); and*

- *the implementation of school policies on drug education and drug-related incidents."*

519 Interpretation will be assisted and the validity of indicators enhanced by using other data, for example from surveys, service audit, research and outcome monitoring. This will be particularly important at a local level as Drug Action Teams begin to devise their own measures to evaluate progress in line with the Statement of Purpose, national objectives (as defined in the White Paper) and local priorities. For example, *Tackling Drugs Together* suggests that Drug Action Teams and Drug Reference Groups may wish to develop *"measures of improvement in access to effective drug counselling, treatment and rehabilitation'*

520 Commissioners and providers will both be interested to monitor progress in this area. First, this requires that separate measures are developed to monitor accessibility and effectiveness. However, simple data on the numbers of referrals to services considered alone is insufficient to assess improvements.

521 Effectiveness of drug counselling, treatment or rehabilitation can only be judged truly by careful analysis of treatment outcome data (see below). However, a limited proxy measure or indicator might be to monitor whether young people are attracted to, and retained within services by examining data on referrals and duration of contact with services.

CONSUMER SATISFACTION SURVEYS AND SURVEYS OF THE GENERAL POPULATION

522 Surveys of the general population, or specific groups within it, can be used to gauge the extent to which services are reaching their intended client groups, the ways in which services are perceived and the extent to which the services are meeting the expressed needs and wishes of the population served. Commonly, surveys of service users are undertaken to determine consumer satisfaction.

523 Surveys might also be undertaken to aid in determining the local prevalence of substance misuse by children and adolescents. Surveys of this type can be time consuming.

524 So, expert advice should always be sought when compiling questionnaires to ensure that the questions are precisely framed and in a manner likely to produce the information required.

525 It should be borne in mind that, while surveys provide opportunities to consult with the population at large, frequently they can exclude the most disadvantaged members of the community. Good examples are people with difficulties in reading and writing and those people for whom English is not their first language.

OUTCOME EVALUATION

526 Assessing treatment outcomes is the only means by which a service can objectively demonstrate that it is effective as a provider of education, prevention, counselling, treatment, rehabilitation or other interventions.

527 Outcome is usually defined as a change in aspects of health, behaviour or social functioning, in a client or patient measured over time, for example at assessment or admission and again at the time of discharge.

528 The Department of Health has used an outcome funding approach to the drug and alcohol specific grant in the last several years and, more recently, has applied this approach to the Young People at Risk from Drugs programme.

529 The outcomes to be measured should be realistic and related to the aims of the intervention delivered, for example outcomes for needle exchange services should be related to injecting behaviour rather than the consumption of drugs.

530 SCODA and Alcohol Concern have produced joint guidance which could be adapted for use in substance misuse services for children and adolescents (*Outcome Monitoring: Practical Advice for Developing Monitoring Systems. Burns,* 1994). Core questions are suggested under the following headings:

- substance using and behaviour;
- social circumstances;
- health status;
- psychological adjustments.

531 Close collaboration between commissioners, purchasers and providers is essential in the development of appropriate evaluation techniques and if the early results of these evaluations are to inform the subsequent planning of services and increasing sophistication in commissioning them.

CHAPTER 17

Checklists

CHECKLIST 1

RISK FACTORS

Societal and Cultural Risk Factors
• The law and societal norms
• Substance availability
• Extreme economic deprivation
• Neighbourhood disorganisation

Individual and Interpersonal Risk Factors
• Physiological factors
• Family attitudes to substance use or misuse
• Use of substances by parents
• Poor and inconsistent family management practices
• Family conflict
• Early and persistent behaviour problems
• Academic problems
• Low commitment to school
• Early peer rejection
• Association with peers who use drugs
• Alienation
• Attitudes favourable to drug use
• Early onset of drug or alcohol use

Protective Factors
• Positive temperament
• Intellectual ability
• A supportive family environment
• A social support system that encourages personal efforts
• A caring relationship with at least one adult

CHECKLIST 2

FACTORS ASSOCIATED WITH THE DIFFICULTIES FACED BY VARIOUS SERVICE PROVIDERS IN MEETING THE NEEDS OF CHILDREN AND ADOLESCENTS

Services for People who Misuse Substances

- patients are too young for the services provided for adults

- the culture is inappropriate to children and adolescents

- lower levels of dependent drug use to which adult services may not be orientated

- fear of the impact of adult patients

Child and Adolescent Mental Health Services

- the problems of managing children and adolescents with substance misuse may be considered to be too difficult

- problems of case-mix within those CAMHS that are more limited in scope and resources

- fear of the impact of substance users on other children

Social Services

- the problems may be considered to be too difficult

- staff may be inadequately trained

- fear of entering a large arena of need for which services have not been planned or financed

Forensic Mental Health Services

- patients are too young for the services provided for adults

- staff are unfamiliar with the client group

- fear of the impact of adults with major problems on children and adolescents

- pressures to provide services for other clients with major but different problems

CHECKLIST 3

A SUMMARY OF PROBLEM ISSUES

• No clear leadership of the commissioning or provision of services
• Lack of systematic planning
• Lack of definition and understanding of the nature of the problem
• Lack of knowledge of the scale of the problem
• Funding responsibilities that are unclear or disputed
• Lack of basic information on existing services
• Poor co-ordination of services
• Lack of trust and the presence of competitiveness between different elements of present services

CHECKLIST 4

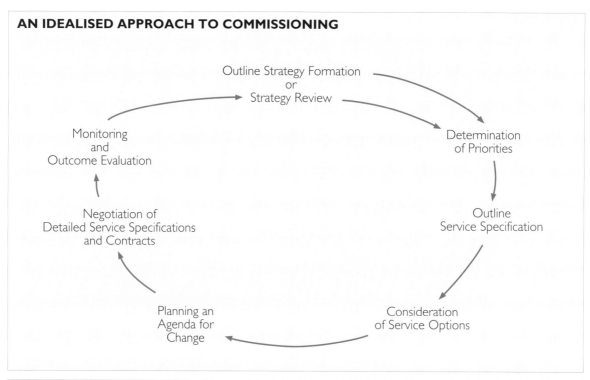

AN IDEALISED APPROACH TO COMMISSIONING

Outline Strategy Formation
or
Strategy Review

Determination
of Priorities

Outline
Service Specification

Consideration
of Service Options

Planning an
Agenda for
Change

Negotiation of
Detailed Service Specifications
and Contracts

Monitoring
and
Outcome Evaluation

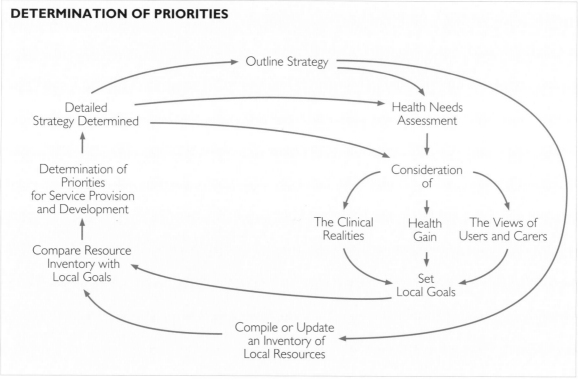

DETERMINATION OF PRIORITIES

Outline Strategy

Detailed
Strategy Determined

Health Needs
Assessment

Determination of
Priorities
for Service Provision
and Development

Consideration
of

The Clinical
Realities

Health
Gain

The Views of
Users and Carers

Compare Resource
Inventory with
Local Goals

Set
Local Goals

Compile or Update
an Inventory of
Local Resources

CHECKLIST 5

A JOINTLY AGREED STRATEGIC FRAMEWORK   149

It is essential that authorities responsible for commissioning substance misuse services for children and adolescents base their approach on a jointly agreed strategic framework. They should:

- build, wherever possible, on existing advisory machinery and previous strategy;

- align their strategic framework with their broader strategies for both child and adolescent mental health services and for substance misuse services for adults;

- include a balance of educational, preventive and treatment-orientated approaches in their strategic framework;

- ensure that the strategic framework is agreed and owned by all potential agencies that have commissioning and purchasing responsibilities, thereby recognising their interdependence in producing an effective system of care;

- identify and prioritise in the strategic framework the high risk groups (eg, intravenous drug users, pregnant drug users and users with a high risk of suicide).

CHECKLIST 6

ROUTES TO AN APPROPRIATE KNOWLEDGE-BASE

Commissioners and purchasers must hold or have access to a sound knowledge-base on the requirements of children and adolescents with problems arising from substance misuse, and the relative effectiveness of potential interventions.

Routes to gaining an appropriate knowledge-base include:
• consultation with non-statutory alcohol and drug agencies on the number of their clients, their patterns of use and misuse, and the nature of the services that they offer;
• information gathering from schools, social services departments, youth justice services, the probation service and the police;
• consultation with community organisations, including any that work within differing ethnic communities;
• understanding the various definitions of use and misuse among local agencies and estimating the way in which these definitions affect both the process of needs assessment and the perceptions of people requiring help;
• awareness of the clinical and social effectiveness of particular services and methods of education, prevention and intervention, that have been conducted locally as well as nationally;
• reviewing research literature from organisations such as the Institute of Substance and Drug Dependency (ISDD), Alcohol Concern, the Standing Conference on Drug Abuse (SCODA) and any academic institutions with an interest in addictions.

CHECKLIST 7

RESPONSIVENESS

Commissioners should be responsive to the needs of their local population to achieve an effective climate for strategic and service development for children and adolescents who misuse substances.

Commissioners should be aware of the following matters and respond appropriately.
• The baseline of public understanding and empathy may be low in this field. Commissioners may choose to invest in, or support the national public education initiatives to counter this.
• There may be a difference of views between users and carers in this field. Each voice needs to be recognised.
• Carers (usually parents) form a distinct constituency which requires services designed to meet its needs, in addition to those of their children.
• The role of the local media is significant in this field. Its contribution can be unhelpful, for example by stigmatising individuals, organisations, including schools or whole localities, or it can be helpful, for example by aiding the public education process. Wherever possible, authorities should try to nurture this more positive approach by maintaining regular contact through briefings and press releases.
• Building contacts with different ethnic groups in the community may well be a slow and sensitive process. It is essential to work towards trusting relationships with the accepted leaders of the different cultural groups, and to be aware of the dangers of racial or cultural stereotyping.
• The user population may be transient, especially in inner city areas. For difficult and high-risk individuals, liaison across geographic boundaries may be essential if services are to be targeted effectively on very vulnerable younger people.

CHECKLIST 8

MATURE COMMISSIONER-PROVIDER RELATIONSHIPS

The development of services for children and adolescents with substance misuse problems will be improved in the context of mature relationships between commissioners, purchasers and service providers.

The following issues are particularly significant in this field.
• There are a wide variety of providers in this field which may result in individual services having infrequent contacts with a small number of cases. Equally, there are many individual GP fundholders who are likely to have infrequent contact with younger people who misuse substances. Steps should be taken to ensure that this unfamiliarity does not jeopardise individual care or threaten monitoring of quality.
• There are three kinds of fundholding. GPs may be *total* fundholders; *standard* fundholders with year-on-year budgets, in line with the original concept; or the more minimal *community* fundholders where groups of practices combine to form consortia. All of them have powers in buying elements of services for young people.
• A number of providers may be in the non-statutory sector. The organisational culture of these agencies may be different to that of the statutory sector. Purchasers should endeavour to understand these differences in order to maximise their contribution to the care of this group of young people.
• There may be different providers or trusts offering different elements of substance misuse services to children and adolescents overall. Commissioners should lead by creating a climate in which all providers operate together in the interests of younger people through effective co-ordination of their contributions to an overarching service.
• Drug Reference Groups, as proposed in *Tackling Drugs Together,* may prove to be a valuable forum for promoting mature and responsible discussion on the commissioning and provision of services for children and adolescents who misuse substances.
• Appropriate sharing of information is enabled by mature organisational relationships. In this setting, providers should not be burdened by requests for information for which they may not be able to see the relevance.

CHECKLIST 9

HEALTHY ALLIANCES

Commissioning authorities should work together with other commissioners and organisations to form healthy alliances that promote consistent and coherent policy aimed at providing integrated and comprehensive prevention and treatment services for children and adolescents with substance misuse problems.

This statement implies the following:
• this field is particularly appropriate to joint commissioning. Key commissioners are: health authorities; social service departments; education departments; schools; GP fundholders; probation services; and other criminal justice agencies;
• a prevention strategy will require effective healthy alliances. Health and social services will require good relationships with: - the youth service (for example, for alternative activities to substance use and education and counselling); - the leisure services (for example, for alternative activities to substance use); - housing departments (for example, for resolutions to problems of homelessness, and those of leaving care); - the prison service (for example, for education and counselling).

CHECKLIST 10

EFFECTIVE CONTRACTS

Commissioning agencies and purchasers should agree effective contracts, with providers which include monitoring procedures.

This means that:
• contracts with non-statutory providers should be based within a robust contracting framework to maximise the contribution of providers (that is, they should be longer-term, three-to five-year agreements which contain negotiated and realistic performance monitoring procedures);
• contracts should be based, wherever possible, on mainstream funding, thus recognising the need to convert short-term and pump-priming finance into robust financial arrangements;
• appropriate contract currencies that recognise the direct service needs of individuals, the needs of generic staff for role support and consultancy, and the importance of training, research and prevention;
• where necessary, commissioners should collaborate on purchasing highly specialised services for children and adolescents who misuse substances. This should offer an effective system of quality control and be capable of sustaining high-cost, low-volume, highly specialised services;
• within the context of the present very low baseline of dedicated specialist (particularly Tier 3 and Tier 4) services, it is important for purchasers to establish contracts that recognise the roles of services that are not specifically dedicated to meeting the needs of children and adolescents who misuse substances but which are used for this purpose.

CHECKLIST 11

ORGANISATIONAL CAPACITY

In order to develop an effective commissioning approach to services for children and adolescents who misuse substances, the commissioning authorities must have the appropriate organisational capacity and capability.

In this respect, commissioners may find it helpful to ask themselves a number of questions.
• Who in the authority has any knowledge of this field?
• Is the organisation aware of its responsibilities as set out in *Tackling Drugs Together*?
• How great is the organisational divide between alcohol and drug misuse services and between the statutory and the non-statutory sectors?
• How senior are the people who have commissioning and purchasing responsibilities for services in this field and what ownership do the authorities have for younger people in need?
• Is the authority showing, or responding to leadership in addressing the issue of substance use and misuse by children and adolescents?
• Are services for children and adolescents who misuse substances lost in the organisational structure, for example, between children's and mental health services?
• Is the authority clear as to whether this is a health promotion issue or one of service provision or both?
• Can the authority identify the resource, if any, it is investing currently in services for children and adolescents who misuse substances, either directly or indirectly?

CHECKLIST 12

THE PRINCIPLES OF GOOD PRACTICE IN THE PROVISION OF INTERVENTION AND TREATMENT SERVICES FOR CHILDREN AND ADOLESCENTS

A. Accessibility

- Where are services provided? Are they convenient to public transport routes?

- When are they open? Are they available out of ordinary office hours?

- Is a service well publicised? Where is it publicised?

- Is the publicity material written in straightforward language? Is it translated into relevant ethnic languages?

- Are there arrangements for providing interpreters?

- Is there access for wheelchairs, buggies and people with limited mobility?

B. Appropriateness

- Is the environment appropriate to younger people?

- Is the service designed to be sensitive to the specific needs of younger people?

- Is the service sensitive to the needs of younger people from an appropriate range of different ethnic and cultural backgrounds and communities?

C. The Operation of Services Within the Spirit and Intentions of the Law

- Does the staff of the service have access to legal advice?

- Are there clear, written policies and guidelines on:
    - the recruitment of staff (including vetting procedures)?
    - obtaining consent to treatment or other interventions?
    - confidentiality?

- Is there a complaints procedure?

- Are adequate individual case records maintained?

D. Staff Competence

- Does the staff, including volunteers, have training and experience in working with younger people and with the issues and problems generated by those younger people who use and/or misuse substances.

- Does the staff have access to expert advice and consultation?
  eg, from:
    - a consultant child and adolescent psychiatrist?
    - a consultant psychiatrist with special experience in substance misuse?
    - a paediatrician?
    - a social services child protection team?
    - a solicitor?
    - an educationalist?

- Does the staff have training in working with people from different ethnic and cultural backgrounds and communities?

- Does the staff have access to regular supervision from a suitably qualified person?

CHECKLIST 12 (cont.)

E. Assessment and Child Protection

- Are there clear, written guidelines, to assist staff in undertaking assessments of the degree of vulnerability of individuals, of the needs (as opposed to wishes) of younger people and of their maturity?

- Are there clear written procedures for child protection which apply to all staff and which are approved by the Area Child Protection Committee?

- Do local criteria for the assessment of risks faced by children and the identification of vulnerable younger people take account of the histories of substance use by the children themselves and by their parents?

F. Collaboration and Consultation

- What arrangements are in place for service providers to consult with young people as service users, with their carers, and with other agencies on the services provided, and on the development of new services?

- Are there opportunities for younger people and their carers to become involved in planning the delivery of services?

G. Co-ordination

- What arrangements are in place to ensure that there are good communications between components of an overall service and that joint work takes place?

- What is the mechanism for ensuring that there is both leadership and management of the shared care that is appropriate for complex cases?

H. Effectiveness and Evaluation

- Does the agency deliver what it sets out to deliver and to the required standard?

- Does the agency achieve its objectives and targets by delivering specified interventions to a specified number of individuals or groups within a defined population?

- Does the agency meet the identified wishes of the target population?

- Does the agency achieve its aims in relation to stimulating lifestyle change, risk reduction, health gain etc?

CHECKLIST 13

THE COMPONENTS OF A COMPREHENSIVE SERVICE

• Health Promotion
• Education
• Prevention
• Information and advice for young people
• Education and support for parents and families
• Peer education
• Alternative activities that are enjoyable
• Direct access and self-referral services
• One-stop shops/comprehensive centres
• Outreach services
• Drop-in community centres
• Outpatient services
• Day care and treatment programmes
• Inpatient services
• Specialist rehabilitation services

CHECKLIST 14

SETTINGS IN WHICH SUBSTANCE MISUSE SERVICES FOR CHILDREN AND ADOLESCENTS SHOULD BE PROVIDED

- The premises of primary healthcare services
- Social services premises
- Schools
- Premises provided by non-statutory agencies
- At the sites of community provision for homeless people, including soup kitchens, night shelters, hostels etc
- Drop-in centres
- Community mental health services
- One-stop shops and comprehensive centres
- Outpatient clinics
- Accident and emergency departments
- Day centres
- Day hospitals
- Medical inpatient facilities and wards
- Psychiatric inpatient wards

CHECKLIST 15

THE ROLES OF PRIMARY LEVEL DIRECT CONTACT SERVICES (TIER 1)

• Providing interventions in a range of accessible and approachable environments
• Providing information, advice and support
• Assessing levels of drug and alcohol use by individuals
• Assessing associated or linked problems
• Assessing other indicators of vulnerability
• Assessing the urgency of problems experienced by individuals and taking appropriate action
• Offering help in the management of crises
• Providing initial counselling
• Making appropriate referrals to specialised services
• Providing support to parents and carers

CHECKLIST 16

A SCHEME FOR RECORDING THE MANAGEMENT OF INDIVIDUAL CASES

The following points should be included in the records of a young person who is receiving any intervention. This is in addition to the basic information ordinarily collected in the course of a clinical contact.
• The problem(s) being addressed should be stated. This may include problems other than those identified by the client/patient.
• The specific nature of the intervention planned should be stated, for example counselling, referral to another agency, within agency and inter-agency discussion, prescription of drugs, admission etc.
• Consideration of the ability of the young person to give consent and the involvement of parents and guardians. This should include opinion on the matters listed in chapter 11.
• The explanation given to the young person.
• Depending on the severity of the problems identified, consideration of the need to involve the following agencies should be recorded: - social services, (eg for child protection issues); - a primary healthcare team; - specialist drug and alcohol services; - child and adolescent mental health services; - child health services; - the housing department; - the school welfare service; - the probation service; - non-statutory agencies; - others.
• The dates decided on for reviews and for updating plans of management, including treatment.
• A record of supervision and of discussions with line managers.

CHECKLIST 17

ASSESSING CHILDREN AND ADOLESCENTS

- **Competence**
  The age, intellectual development and level of emotional maturity of the young person must be ascertained. These contribute to the assessor's judgement of:
  - the young person's understanding of the issues involved;
  - the competence of the young person to make a decision about the problem.

- **Truthfulness**
  The accuracy and veracity of the young person's information, including reasons for refusal of consent to inform the responsible parent, must be assessed. Assessment of both competence and truthfulness may need to be cross-referenced with information from other informants and contacts with other agencies.

- **The Needs and the Wishes of the Child or Young Person**
  Any difference of opinion among staff about the young person's needs as opposed to the wishes of that young person should be overtly stated and considered.

CHECKLIST 18

TYPICAL CHALLENGES FACED WHEN ASSESSING THE NEEDS OF CHILDREN AND ADOLESCENTS AND THE INTERVENTIONS THEY REQUIRE

- Lack of knowledge is the simplest type of problem and can generally be overcome with accurate information.

- Many needs and problems require discussion at some length. This may involve formal counselling when there are choices that a young person can make.

- The assessment of some problems necessitates involving other agencies and disciplines because of their severity and complexity.

- Some of the more complex and severe problems may require the involvement of procedures provided for by one or more of the following:
  - the Children Act 1989;
  - the Mental Health Act 1983;
  - criminal justice procedures;
  - the Education Act 1981;
  - the Education Act 1993 and its Code of Practice.

- A young person may be a victim or perpetrator of physical, sexual or emotional abuse and others may be at risk.

- A judgement must be made about the potential damage that might be done by withholding or giving services requested by a young person. In some situations, the provision of services may accentuate existing problems or even create new ones and problems resolved in the short-term can lead to longer-term difficulties.

- Staff must invoke and operate within the guidelines and procedures set by the local Area Child Protection Committee, when these are appropriate.

- Staff must consider what action may need to be taken when dealing with illicit or illegal behaviours.

CHECKLIST 19

STAFF TRAINING

Level 1 - General Training - Core Knowledge, Attitudes and Skills

- A basic knowledge of the physical, psychological and social effects of mood-altering drugs and alcohol, including the impacts of substance misuse by parents on children and adolescents.

- Awareness of the professional's own attitudes towards, and experiences of substance use and misuse and how these may impact on their work with young people who use and/or misuse substances.

- The ability to recognise substance misuse by young people.

- Assessment skills, with particular reference to the ability to distinguish between substance use, for example of an experimental nature, and harmful substance use.

- Basic life support skills.

- The ability to deliver simple interventions, for example information or advice about withdrawal from substance use and harm-minimisation, when appropriate.

- Information on local specialist substance misuse agencies and their specialist staff and about when and how to refer.

Level 2 - Advanced Training - Knowledge, Attitudes and Skills

- The core basic knowledge, attitudes and skills summarised at Level 1.

- Skills in communicating with and counselling young people and/or their parents.

- Knowledge of, and skills in therapeutic interventions, including those that are brief and focused, and knowledge of the indications for longer-term and more specialised interventions.

- Skills in multi-disciplinary working in a range of different contexts.

- Skills of managing conflict in attitudes, opinions and beliefs.

- Knowledge of when to inform parents or the authorities and when to offer confidentiality.

- Knowledge of the law relating to purchasing and consuming drugs, alcohol and other substances with particular reference to young people.

- The ability to construe and manage the boundaries of staff members' expertise.

- Record-keeping skills - awareness of the needs for and methods of keeping detailed contemporaneous records.

- The skills of contributing to the development of services for managing people who misuse substances.

CHECKLIST 19 (cont.)

Level 3 - Specialist Training for the Staff of Substance Misuse Services

- The core knowledge, attitudes and skills outlined at Levels 1 and 2.

- A working knowledge of child and adolescent development.

- Understanding of the particular impact of major events on the lives of children and adolescents, for example, abuse, bereavement and major traumatic events.

- Skills in communicating with and counselling young people and their parents.

Level 3 - Specialist Training for the Staff of CAMHS

- The core knowledge, attitudes and skills outlined at Levels 1 and 2.

- The ability to conduct therapeutic interventions (including brief focused practical work) with people who misuse substances, and knowledge of the indications for longer-term and more specialised interventions.

Level 3 - Additional Joint Specialist Training - for the Staff of Substance Misuse Services and CAMHS

- The skills of multi-disciplinary work and those of leading and managing shared care, including managing conflict in attitudes, opinions and beliefs.

- The knowledge and skills to handle issues of confidentiality and consent to treatment that involve the rights of young people, and the responsibilities of parents and professionals.

- Assessment skills, with particular reference to the ability to discern the severity and risks of substance misuse, the complexity of any planned intervention and the competence of a young person to consent to treatment or intervention.

- The law relating to drugs, alcohol and other substances, with particular reference to young people.

- The ability to manage and work with child protection issues including those that concern the relationship between substance misuse and the vulnerability of children and young people.

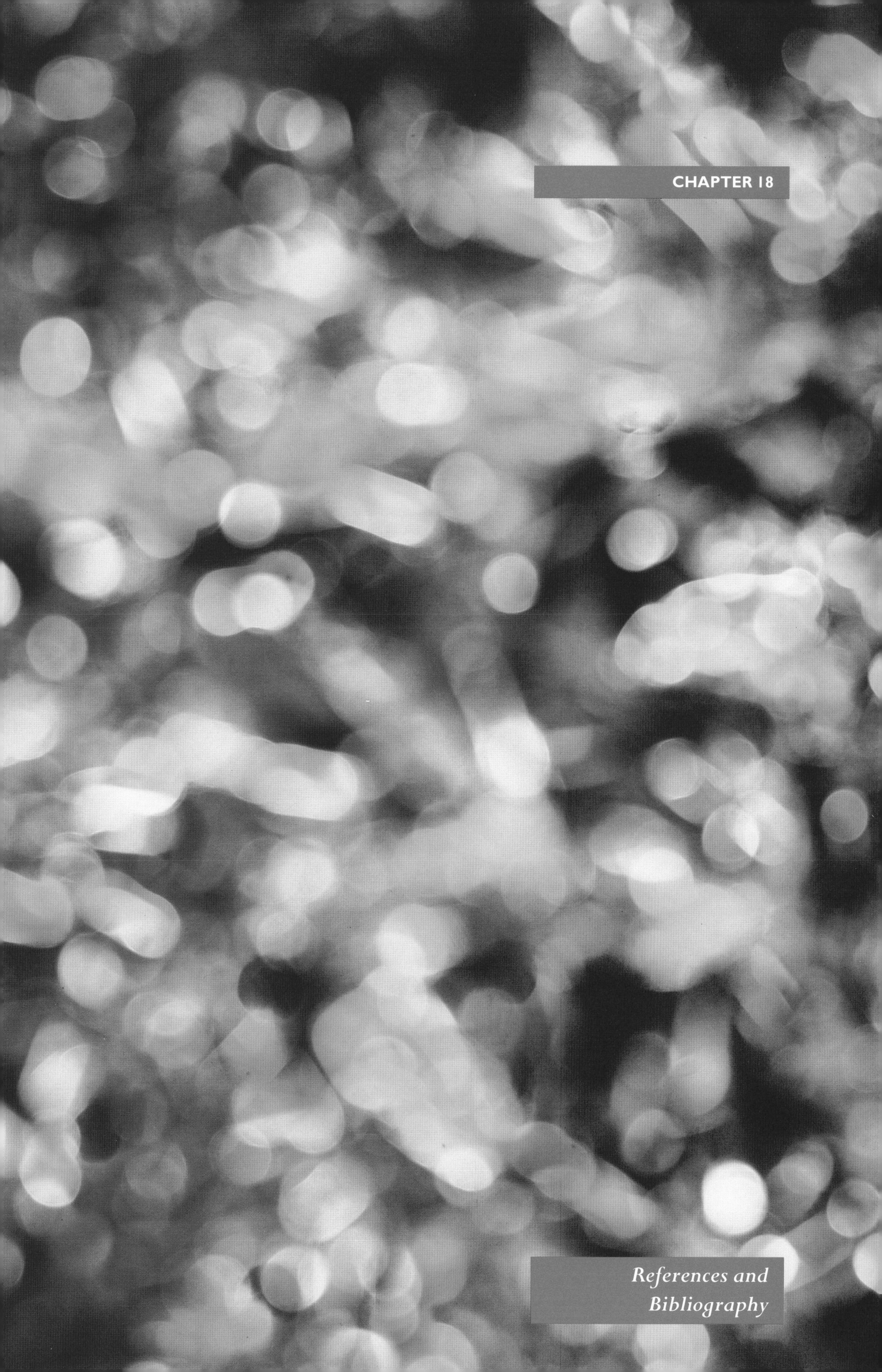

CHAPTER 18

References and Bibliography

MAJOR RELEVANT LEGISLATION AND GUIDANCE DOCUMENTS

The Children and Young Persons Act, 1969. London, HMSO.

The Misuse of Drugs Act 1971. London, HMSO.

The Education Act 1981. London, HSMO.

The Children Act 1989, London, HMSO.

Guide to the Misuse of Drugs Act 1971 and the Misuse of Drugs Regulations, (1989).

The NHS and Community Care Act 1990. London, HMSO.

The Criminal Justice Act 1991. London, HMSO.

Health of the Nation, (1992). London, HMSO.

Protection of Children: Disclosure of Criminal Background of those with Access to Children, HOC 47, 93, (1993). Home Office.

The Education Act 1993 and the Code of Practice on the Identification and Assessment of Special Needs, (1994), London, HMSO.

Tackling Drugs Together - A Strategy for England 1995-1998, (1995). London, HMSO.

Forward Together - A Strategy to Combat Drug and Alcohol Misuse in Wales, (1995). Welsh Office

Reviewing Shared Care Arrangements for Drug Misusers, EL(95) 114, (1995). NHS Executive.

REFERENCES

ACTION's Drug Prevention Program, (1984b). *Idea Exchange - Young Volunteers in Action.* Adolescent Health Vol.1, Summary and Policy OTA-H-468. Washington DC, US Government Printing Office.

Advisory Council on the Misuse of Drugs, (1982). *Treatment and Rehabilitation.* London, HMSO.

Advisory Council on the Misuse of Drugs, (1984). *Prevention.* London, HMSO.

Advisory Council on the Misuse of Drugs, (1988). *AIDS and Drug Misuse: Part 1.* London, HMSO.

Advisory Council on the Misuse of Drugs, (1989). *AIDS and Drug Misuse: Part 2.* London, HMSO.

Advisory Council on the Misuse of Drugs, (1990). *Problem Drug Use: A Review of Training.* London, HMSO.

Advisory Council on the Misuse of Drugs, (1991). *Drug Misusers and the Criminal Justice System Part 1: Community Resources and the Probation Service.* London, HMSO.

Advisory Council on the Misuse of Drugs, (1993). *Drug Education in Schools: The Need for New Impetus.* London, HMSO.

Advisory Council on the Misuse of Drugs, (1993). *AIDS and Drug Misuse Update.* London, HMSO.

Advisory Council on the Misuse of Drugs, (1994). *The Police, Drug Misusers and the Community.* London, HMSO.

Advisory Council on the Misuse of Drugs, (1995). *Volatile Substance Abuse.* London, HMSO.

Aitken P, (1978). *Ten-to-Fourteen-year-olds and Alcohol: a Developmental Study in the Central Region of Scotland.* London, HMSO.

Alcohol Concern (1992). *Quality in Alcohol Services; Minimum Standards for Good Practice and General Principles of Good Practice.* Alchohol Concern.

American Psychiatric Association *Diagnostic and Statistical Manual of Mental Disorders Fourth Edition (DSM-IV),* (1994). . American Psychiatric Association, Washington DC.

Andresson S, Allbreck P, Engstrom A, Romelsjo A, (1987). *Antecedents and Covariates of High Alcohol Use in Young Men. Alcoholism: Clinical and Experimental Research,* 16, 708-713.

Awiah J, Butt S, Dorn N, (1992). *Race, Gender and Drug Services,* London. Monograph 6. The Institute for the Society of Drug Dependence Research.

Bagnall G, (1990). *Alcohol Education for 13 Year Olds - Does it Work?* Results from a controlled evaluation. British Journal of Addiction, 85,89-96.

Bailey V, (1995). *Personal Communication.*

Bell T, Hein K, (1984). *The Adolescent and Sexually Transmitted Disease.* In: K.Holmes (ed). Sexually Transmitted Diseases, pp 73-84 New York, McGraw and Hill.

Benson G, Holmberg M B, (1984). *Drug-Related Mortality in Young People.* Acta Psychiatrica Scandinavica; 70:525-34.

Bernard P, Garralda M E, (1995). *Child and Adolescent Mental Health Practice in Primary Care.* Current Opinion in Psychiatry, 8, 4, 206-209.

Beschner G M, Friedman A S, (1979). *Youth Drug Abuse: Problems, Issues and Treatment.* Lexington, MA: D.C.Heath.

Beschner G M, Friedman A S, (1985). *Treatment of Adolescent Drug Abusers.* International Journal of the Addictions, 20(6 and 7), 97-99.

Bosworth K, Sailes J, (1993). *Content and Teaching Strategies in 10 Selected Drug Abuse Prevention Curricula.* Journal of School Health, 63,247-253.

Botvin G J, Baker E, Filazzola A D, Botvin E M, (1990). *A Cognitive Behavioural Approach to Substance Abuse Prevention: One Year Follow-up.* Addictive Behaviours, 15:47-63.

Botvin G J, Dusenburg L, (1989). *Preventing Tobacco, Alcohol and Drug Abuse.* Paper presented at the 5th International Symposium on Prevention and Intervention, Brelegel.

Brent D, (1987). *Correlates of Medical Lethality of Suicide Attempts in Children and Adolescents.* Journal of the American Academy of Child and Adolescent Psychiatry, 26,87-91.

British Paediatric Association and the Royal College of Physicians, (1995). *Alcohol and the Young.* London, Royal College of Physicians.

Brook D, Brook J, (1990). *The Etiology and Consequences of Adolescent Drug Use:* In: Watson R, (ed). Drug and Alcohol Abuse Prevention, pp339-362. Humana Press, Clifton, New Jersey.

Brown H, (1991). *Report on Services for Adolescents with Drug-Related Problems,* Taskforce Community Involvement Centre, Prahran, Victoria.

Buholz K K, (1990). *A Review of Correlates of Alcohol Use and Alcohol Problems in Adolescence.* In: Galonte M, (ed). Recent Developments in Alcoholism, 8:111-124.Plenum, New York.

Bukstein O G, Brent D A, Kaminer Y, (1989). *Comorbidity of Substance Abuse and Other Psychiatric Disorders in Adolescents.* American Journal of Psychiatry, 146:1131-1141.

Bukstein O G, (1995). *Influences on the Risk and Cause of Substance Use and Abuse in Adolescents.* Current Opinion in Psychiatry, 8,4,218-221.

Burns S, (1994). *Outcome Monitoring: Practical Advice for Developing Monitoring Systems.* Alcohol Concern/Standing Conference on Drug Abuse.

Bury J, (1991). *Teenage Sexual Behaviour and the Impact of AIDS.* Health Education Journal, 50,43-48.

Cadoret R J, O'Gorman T, Troughton E, (1989). *Alcoholism and Antisocial Personality: Interrelationships, Genetic and Environmental Factors.* Archives of General Psychiatry, 42, 161-167.

Carpenter C, Glassner B, Johnson B D, Laughlin J, (1988). *Kids, Drugs and Crime,* Lexington MA, Lexington Books.

Casswell S, Gilmore L, (1989). *An Evaluated Community Action Project on Alcohol.* Journal of Studies on Alcohol, 50, 339-346.

Center for Substance Abuse Prevention, (1993). *Signs of Effectiveness in Preventing Alcohol and other Drug Problems.* DHHS Publication No. SAM 93-2001. Washington, DC: US Department of Health and Human Services.

Challen A H, Davies A G, Williams R J W, Haslum M N, Baum J, (1988). *Measuring Psychosocial Adaptation to Diabetes in Adolescence.* Diabetic Medicine, 5, 739-746.

Challen A H, Davies A G, Williams R J W, Baum J D, (1992). *Hospital Admissions of Adolescent Patients with Diabetes.* Diabetic Medicine 9. 850-854.

Chambers G, Tombs J, (1984). *The British Crime Survey.* Scotland: a Scottish Research Study. Edinburgh, HMSO.

Chief Medical Officer, (1993). *On the State of the Public Health 1993. The annual report of the Chief Medical Officer for the Department of Health 1993.* HMSO London.

Coggans N, Shewan D, Henderson M, Davies J B, (1991). *National Evaluation of Drug Education in Scotland.* London, Institute for the Study of Drug Dependence.

Coggans N, McKellar S, (1994). *Drug Use Amongst Peers: Peer Pressure or Peer Preference?* Drugs: Education, Prevention and Policy. Volume I, 1: 15-26.

Coleman J C, (1989). *The Focal Theory of Adolescence: A Psychological Perspective.* In: The Social World of Adolescents: International Perspectives, Humelman K, and Engel U (Eds), pp 43-56. Berlin, De Gruyter

Cooney A, Dobbinson S, Flaherty B, (1993). *Drug Use by NSW Secondary School Students:* 1992 Survey Sydney: NSW Department of Health, Drug and Alcohol Directorate.

Cripps C, Craig D, Reid V, (1991). *Providing a Drug Service for Young People.* Newham Drugs Advice Project.

Davies J B, Stacey B, (1972). *Teenagers and Alcohol: A Development Study in Glasgow.* London, Croom Helm.

DeMilio L, (1989). *Psychiatric Syndromes in Adolescent Substance Abusers.* American Journal of Psychiatry, 146, 1212-1214.

Department for Education, 1994. *Drug Prevention and Schools.* London, HMSO.

Department of Health, (1991). *Drug Misuse and Dependence: Guidelines on Clinical Management.*

Department of Health, (1992). *Children's Services Plans,* Local Authority Circular LAC(92)18.

Department of Health, (1994). *Substance Misuse Detainees in Police Custody: Guidelines for Clinical Management.* London, HMSO.

Department of Health and Community Services, (1993). *1992 Survey of Alcohol, Tobacco and other Drug Use among Victorian Secondary School Students.* Victoria.

Department of Transport, (1990). *Blood Alcohol Levels in Fatalities in Great Britain 1988.* Transport and Road Research Laboratory.

Deykin E Y, Levy J C, Wells V, (1987). *Adolescent Depression, Alcohol and Drug Abuse.* American Journal of Public Health, 77:178-182.

Diekstra R F, (1989). *Suicidal Behaviour in Adolescents and Young Adults: The International Picture.* Crisis,10,16-35.

Dorn N, Murji K, (1992). *Drug Prevention: a Review of the English Language Literature.* Institute for the Study of Drug Dependency Research Mongraph 5

Douglas R R, (1990). *Formulating Alcohol Policies for Community Recreation Facilities: Tactics and Problems.* In: Giesbrecht N, Conley P, Denniston R, Gliksman L, Holder H, Pederson A, Room R, Shain M, (eds). Research, action and community: experiences in the prevention of alcohol and other drug problems (OSAP Prevention Monograph-4), pp61-67. Washington DC, US Government Printing Office.

Dufficy H, Hager K, (1993). *Standard Setting in Audit.* SCODA Audit Working Groups 1993. Standing Conference on Drug Abuse.

Duffy J C, *Trends in Alcohol Consumption Patterns 1978-1989.* Henley-on Thames. NTC Publications.

Edeh J, (1989). *Volatile Substance Abuse in Relation to Alcohol and Illicit Drugs: Psychosocial Perspectives.* Human Toxicology, 8, 313-317.

Edwards G, et al. (1994). *Alcohol and the Public Good.* World Health Organisation, Europe. Oxford University Press.

Elliot D S, Ageton A R, (1976). *The Relationship between Drug Use and Crime in Adolescents.* In: Research Triangle Institute, Appendix to Drug Use and Crime: Report of the Panel on Drug Use and Criminal Behaviour. Springfield, VA: National Technical Information Service, pp297-322.

Elliott D S, Huizinga D, Ageton S S, (1985). *Explaining Delinquency and Drug Use.* London, Sage.

Elliott D S, Huizinga D, (1984). *The Relationship Between Delinquent Behaviour and ADM Problems.* The National Youth Survey Project Report no.28, Behavioural Research Institute. Colorado, Boulder.

Falck R, Craig R, (1988). *Classroom-Oriented Primary Prevention Programming for Drug Abuse.* Journal of Psychoactive Drugs, 20,4, 403-408.

Farrell M, (1989). *Ecstasy and the Oxygen of Publicity.* British Journal of Addiction, 84, 943.

Farrington D P, (1991). *Antisocial Personality from Childhood to Adulthood*. The Psychologist. Bulletin of the British Psychological Society, 4, 389-394

Faupel C E, (1988). *Heroin Use, Crime and Employment Status*. Journal of Drug Issues, 18, 467-479.

Findlay J, Bright J, Gill K, (1990). *Youth Crime Prevention: A Handbook of Good Practice*. Swindon, Crime Concern.

Foster K, Wilmot A, Dobbs J, (1990). *General Household Survey, 1988*. London, HMSO.

Friedman A S, Glickman N W, Morrissey M R, (1986). *Prediction of Successful Treatment Outcome by Client Characteristics and Retention in Adolescent Drug Treatment Programs: A large-scale cross-validation*. Journal of Drug Education, 16, 149-165.

Garfinkel B D, Froese A, Hood J, (1982). *Suicide Attempts in Children and Adolescents*. American Journal of Psychiatry, 139, 1257-1261.

Gilvarry E, McCarthy S, McArdle P, (1995). *Substance Use Among School Children in the North of England*. Drug and Alcohol Dependence, 37, 255-259.

Gilvarry E, Tayler P and Murphy M, (1994). *Vulnerable Children/Young People - Principles for Good Practice*. Northern Regional Health Authority.

Gorman D M, (1992). *Using Theory and Basic Research to Target Primary Prevention Programs: Recent Developments and Future Prospects*. Alcohol and Alcoholism, 27,583-594.

Giesbrecht N, Gonzalez R, Grant M, Osterberg E, Room R, Rootman I, Towle L, (eds), (1989). *Drinking and Casualties: Accidents, Poisonings and Violence in an International Perspective*. London, Tavistock/Routledge.

Giesbrecht N, Douglas R, (1990). *The Demonstration Project and Comprehensive Community Programming: Dilemmas in Prevention Alcohol-Related Problems*. Contemporary Drug Problems, 17, 421-459.

Goddard E, Iken C, (1988). *Drinking in England and Wales in 1987*. London, HMSO.

Goodstadt M, (1986). *Factors Associated with Non-use and Cessation of Use : Between and Within Survey Replication of Findings*. Addictive Behaviours, 11, 275-286.

Gorman D M, (1992). *Using Theory and Basic Research to Target Primary Prevention Programmes: Recent Developments and Future Prospects*. Alcohol and Alcoholism, 27, 583-594.

Gottfredson D C, (1988). *An Evaluation of an Organisation Development Approach to Reducing School Disorder*. Evaluation Review, 11, 739-763.

Graham P J, (1986). *Behavioural and Intellectual Development in Childhood Epidemiology*. British Medical Bulletin, 42, 2, 155-62

HM Government Statistical Service, (1992). *Statistics of Drug Seizures and Offenders Dealt With, United Kingdom (1991)*. Home Office Statistical Bulletin, 25/92.

HM Government Statistical Service, (1994). *Statistics of Drug Addicts Notified to the Home Office, United Kingdom, (1993)*. Home Office Statistical Bulletin, 10/94,

HM Government Statistical Service, (1994). *Statistics of Drug Seizures and Offenders Dealt With, United Kingdom, (1993)*. Home Office Statistical Bulletin, 28/94.

HM Prison Service, (1995). *Briefing Paper No. 81.*

Hager K, (1993). *Audit for Drug Services (Drugs Work 4).* Institute for the Study of Drug Dependence.

Hammersley R, Morrison V, Davies J B, Forsyth A, (1989). *Heroin Use and Crime: A Comparison of Heroin Users and Non-Users in and out of prison.* Report to the Criminological Division, Scottish Home and Health Department.

Hammersley R H, Forsyth A, Morrison V, Davies J B, (1989). *The Relationship Between Crime and Opioid Use.* British Journal of Addiction, 84, 1029-1043.

Hammersley R, Forsyth A, Lavelle T, (1990). *The Criminality of New Drug Users in Glasgow.* British Journal of Addiction 85, 1583-1594.

Hando J, Hall W, (1993). *Amphetamine Use Among Young Adults in Sydney, Australia* (Report B93/2). Sydney, New South Wales Department of Health, Drug and Alcohol Directorate.

Hartup W, (1970). *Peer Interaction and Social Organisation.* In: P Mussen, (ed.). Carmichael's manual of child psychology. New York, John Wiley.

Hawker A, (1978). *Adolescents and Alcohol.* London, Edsall.

Hawkins J D, Jenson J M, Catalano R F, Lishner D, (1988). *Delinquency and Drug Abuse: Implications for Social Services.* Service Review, 62, 258-284

Hawkins J, Lishner D, Catalano R, Howard M, (1985). *Childhood Predictors of Adolescent Substance Abuse: Towards an Empirically Grounded Theory.* Journal of Children in Contemporary Society, 18(1&2), 11-48.

Hawton K, Osborn M, O'Grady J, Cole D, (1982). *Classification of Adolescents Who Take Overdoses.* British Journal of Psychiatry, 140, 124-131.

Health Education Authority, (1989). *Young People's Health and Lifestyles Survey (9-15 year-olds).* London, MORI.

Health Education Authority, (1990). *Young People's Health and Lifestyles Survey (16-19 year-olds).* London, MORI.

Health Education Authority, (1992). *Tomorrow's Young Adults 9-15 year-olds look at Alcohol, Drugs,Exercise and Smoking.* London, MORI

Helzer J E, Pryzbeck T R, (1988). *The Co-occurrence of Alcoholism With Other Psychiatric Disorders in the General Population and its Impact on Treatment.* Journal for the Study of Alcoholism 49, 219-224.

Hill P, (1995). *Personal Communication.*

Hingson R, Howland J, (1993). *Alcohol and Non-traffic Unintended Injuries.* Addiction, 88, 877-83.

Hofferth S, Kahn J, Baldwin W, (1987). *Premarital Sexual Activity Among US Teenage Women Over the Past Three Decades.* Family Planning Perspectives, 19, 46-53.

Hu T, McDonnell N S, Swisher J, (1981). *The Application of Cost-Effectiveness Analysis to the Evaluation of Drug Abuse Prevention Programs: an Illustration.* Journal of Drug Issues, 11,125-138.

Hurrelmann K, (1990). *Health Promotion for Adolescents. Preventative and Corrective Strategies Against Problem Behaviour.* Journal of Adolescence, 13, 231-250.

Hyndman B, Giesbrecht N, (1993). *Community Based Substance Abuse Prevention Research; Rhetoric and Reality (editorial)*. Addiction, 88, 1613-1616.

Jahoda G, Cramond J, (1972). *Children and Alcohol: a Developmental Study in Glasgow*. London, HMSO.

Jessor R, (1976). *Predicting Onset of Marijuana Use: A Development Study of High School Youth*. In: D J Lettaeri, (ed). Predicting adolescent drug abuse: A review of issues, methods and correlates. Research Issues 11. (DHEW Publication No.ADM 77-299). Washington DC, US Government Printing Office.

Jessor R, Jessor S L, (1977). *Problem Behaviour and Psychosocial Development: A Longitudinal Study*. New York, Academic Press.

Johnson L D, O'Malley P M, Bachman J G, (1989). *Drug Use, Drinking and Smoking: National Survey Results From High School, College, and Young Adults Populations 1975-1988*. National Institute on Drug Abuse. Washington DC, US Government Printing Office.

Johnson B D, Goldstein P J, Preble E, Schmeidler J, Lipton D S, Spunt B, Miller T, (1985). *Taking Care of Business. The Economics of Crime by Heroin Abusers*. Lexington, MA, Lexington Books.

Johnston L, O'Malley P, Bachman J, (1986). *Drug Use Among High School Students, College Students and Other Young Adults : National Trends Through 1985*. Rockville, MD, National Institute on Drug Abuse.

Johnston L D, O'Malley P M, (1986). *Why Do The Nation's Students Use Drugs and Alcohol? Self-reported Reasons From Nine National Surveys*. Journal of Drug Issues, 16, 29-66.

Kaminer Y, (1991). *Adolescent Substance Abuse*. In: Frances R J, Miller R I, (eds). Clinical Textbook of Addictive Disorders, pp.320-346. New York, Guildford Press.

Kandel D B, (1980). *Drug and Drinking Behaviour Among Youth*. Annual Review of Sociology 6, 235-285.

Kandel D B, (1985). *On Processes of Peer Influences in Adolescent Drug Use :a Developmental Perspective*. Alcohol and Substance Abuse (in Adolescence), 4, 3/4, 139-163

Kazdin A, Esveldt-Dawson K, French N, Unis A, (1987). *Effects of Parent Management Training and Problem-solving Skills Training Combined in the Treatment of Anti-social Child Behaviour*. American Journal of Child and Adolescent Psychiatry, 26, 2, 414-416.

Kerfoot M, Huxley P, (1995). *Suicide and Deliberate Self-Harm in Young People*. Current Opinion in Psychiatry, 8,4,214-217.

Kokkevi A, (1990). *Illicit Drug Use Among Adolescents in Western European Countries*. In: Stefans C N, (ed). Psychiatry: A World perspective-Vol 1. Elsevier Science Publishers BV.

Kolvin I, Garside R, Nicol A, Macmillan A, Wolstenholme F, Leitch I, (1981). *Help Starts Here: The Maladjusted Child in the Ordinary School.*, London, Tavistock

Kolvin I, Miller F, McI-Scott D, Gatzonis S, Fleeting M, (1990). *Continuation of Deprivation? The Newcastle 1000 Family Study. Studies in Deprivation and Disadvantages*. Aldershot, Avebury.

Kumpfer K, Turner C, (1991). *The Social Ecology Model of Adolescent Substance Abuse: Implications for Prevention.* International Journal of the Addictions, 254A, 435-463.

Lavik N, Clausen S, Pedersen W, (1991). *Eating Behaviour, Drug Use Psychopathology and Parental Bonding in Adolescents in Norway.* Acta Psychiatrica Scandanavica, 84, 387-390.

Lawson G, Ellis D, Rivers C, (1984). *Essentials of chemical dependency counselling.* Gaithersburg, MD, Aspen Publishers.

Lindebaum G, (1989). *Pattern of alcohol and drug abuse in an urban trauma centre: the increasing role of cocaine abuse.* The Journal of Trauma, 29, 1654-1658.

Maccoby E, Masters J, (1970). *Attachment and Dependency.* In: P. H. Mussen, (ed). Carmichael's manual of child psychology, 3rd ed., Vol.2. New York, John Wiley.

Malvin J H, Moskowitz J M, Schaps E, Schaeffer G A, (1985). *Evaluation of Two School Based Alternatives Programs.* Journal of Alcohol and Drug Education, 30, 98-108.

Mannuzza S, Gittelman Klein R, Bonagura N, Malloy P, Giampino T, Addali K, (1991). *Hyperactive Boys Grow Up V Replication of Psychiatric Status.* Archives of General Psychiatry 48, 77-83.

Marques J K, et al, (1993). *Findings and Recommendations from California's Experimental Treatment* In: Sexual Aggression, Issues in Etiology, Assessment and Treatment. Eds: Nagayama Hall G C, et al, Taylor and Francis, Washington.

Marsh A, Dobbs J, White A, (1986). *Adolescent Drinking.* London, HMSO.

Mawhinney R, Nichol D, (1993). *Purchasing for Health: A Framework for Action.* The Health Publications Unit.

Mauss A L, Hopkins R H, Weisheit R A, Kearney K A, (1988). *The Problematic Prospects for Prevention in the Classroom: Should Alcohol Education Programs Be Expected To Reduce Drinking By Youth.* Journal of Studies on Alcohol, 49, 1, 51-61

May C, (1991). *Research on Alcohol Education for Young People: a Critical Review of the Literature.* Health Education Journal, 50, 195-199.

May C, (1992). *A Burning Issue? Adolescent Alcohol Use in Britain 1970-1991.* Alcohol and Alcoholism, 27, 2, 109-115.

Measham F, (1993). *The Post-Heroin Generation.* Drug Link, May/June.

Meyer R E, Mirin S M, (1979). *The Heroin Stimulus: Implications for a Theory of Addiction.* New York and London, Plenum Medical Book Co.

Milin R, Halikas J A, Meller J, Morse C, (1991). *Psychopathology Among Substance Abusing Juvenile Offenders.* Journal of the American Academy of Child and Adolescent Psychiatry, 30, 4, 569-574.

Mott J, (1985). *Self-report Cannabis Use in Great Britain in 1981.* British Journal of Addictions, 84, 1433-1440.

Mullaney J A, Trippett C J, (1979). *Alcohol Dependence and Phobias: Clinical Description and Relevance.* British Journal of Psychiatry, 41, 934-941.

Murdoch D, Pihl R O, Ross D, (1990). *Alcohol and Crimes of Violence: Present Issues.* International Journal of Addictions. 25, 1065-81.

Mussen P, Conger J, Kagan J, (1974). *Child Development and Personality* 4th ed. New York, Harper and Row.

NHS Executive, (1994). *EL(94)79, Towards a Primary Care-Led NHS.* Department of Health.

NHS Executive, (1995). *An Introduction to Joint Commissioning.* Department of Health.

NHS Executive, (1995). *Practical Guidance on Joint Commissioning for Project Leaders.* Department of Health.

NHS Executive, (1995). *EL(95)68, Priorities and Planning Guidance 1996-97.* The Department of Health.

NHS Health Advisory Service, (1994), *Suicide Prevention: The Challenge Confronted,* London, HMSO.

NHS Health Advisory Service, (1995a). *Together We Stand: The Commissioning, Role and Management of Child and Adolescent Mental Health Service.* London, HMSO.

NHS Health Advisory Service, (1995b). *A Place in Mind: Commissioning and Providing Mental Health Services for People who are Homeless.* London, HMSO.

NHS Management Executive, (1992). *EL(92)18, Support for Pharmacy Based Needle Exchange Schemes.* Department of Health.

National Curriculum Council, (1990). *Curriculum Guidance 5: Health Education.*

National Insititute on Drug Abuse, (1983). *Communities: What You Can Do About Drug and Alcohol Abuse.* Rockville. MD

National Institute on Drug Abuse, (1986). *A Guide To Mobilising Ethnic Minority Communities for Drug Abuse Prevention.* Rockville MD.

National Institute on Drug Abuse, (1990). *Overview of the 1990 National Household Survey on Drug Abuse* Rockville MD.

National Institute on Drug Abuse, (1991). *National Household Survey on Drug Abuse: Population Estimates 1991.* Rockville MD.

Newcomb M D, Maddahian E, Bentler P M, (1986). *Risk Factors for Drug Use Among Adolescents: Concurrent and Longitudinal Analyses.* American Journal of Public Health, 76,525-530.

Newcomb M D, Bentler P M, (1988). *Consequences of Adolescent Drug Use: Impact on the Lives of Young Adults.* Beverly Hills, California, SAGE.

Newcomb M D, Bentler P M, (1989) *Substance Use and Abuse Among Children and Teenagers.* American Psychologist, 44, 2, 242-248.

Newcombe R, Measham F, Parker H, (1994). *A Survey of Drinking and Deviant Behaviour Among 14/15 Year Olds in North West England.* Addiction Research, 1, 1-23.

Nurco D N, (1987). *Drug Addiction and Crime: A Complicated Issue.* British Journal of Addiction, 82, 7-9

Office of Population Censuses and Surveys, (1995). *The Health of Our Children: Dicennial Supplement.* London HMSO.

O'Halloran A, (1990). *Don't Pressure Me: Report by the Youth Accommodation Group on the Needs of Drug and Alcohol Affected Young People in the ACT.* Canberra, YAC.

Parker H, Bakx K, Newcombe R, (1986). *Drug Use in Wirral: The First Report of the Wirral Misuse of Drugs Project.* Sub-department of Social Work Studies, University of Liverpool, Liverpool.

Parker H, Newcombe R, (1987). *Heroin Use and Acquisitive Crime in an English Community*. British Journal of Sociology, 38, 331-350.

Paykel E, Myers J K, Lindenthal J J, Tanner J, (1974). *Suicidal Feelings in the General Population: A Prevalence Study*. British Journal of Psychiatry, 124, 460-9.

Pearson G, (1987). *The New Heroin Users*. Oxford, Blackwell.

Piacentini J, Rotheram-Borus M J, Trautman P, Graae F, (1991). *Psychosocial Correlates of Treatment Compliance in Adolescent Suicide Attempters*. Presented at the Association for Advancement of Behaviour Therapy Meeting, New York.

Pithers W D, et al (1989). *Identification of Risk Factors Through Clinical Interviews and Analysis of Records in Relapse Prevention with Offenders*. Richard Laws (ed). The Guildford Press.

Plant M A, Peck D F, Samuel E, (1985). *Alcohol, Drugs and School-Leavers*, London. Tavistock.

Plotnick R D, (1994). *Applying Benefit-cost Analysis to Substance Use Prevention Programs*. International Journal of the Addictions, 29, 339-359.

Porritt J, (1991). *Report on a Survey Among Street Kids in Sydney*. Sydney, Australian Social Issues Research.

Power R, (1989). *Drugs and the Media: Prevention Campaigns and Television. In: McGregor S, (ed). Drugs and British Society*. London, Routledge.

Rayner G, *Assessment and Community Care: The Views of Drug and Alcohol Community Services: April-June 1993*. SCODA/Alcohol Concern Joint Contracts and Community Care Project. Standing Conference on Drug Abuse.

Robbins D R, Alessi N E, (1985). *Depressive Symptoms and Suicidal Behaviour in Adolescents*. American Journal of Psychiatry 142, 588-92.

Robins L M, McEvoy L, (1990). *Conduct Problems as Predictors of Substance Misuse*. In: Robins L N, Rutter M, (eds). Straight and Deviant Pathways from Childhood to Adulthood. New York, Cambridge University Press.

Robins L N, Przybeck T R, (1985). *Age of Onset of Drug Use as a Factor in Drug and Other Disorders*. In: NIDA Research Monograph No.56. Aetiology of Drug Abuse, Implications for Prevention. Rockville M.D, National Institute on Drug Abuse.

Robins L N, (1991). *Conduct Disorder*. Journal of Child Psychology and Psychiatry, 32, 1, 193-212.

Robins L N, Ratcliff K S, (1979). *Continuation of Antisocial Behaviour into Adulthood*, International Journal of Mental Health, 7, 96-116.

Ross H E, Glaser F R, Germanson T, (1988). *The Prevalence of Psychiatric Disorders in Patients with Alcohol and Other Drug Problems*. Archives of General Psychiatry, 45, 1023-1031.

Royal College of Psychiatrists, (1987). *Drug Scene: a report on drugs and drug dependence*. Gaskell.

Rutter M, (1980). *Changing Youth in a Changing Society*. Cambridge, MA, Harvard University Press.

Rutter M, (1985). *Resilience in the Face of Adversity: Protective Factors and Resistance to Psychiatric Disorder.* British Journal of Psychiatry, 147, 598-611.

Schaps E, Churgin S, Palley C S, Takata B, Cohen A Y, (1990). *Primary Prevention Research: A Preliminary Review of Programs Outcome Studies.* International Journal of Addictions 15, 5, 657-676.

Scottish Affairs Committee, (1994). *Drug Abuse in Scotland, Report, Together with the Proceedings of the Committee, Vol.1.* London, HMSO.

Shaffer D, Gould M, Fisher P, Trautman P, Kleinman M, Moroshima A. *An Epidemiological Study of Child and Adolescent Suicide.* 11 Clinical Diagnosis. (In preparation)

Sharp C, (1993). *Alcohol Education for Young People: A Review of the Literature from 1983-1992.* A Report for the Alcohol Education and Research Council and the Portman Group. National Foundation for Educational Research.

Shelder J, Block J, (1990). *Adolescent Drug Use and Psychological Health: A Longitudinal Inquiry.* The American Psychologist, 45, 5, 612-630.

Sonenstein F, Pleck J, Ku L, (1989). *Sexual Activity, Condom Use and AIDS Awareness Among Adolescent Males.* Family Planning Perspectives, 21, 152-158.

Spirito A, Brown L, Overholser J, Fritz G, (1989). *Attempted Suicide in Adolescence: A Review of the Literature.* Clinical Psychology Review, 9, 335-363.

Standing Conference on Drug Abuse, *Standard Setting and Audit.*

Stein J A, Swisher J D, Hu T, McDonnell N, (1984). *Cost-effectiveness of a Channel One Program.* Journal of Drug Education, 14, 251-269.

Swadi H, (1988). *Drug and Substance Use Among 3,333 London Adolescents.* British Journal of Addictions, 83, 935-942.

Swisher J, Hu T, (1983). *Alternatives to Drug Abuse: Some Are and Some Are Not.* In: Glynn, Lenkejeld, Ludford (eds). Preventing Adolescent Drug Abuse: Intervention Strategies (pp 93-117). Washington DC, US Government Printing Office.

Tobler N S, (1986). *Meta Analysis of 143 Adolescent Drug Prevention Programmes: Quantitative Outcome Results of Program Participants Compared to a Control or Comparison Group.* Journal of Drug Issues 16, 4, 547-567.

US Congress, Office of Technology Assessment, (1991). *Ottawa Charter for Health Promotion, Health Promotion 1,4,3-5, 1987.* Adolescent Health Vol. 1 Summary and Policy Options, OTA-H-468. Washington DC, US Government Printing Office.

US Department of Education and US Department of Health and Human Services, (1987). *Report to the Congress and the White House on the Nature and Effectiveness of Federal, State, and Local Drug Prevention/Education Programmes.* Washington DC, US Government Printing Office.

Wallack L, Barrows D C, (1982/1983). *Evaluating Primary Prevention; the California Winners Alcohol Program.* International Quarterly of Community Health Education, 3, 307-336.

Walters R, Marshall W, Shooter J, (1960). *Anxiety, Isolation, and Susceptibility to Social Influence.* Journal of Personality, 28, 518-529.

Weatherburn P, Davies P, Hickson F, Hunt A, McManus T, Coxon A, (1993). *No Connection Between Alcohol Use and Unsafe Sex Among Gay and Bisexual Men.* AIDS, 7, 115-119.

Weisman C S, Plichta S, Nathanson C A, Ensminger M, Robinson J C, (1991). *Consistency of Condom Use For Disease Prevention Among Adolescent Users of Oral Contraceptives.* Family Planning Perspective, 23, 71.

Weiss W, (1990). *User Careers: Implications for Preventing Drug Misuse.* In: Plant M, Goos C, Kuep W, Osterberg E, (eds). Alcohol and Drugs: Research and Policy, Edinburgh. Edinburgh University Press, 142-154.

Weiss G, pp 142-154. Hechtman L T, (1986). *Hyperactive Children Grown Up.* New York: Guildford Press.

Weissman M M, Myers J K, (1980). *Clinical Depression in Alcoholism.* American Journal of Psychiatry 137, 372-373.

Welsh Health Planning Forum, (1993). *Protocol for Investment in Health Gain - Mental Health.* Welsh Office NHS Directorate.

Williams R, (1994). *Commissioning Services for Vulnerable People.* British Geriatric Society.

Williams R, (1995). *Improving the Mental Health of Children and Adolescents - Using Research in Developing Knowledge and Concepts of Service Delivery.* Current Opinion in Psychiatry, 8, 203-205.

Williams R, Avebury K, (1995). *A Place in Mind - Commissioning and Providing Mental Health Services for People Who Are Homeless.* NHS Health Advisory Service, London, HMSO.

Williams R, Farrar M, (1994). *Commissioning Child and Adolescent Mental Health Services.* In: Dean C, (ed). *A Slow Train Coming - Bringing the Mental Health Revolution to Scotland.* Glasgow, Greater Glasgow Community and Mental Health Services NHS Trust.

Williams R, Morgan H G, (1994). *Suicide Prevention - The Challenge Confronted.* NHS Health Advisory Service, London, HMSO.

Williams R, Ponton L, (1992). *HIV and Adolescents: An International Perspective.* Journal of Adolescents 15, 335-343.

Williams R, Richardson G, (1995). *Together We Stand - The Commissioning, Role and Management of Child and Adolescent Mental Health Services.* NHS Health Advisory Service, London, HMSO.

Williams R, White R, (eds), (1992). *A Concise Guide to the Children Act 1989.* London, Gaskell. (2nd Edition in press).

World Health Organisation, (1991). *Assessment of Standards of Care in Drug Abuse Treatment. Programme on Substance Abuse.* Geneva, World Health Organisation.

World Health Organisation, (1981). *Documents on Nomenclature and Classification.* Geneva, World Health Organisation.

World Health Organisation. *Ottawa Charter for Health Promotion.* Health Promotion 1(4): iii-v, 1987. Geneva, World Health Organisation.

World Health Organisation, (1992). *The ICD-10 Classification of Mental and Behavioural Disorders: Clinical Descriptions and Diagnostic Guidelines.* Geneva, World Health Organisation.

Wright J D, Pearl L, (1990). *Knowledge and Experience of Young People Regarding Drug Abuse. 1969-1989.* British Medical Journal, 300, 99-103.

Yamaguchi K, Kandel D, (1984). *Patterns of Drug Use From Adolescence to Young Adulthood: Sequences of Progression, Predictors of Progression.* American Journal of Public Health, 74, 668-681.

PART G

Annexes

The Methodology of the
Review

THE ORIGINS OF THE REVIEW

1 This thematic review of Services for Children and Adolescents who Misuse Substances, including particularly alcohol and drugs, is one of a series of thematic reviews prepared by the NHS Health Advisory Service (HAS).

2 *Suicide Prevention - The Challenge Confronted*, highlights the strong influence of alcohol and substance use and misuse on suicide and in deliberate self-harm by young people.

3 In *Together We Stand*, the HAS identified that by 1993 75% of health authorities had proposals for alcohol and substance misuse services which could include provision for young people. The same review highlighted the significance of substance use and misuse for the mental health problems and disorders experienced by this population.

CONDUCTING THE REVIEW

4 The director of the HAS established a single steering committee to advise him in conducting the thematic reviews relating to mental health services for children and adolescents. This committee divided into two groups. One concentrated on conducting the work published in *Together We Stand* while the second carried out a series of literature reviews and service visits related to alcohol and substance misuse which formed the backbone of the work for this review. It also orchestrated a multi-disciplinary conference of experts .

5   The methodology of the review is outlined in the schematic diagram below:

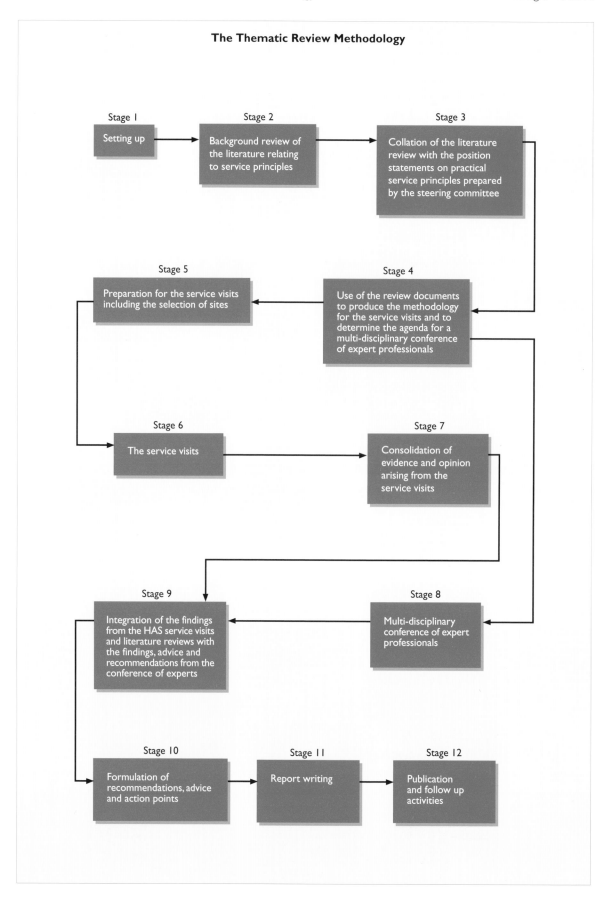

The Thematic Review Methodology

Stage 1
Setting up

Stage 2
Background review of the literature relating to service principles

Stage 3
Collation of the literature review with the position statements on practical service principles prepared by the steering committee

Stage 5
Preparation for the service visits including the selection of sites

Stage 4
Use of the review documents to produce the methodology for the service visits and to determine the agenda for a multi-disciplinary conference of expert professionals

Stage 6
The service visits

Stage 7
Consolidation of evidence and opinion arising from the service visits

Stage 9
Integration of the findings from the HAS service visits and literature reviews with the findings, advice and recommendations from the conference of experts

Stage 8
Multi-disciplinary conference of expert professionals

Stage 10
Formulation of recommendations, advice and action points

Stage 11
Report writing

Stage 12
Publication and follow up activities

6   Specific commissioning of services targeted towards children and adolescents who use and misuse alcohol and drugs appeared to be largely non-existent at present. Examination by the HAS of the strategy documents, contracts and service specifications prepared by 90% of the health authorities in England and Wales that provided documents to the HAS Library of Commissioning Documentation for 1993-94 showed no mention of such specific services. In this circumstance it stands out that two health authorities did mention that they provided such services for children and adolescents within their mainstream provision for adults.

7   A review of the general literature was conducted, as was a retrospective inspection of the reports of the NHS Drug Advisory Service (DAS) for the last three years. Visits were carried out in conjunction with those made to review mental health services for children and adolescents by the HAS. They were also made to selected voluntary agencies that work with young people in relation to substance misuse. Given the known lack of specially designated services for this age group, found in other surveys, and the concerned comments which are frequently made in DAS reports, any form of random selection of services for specific visits to view good practice was not considered to be a viable option. Instead, a selection was made of services known to the authors, who are collectively very familiar with service provision in the UK.

8   The review also took account of contributions made by delegates at a special conference held by the HAS to consider the problems presented by use, misuse and abuse by younger people. These are reflected in the contents of this report. It also uses information based upon the returns of district health authorities on their strategies for adult mental illness, drug and alcohol services and child and adolescent mental health services. These were examined to determine what strategies these authorities had for children and young people with problems arising from alcohol and substance misuse.

9   The range of substances considered in this review, and to which the recommendations apply, include alcohol, tobacco, use of illicit and prescribed drugs, including steroids, and volatile substances.

10   Members of the group drawn from the steering committee for this thematic review carried out eight visits to selected services for children and young people in England and Wales. In addition, they visited a range of non-statutory agencies that provide services to younger people with alcohol and substance abuse problems. Before undertaking the fieldwork, the review group formulated a number of specific questions and identified broad areas which it considered should be addressed in each of the visits. These considerations shaped the programme for the visits. The principal questions that service visitors posed are listed here.

- How many detoxifications of younger people of less than 20 years of age relating to the use of alcohol and drugs have been conducted in the last two years: a. as an inpatient; b. as an outpatient?

- What special provision is provided for people in ethnic groups who have problems with drinking or drugs in your community?

- What strategy do you have for facilitating access to services for mobile, migrant and homeless young people with problems with drinking or drugs?

- What are your recommendations for emergency responses for young people at rave parties and festivals?

- What have been your recommendations for outreach intervention and harm reduction for young people who use drugs? Which of these recommendations have been implemented in the last two years?

- What fast-track arrangements are in place for assessing young people with problems with the use of substances? Who carries out the assessments?

- How many under 20 year-olds have been funded by the social services department for drug and alcohol rehabilitation programmes? How many have been assessed under the community care arrangements?

- What are your recommendations for needle and syringe exchange provision for under 16 year-olds? Have you a written policy? If yes, please enclose a copy?

- What advice have you given to service commissioners on the needs of young people with drug and alcohol problems and their prioritisation? What specific advice have you given regarding the funding of these services?

11   A particularly important part of the work was drawing together the findings from the variety of sources outlined above. These, and the work which the HAS has in hand in guiding commissioners and purchasers (including GP fundholders), generated a picture of the misuse of alcohol, drugs and other substances. This also led to the development of a strategic approach to service strategy and delivery. These considerations form the basis of the approach recommended in this review.

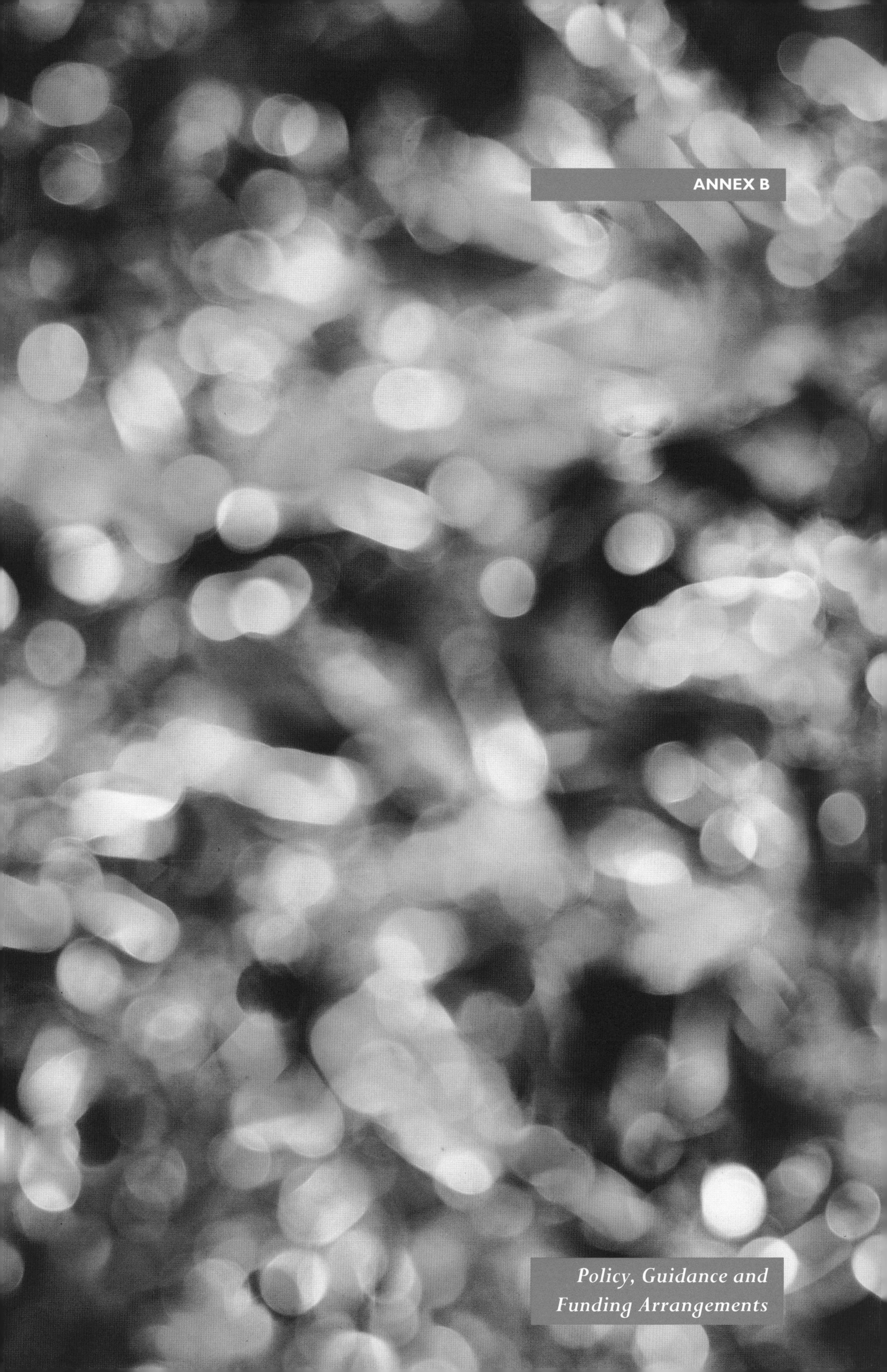

ANNEX B

Policy, Guidance and Funding Arrangements

1   There are many reports from the Advisory Council on the Misuse of Drugs (ACMD), the Department of Health and the Home Office offering guidance to all those involved in purchasing and providing substance misuse services to young people. In the period when this report was being written, the Government produced its inter-departmental strategy as the White Paper - *Tackling Drugs Together*, (1995).

POLICY, GUIDANCE AND FUNDING ARRANGEMENTS

POLICY

Tackling Drugs Together - A Strategy For England 1995-98

2   This White Paper sets out a new strategy to tackle drug misuse. The Government recognises that, while the focus of the strategy is on substances controlled under the Misuse of Drugs Act 1971, much prevention and treatment is carried out within a *"broader context of tackling alcohol and other substance misuse."* The report also states: *"At local level, arrangements for Drug Action Teams can certainly include action in relation to other substances."*

3   The strategy is driven by the Statement of Purpose in the White Paper:
"To take effective action by vigorous law enforcement, accessible treatment and a new emphasis on education and prevention to:

- *increase the safety of communities from drug-related crime;*

- *reduce the acceptability and availability of drugs to young people; and*

- *reduce the health risks and other damage related to drug misuse.'*

4   This focus on young people, crime and public health is welcomed. Achieving the aims of the White Paper will require multi-agency collaboration and co-ordination. The strategy sets out national priorities, objectives and timetables. It offers guidance on the establishment of Drug Action Teams and Drug Reference Groups that will deliver the strategy.

Forward Together - A Strategy to Combat Drug and Alcohol Misuse

5   This Welsh Office document was issued for consultation in October 1995 and comments were invited by 31 December 1995.

6   The statement of purpose in the strategy is intended to stimulate vigorous action and it places new emphasis on:

- preventing the misuse of drugs and alcohol, particularly among younger people;
- providing treatment, support and rehabilitation for those people who misuse drugs and alcohol.

7   The Statement of Purpose in this draft document of guidance complements that in the Government's White Paper *Tackling Drugs Together*. In addition, that document requires criminal justice agencies, including those in Wales, to seek to increase community safety from drug related crime.

8   The objectives of the Welsh strategy are to:

- increase prevention activity in schools and elsewhere in order to reduce the acceptability to young people and others, of taking drugs and of excessive or inappropriate drinking;
- reduce health-related and other risks caused by drug and alcohol misuse;
- increase co-operation between agencies working to combat drug and alcohol misuse.

9   It has been recognised that no single individual or agency can tackle the tasks of: putting young people and others in possession of the facts about drugs and alcohol, equipping them to make the right choices; and offering them the support and treatment needed to overcome the problems that misuse can cause.

10 Therefore, this strategy places heavy emphasis on inter-agency working and calls upon chief officers of health and local authorities together with education departments, and social, probation, prison and police services to come together to form Drug and Alcohol Action Teams.

11 While the Welsh Office will continue to have responsibility for setting policy and monitoring implementation, it will be supported by the Welsh Drug and Alcohol Unit. This is a specialist body charged with providing expertise, advice and services in relation to drug and alcohol misuse. Additionally, the Welsh Office will be supported by the Welsh Committee on Drug and Alcohol Misuse. This is an advisory body that offers advice and information to the Secretary of State and the Welsh Office, service commissioners and service providers.

GUIDANCE FROM CENTRAL GOVERNMENT

The Department of Health

Drug Misuse and Dependence - Guidelines on Clinical Management, 1991.

12 These guidelines were based on a revision of the *Guidelines of Good Clinical Practice in the Treatment of Drug Misuse* and were produced in the light of developments since the publication of the original guidelines in 1984. The guidelines of 1991 were written for GPs and those likely to see people who use drugs (eg, the staff of accident and emergency departments, general hospital staff, and the staff of neonatal care services). The guidelines give advice on the principles of clinical midwifery, obstetrics and assessment, management and treatment, and on harm-minimisation and specialist referral.

Substance Misuse Detainees in Police Custody - Guidelines for Clinical Management, 1994.

13 These guidelines are *intended to supplement* the guidance summarised above. They specifically address the issues that arise for doctors in forensic practice when caring for those people who use drugs and while they are detained in custody.

Children's Services Plans - Local Authority Circular LAC(92)18

14 This circular establishes a requirement on social services departments to draw up Children's Services Plans:

- in collaboration with a wide number of interested organisations including health authorities, local education authorities and the non-statutory sector;

- that reflect the policies of central government;

- in accordance with the legal requirements imposed upon local authorities, in particular the requirements of the Criminal Justice Act 1991.

15   In discharging this role, social services departments are expected to draw upon the following information:

- the demography of the child population in the local area;

- the number of children in local authority care, including the ages of the children, the length of time in care and the reasons for them being there;

- the number of children on the child protection register, including their ages, length of time on the register and the reasons for their inclusion;

- the range of foster places available and whether the number meets the demand;

- the range of children's homes placements provided and the occupancy levels of the homes;

- the number of core staff available to provide children's services, the qualifications of the staff and details relating to staff turnover etc.;

- the range of family support services provided, including family centre places etc.;

- the number of young people leaving care each year, and the services provided for them, including housing;

- the educational requirements of children in care and the services available to them;

- the number of children excluded from school, including whether the exclusion is permanent, fixed-term or indefinite;

- an explanation of any regulatory policies that the local authority is required to follow over and above those required by the Department of Health.

16   The HAS is aware that currently the Department of Health is reviewing the guidance contained in circular LAC(92)18. This is being done in the light of the Audit Commission report, *Seen but not Heard,* and a number of recent reviews of Children's Services Plans undertaken by the Social Services Inspectorate of the Department of Health.

17   It is likely that the results of this review will require social services departments to pay particular attention to the needs of vulnerable children and their families when constructing Children's Services Plans. Additionally, it is expected that the revised guidance will require social services departments to clarify what services are provided and to ensure that the plans are drawn up in accordance with the *Citizen's Charter.* Thus, one requirement will be that the plans should be drawn up in consultation with the users of services, whose views should be taken into account.

The Department for Education and Employment

18   Two policy documents from the then Department for Education are surveyed below.

Drug Prevention and Schools, Circular Number 4/95

19   This circular:

- offers advice on the principles that should inform drug education;

- offers guidance on the development and implementation of education on drugs and related issues;

- offers guidance on the effective and consistent management of drug-related incidents;

- includes advice on smoking, volatile substance misuse, alcohol, anabolic steroids and other substances as well as illicit drugs.

20   Within its annexes it refers to:

- *Tackling Drugs Together* - a Strategy for England 1995-1998;

- The extent of drug misuse among young people;

- *Drug Education in Schools: The Need for New Impetus;*

- Use of visitors and outside agencies;

- A Draft Policy on Substance Use and Misuse;

- *Drug Misuse and the Young - A Guide for the Education Service,* 1992 Department for Education/Welsh Office;

- A summary of an LEA's Schools Drug Prevention Charter 1994;

- *Smoking Policies in Schools: Guidelines for Policy Development,* HEA Booklet, 1993.

Drug proof - Protecting Children Through Education (1995)

21   This guidance, given by the School Curriculum and Assessment Authority (SCAA), reflects the broad principles outlined in the Department for Education's document, *Drug Prevention and Schools.* It gives guidance on:

- the approaches, aims and principles of education on drugs and related issues;

- the development of a drug education programme;

- the content of drug education programmes;

- the options available for organisation of the curriculum;

- the availability and use of teaching materials and approaches;

- the training and support needed for teachers.

The Welsh Office

22   In parallel with the guidance issued to schools in England, the Welsh Office has issued advice to schools in Wales in its circular 54/95 *Drug Misuse: Prevention and Schools.* This circular provides guidance on the provision of drug education in the school curriculum and the management of illegal drug-related incidents on school premises.

Protection of Children: Disclosure of the Criminal Background of those with Access to Children HOC 47/1993, DFE 9/93, DH LAC 93(17), WOC 54/93

23   This Home Office, Department for Education, Department of Health and Welsh Office circular was drawn up in conjunction with the Association of Chief Police Officers, representatives of local authorities' associations and other government departments. It provides guidance on the arrangements for checking the background of people who apply to work with children and so it is essential that this circular is fully addressed by all organisations that come into contact with children and young people.

24   Checks of criminal records are especially important where the children involved are the most vulnerable or where supervision of staff is difficult or impossible. Checks are less crucial where staff do not work alone or where work is undertaken with larger groups of less vulnerable children. Nevertheless, effective management and supervision of staff should be maintained in all circumstances and conducting checks prior to employment is not an alternative to proper supervision.

25   Posts which entail *"a substantial level of access to children which may also be unsupervised, and will be regular or sustained"* qualify applicants for a check of a possible criminal record by the police. The guidance in the circular defines how the statement quoted above should be interpreted and it lists the main groups of people for which checks should be considered. In the main, these are people engaged by statutory local authorities, for example in childcare or educational establishments. The guidelines do not apply to voluntary organisations unless they are specifically contracted to undertake work which meets the above criteria on behalf of local authorities. Separate guidance for the non-statutory sector is contained in HOC 117/92.

26   Checks made by the police must not take the place of normal personnel procedures and safeguards such as references, verification of qualifications and clarification of gaps in employment history.

ADVICE FROM NON-STATUTORY BODIES

Action For Sick Children

27   A longstanding policy of Action for Sick Children, (formerly the National Association for the Welfare of Children in Hospital) is that adult settings are inappropriate for children and adolescents. The policy lays down an important principle of service delivery: *"It is the responsibility of health authorities and social services departments to provide an environment for children and young people which is appropriate to their age group and takes account of the emotional and physical needs of the young person and those with disability and special needs."* It is important to recognise that the provision of an adult-oriented drug and alcohol service is inappropriate to meet the needs of young people and steps should be taken to ensure that appropriate environments for assessment and treatment are provided separate from adult services.

28   At the time this report was being written, the Department of Health was consulting on *The Patient's Charter - Services for Children and Young People*. This consultation document endorses the view of Action for Sick Children that adult settings are inappropriate for children and adolescents.

The Reports of The Advisory Council on the Misuse of Drugs (ACMD)

Treatment and Rehabilitation, 1982

29   This report recommended:

- monitoring the extent of the drug problem;

- the establishment of regional drug problem teams, district drug advisory committees and district drug problem teams;

- that training should be developed in an integrated way;

- that there should be more research into service policy and the factors that influence users to seek treatment.

30   Not least, it called for tighter safeguards on prescription and for guidelines on good medical practice in the treatment of problem drug users.

Prevention, 1984

31   This report endorsed the trend away from drug education based solely on information, towards broader programmes which focus more on social and cultural factors, and which aim to promote healthy living. Among some of its recommendations were:

- media coverage of drugs matters to be better informed;

- preventive measures in local communities should be part of a wider objective of achieving a healthier community;

- national campaigns aimed specifically at reducing the incidence of drug use should not be attempted;

- inter-agency and multi-disciplinary liaison and co-operation is crucial;

- training should be provided for all professionals;

- improved co-ordination of prevention at national and local levels;

- a need for further research on measures that affect supply;

- evaluation of health and social education programmes.

AIDS and Drug Misuse

32   These four reports, published in 1988, 1989, 1990 and 1993, affirm that drug use and drug injecting can result in major health problems for individual drug users, for families and friends, and for society as a whole. HIV-related disease has significantly increased the risks of harm, arising from injecting drugs, to individuals and to society. In the past decade, harm-reduction strategies have been a major focus of care. These reports recommended greater action to reduce the extent of drug use, to identify users early on, and for early and effective interventions to encourage individuals to cease their use of drugs and to discourage drug-related risk-taking behaviour and unsafe sexual practices.

33   Evidence demonstrates that the public is well aware of the risks involved. Needle-sharing appears to have reduced and the targeted interventions of community-based agencies and needle-syringe exchanges have contributed to the reduction of risk. The lower levels of risk-taking and low prevalence of HIV among drug users in the UK suggest the success of the strategies which have been adopted.

Recent recommendations of the ACMD about strategy include:

- the twin objectives of reducing sexual and injecting risk behaviour among drug users and of working towards a reduction in problem drug use;

- a broader response to outreach work (or activities) which incorporates a range of early interventions;

- thorough evaluation of the achievements to date in service development and working methods as a step towards the consolidation of good practice and improvement in agency efficiency.

Key recommendations of the ACMD include:

- Establishment of methadone prescribing programmes with evaluation;

- Promotion of safer sexual practices;

- Promotion of early testing for HIV serum positivity;

- Recognition of the central role in service provision of GPs who need adequate support from more specialised drug services;

- A focus on drug use and services in the criminal justice system and, in particular, prisons;

- An emphasis on the need for continuing liaison and the co-ordination of services.

Problem Drug Use - A Review of Training, 1990

34 This report recommended that training should be delivered in an integrated way (ie, to include training on all substances including alcohol, solvents and tobacco), particularly for those who work with young people. It recommends that all professionals who are in any contact with people who use drugs should have basic awareness training and that government health departments should establish one or more intensive multi-disciplinary courses for trainers and consider national training facilities. The recommendations for training are aimed at four target levels:

- courses for non-specialist, non-professional workers;

- initial professional qualifying courses;

- post-basic qualification courses;

- courses for staff who work in specialist drug use and misuse agencies.

Drug Misusers and the Criminal Justice System, 1991

35 This report considers aspects of the criminal justice system which affect people who misuse drugs. Among its recommendations are:

- adoption of the principles of harm-reduction;

- attempts to attract misusers from ethnic minorities to services;

- better identification of those with drug problems, particularly women and ethnic minorities;

- partnerships between the probation services and other agencies which deal with drug misusers;

- full assessment of each person's drug use prior to recommendations being made to the courts for probation orders and the subsequent inclusion then of a condition of treatment;

- promotion of links between duty solicitors and local drug misuse services;

- the need for the training of probation officers in respect to drug use and misuse;

- the need for organisational changes in response to the recommendations;

- the need for the improved availability of treatment facilities for work with probation service and others in the criminal justice system; and

- the needs of magistrates and the judiciary for information on drugs and for training on issues relating to drug use and misuse.

Drug Education in Schools: The Need for New Impetus, 1993

36   This report recommended the development of a national strategy for drug education that is integrated at national and local levels. It also recommends the provision of accurate prevalence figures, evaluation of education programmes, the development of national standards and guidelines and the setting of targets which focus on the implementation of education programmes, teacher training, school drug policies, the involvement of parents and the reduction of the national prevalence of drug misuse among children of school age. It argues that national standards and guidelines need to be established and reviewed regularly and that, while guidelines should be flexible, specific targets should be set which are capable of being audited.

The Police, Drug Misusers and the Community, 1994

37   This report focuses on the interaction between people who misuse drugs and the enforcement and prosecution agencies, drug services and the general community. Its principal recommendations include:

- the development of street-level strategies by the police with community consultation;

- the adoption of principles of harm-reduction in relation to both users and the community;

- effective joint working to include regular monitoring and progress reports;

- establishment of criteria for granting licences for raves and other such events;

- the production of national guidelines for cautioning those who commit offences relating to drugs;

- the development of agreed guidelines for the treatment in custody of people who misuse drugs;

- further research into the treatment of people from ethnic minorities within the criminal justice system.

Volatile Substance Abuse, 1995

38   This report presents *"ideas about how to confront this deadly and socially damaging problem."* It advises on:

- prevalence and patterns of volatile substance abuse (VSA);

- preventive strategies for carers, parents, trade associations and government;

- a strategy to provide appropriate and flexible advice and intervention for users and their families;

- the need for a strong organisational base for drug education in schools;

- the inclusion of VSA in training programmes on drug issues;

- proposals for a co-ordinated response to the training needs of various professionals;

- an effective mechanism for planning an overall response to VSA at local level.

CONTRACTUAL AND FUNDING ARRANGEMENTS

39   Services provided by the NHS are usually financed from mainstream budgets for mental health services, with input from social services departments in the form of time allocated from social workers. Therefore, they form part of the contract for mental health services between the local health commission and a local trust. The extent to which contracts are placed with other providers, for example those in the non-statutory sector, is substantially dependent upon the availability of specific central allocations of money. The following paragraphs describe the various sources of the allocations which have defined the pattern of services and the placing of contracts in many areas.

Central Government Funding for Services for Drug Misusers

40   Statutory and non-statutory substance misuse services, have benefited from special allocations made available centrally to encourage the development of services for drug misusers and initiatives relevant to substance misusers directed at preventing the spread of HIV. The money has followed the publication of guidance to health and local authorities. These include: *HC(86)3 - Services for Drug Misusers; HC(87)8 and HC(88)26 - Services for Drug Misusers - Curbing the Spread of AIDS and HIV Infection; HC(88)53 - Preventing the Spread of HIV Infection Among and From Injecting Drug Misusers.* So far, finance from these sources has remained ring-fenced. These special allocations are renewed annually and therefore have been treated as non-recurring finance by some authorities. For many non-statutory agencies, this has resulted in contracts being placed for one year only with renewal being subject to the continued availability of central finance. In many instances, the degree of uncertainty about continued availability of this money has inhibited forward planning.

The Department of Health

41   In recent years, monies have also been released by the Department of Health for specific purposes:

- to assist with the cost of methadone-prescribing (EL(92)18)

- to support pharmacy-based needle exchange schemes (EL(92)49)

42   In 1995, the Department of Health allocated and distributed £1 million pounds for the development of services offering a variety of styles of work with young people who use and misuse substances. The range of projects is very diverse and their evaluations are being considered by the Department of Health's Effectiveness Review. Additionally, this body has commissioned further reviews to inform its deliberations.

The Home Office

43   The Home Office provides finance for the *Drugs Prevention Initiative,* which has led to the development of *Drugs Prevention Teams* in urban areas.

44   Drugs Prevention Teams were set up in 1990 to work in 20 areas in England, Wales and Scotland. In each area, they worked with local people, voluntary agencies and community groups to promote drug prevention activities. Each team has a small budget for supporting local initiatives. Many of these prevention activities target young people, have included peer education projects, and diversionary activity schemes and have stimulated the provision of a range of training and education programmes. All the work is subject to external evaluation and some of the evaluation reports have been published.

45   In April 1995, funding for the Drugs Prevention Teams was renewed for a further four years. Twelve new larger teams have been set up to cover a wider area of England.

The Department for Education and Employment

46   The Department for Education and Employment has made funding available to local education authority maintained schools, under the Grants for Education Support and Training (GEST) programme, to support staff training and the development of innovative preventive programmes. The total amount of funding available in each year is £5.9 million. The Department has published guidance in the form of a circular *Drug Prevention and Schools* (1994) to assist with this.

47   The GEST provided seed-corn finance for Drug Education Co-ordinators, which many local education authorities continue to support through advisory teacher posts for personal, social and health education.

Tackling Drugs Together - A Strategy for England 1995-1998

48   The pattern in which finance is pledged in parallel with strategy developments has continued with the publication of this White Paper. This has brought in its wake the following:

- £1 million for one year for young people at risk from drugs;

- £8.8 million over three years to assist with the development of local co-ordination arrangements (eg, administrative support, research, advice and training, commissioning local needs assessments and mobilising community involvement);

- £5.9 million for one year under the GEST programme to train teachers and to support innovative projects in education and prevention on drugs.

Funding for Services for People who Misuse Alcohol

49 Services for people who misuse alcohol have not benefitted in the same way from the allocation of central funding. Despite the complexity and time-limited nature of much of the funding for drug misuse services, in recent years, it has stimulated a considerable growth in the number and range of services for people who misuse drugs. Centrally sourced funds that are available for alcohol services, in so far as they exist at all, tend to be provided only to the non-statutory sector. One example is the Drug and Alcohol Specific Grant, which is administered by social services departments, either on a grant aid or contractual basis. This circumstance has led to under-development of services for people who misuse alcohol relative to the known level of need when compared with services for people who misuse drugs.

50 Where alcohol services have developed, local commissioners have been more imaginative, by making use of joint finance and health-gain monies, by developing schemes in support of the *Health of the Nation* initiative and, by adding them to schemes for drug and HIV prevention.

51 Much of the cost of providing health services for people with problems in the use of alcohol is hidden. It is estimated that as many as 40% of acute hospital beds in surgical, renal, and general medical wards, are occupied by people with alcohol-related medical problems. Alcohol use is a factor leading to many GP consultations and is frequently related to deliberate self-harm. There is an argument for urging health commissioners to re-direct finance currently spent on acute hospital services to contracts which more directly recognise this area of need, by commissioning specialist alcohol services. Such a radical step could do much to prevent alcohol-related ill-health, which is very costly to the health service and often not visible.

The Single Regeneration Budget

52 A more immediate solution, potentially available for both drug and alcohol services, is provided by the Single Regeneration Budget.

53 The Single Regeneration Budget brings together 20 existing funding programmes from five government departments to provide flexible support for local initiatives. The aim of the programmes is to achieve physical, economic and social regeneration within a specific geographical area, through projects that address issues such as community safety, employment and training opportunities, housing improvements, economic development, and health and the quality of life. Successful schemes have to attract significant contributions from both public and private sectors as a condition of their application for Single Regeneration Budget funding. Projects which address substance misuse could clearly have a part to play in regeneration schemes of this nature that are likely to receive financial support for a number of years.

Funding for Residential Rehabilitation

54   Residential rehabilitation services for people who misuse substances are funded in an aggregated way. A package of funding is organised for each individual who is placed in a residential rehabilitation service, following a comprehensive assessment of the needs of that individual. The package is likely to include contributions from:

- the individual, either personally or via their benefit payments (including housing benefit);

- the local authority drawn from the community care grant allocated to the social services department;

- the local health authority in respect of any health service provided, including detoxification services;

- a top-up element from the local authority, probation service or charitable sources, to meet any cost, which exceeds the local authority's target for weekly placement fees.

55   In some instances, residential projects may also attract grants which contribute to their overall running costs or which enable them to undertake specific projects, such as skills training.

Funding under the NHS and Community Care Act 1990

56   Special Transitional Grant (STG) funding is available for services for adults and therefore can only be used to finance placements for young people over the age of 18. Funding for those aged 17 or under, or for any children involved in family placements must be provided from the social services department's budget for children's services. There is considerable pressure on these budgets and in general money will only be available for those clients who fall within individual department's priority groups. Vulnerable children who require child protection services will be included in this category. As a result, there may be many calls and pressures on the budget and obtaining funding for residential rehabilitation placements for young people under 18 is extremely difficult.

57   Increasingly, agencies that provide community care, whether in a residential or day care setting, receive a payment for each individual placed rather than for providing a block quantum of service. This finance, found from the community care or special transitional grant allocation, is then applied directly to meeting the assessed needs of the individual. Experience indicates new projects are likely to require pump-priming, perhaps via the joint commissioning process, if they are to become sufficiently established to be able to rely on individual placement fees to meet their revenue costs. Nonetheless, a balance is necessary as experience also indicates that services should not become over-reliant on relatively small injections of pump-priming finance. Rather, they should work to achieve commitments to longer-term financial support that will enable them to develop in stable and predictable ways.

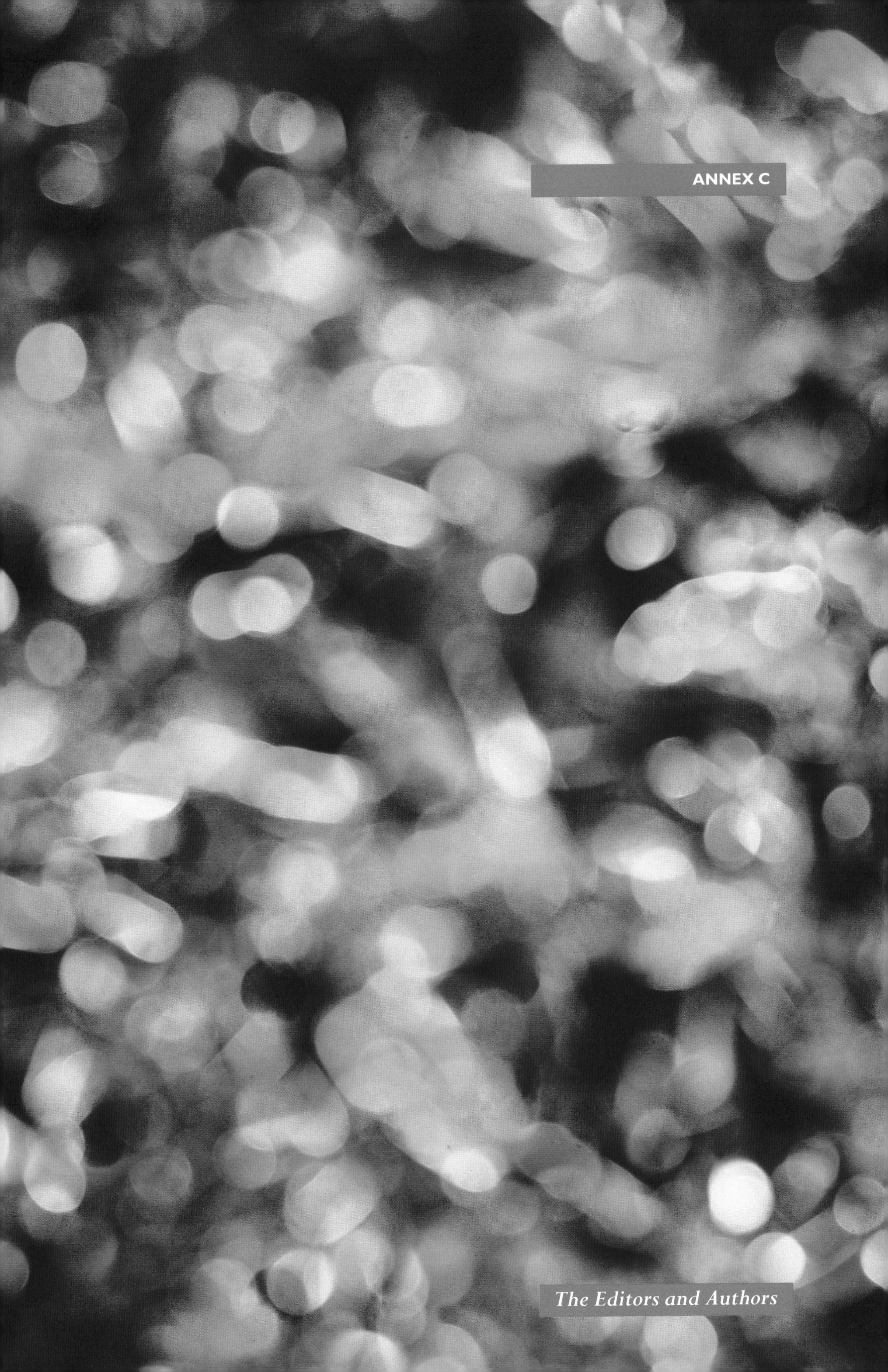

ANNEX C

The Editors and Authors

THE EDITORS

Ms Kina Avebury

Ms Kina Avebury works as an independent consultant in mental health and related fields. She was previously an assistant director of MIND with responsibility for regional and community development. She subsequently worked in the Department of Psychiatry, Tower Hamlets Health Authority and latterly for the London Borough of Tower Hamlets as principal officer for mental health. She was the social services manager of the East London and the City HHELP team, which provides primary and mental health care to homeless people. She has worked extensively in the fields of homelessness, supported housing, and alcohol misuse. She is a former council member of CCETSW, co-author of *Home Life - Code of Practice for Residential Care* 1984 and a former member of a Mental Health Review Tribunal.

Ms Jane Christian

Ms Jane Christian has worked in the field of non-statutory provision of services for people who misuse substances since completing a degree in social policy and administration in 1979. The following year she joined Turning Point, the UK's largest charity providing alcohol, drugs, mental health and learning disabilities services. Jane Christian has worked in a range of drugs misuse services: a residential rehabilitation project; a central London street agency; and in a partnership project with health authority, social services department and probation services. Currently, she is the manager of community drugs services in Staffordshire, placing a particular emphasis on developing services to meet the needs of young people. Jane has been involved in the work of the NHS Drug Advisory Service since 1988.

Mr Giles Emerson

Giles Emerson is a professional writer whose clients include most of the major government departments, as well as corporations in the private sector. He writes occasionally for *The Times* and *The Independent*, usually but not exclusively on the subject of the use and abuse of English, advocating a simple and direct approach. He has recently been commissioned to write a book on how to survive as a professional writer. Giles was educated at Exeter School in Devon and at Exeter College, Oxford, where he read English Language and Literature, graduating in 1978. He subsequently worked as a sub-editor on magazines about DIY, Gardening, War, and Sex among other subjects for Marshall Cavendish Partworks in London. In 1980, he joined the Central Office of Information as a writer and editor, where he gained much of his experience of writing for government organisations. In September 1984, Giles left the COI to learn more about the private sector and worked as a writer in a leading public relations company in Fleet Street for a year. In September 1985, he left London to set up his own business in Shropshire, where he works today.

Dr Martyn Gay

Dr Gay is a Consultant Child and Adolescent Psychiatrist based in the Department of Family Psychiatry at the Royal Hospital for Sick Children and in the Weston Health NHS Trust. He is also a consultant to the Regional Secure Unit at Kingswood, Bristol and has a special interest in child and adolescent forensic psychiatry services and in the delivery of drug and alcohol services to children and adolescents. He previously worked in the prison and probation service in the United States of America at Temple University, Philadelphia prior to coming to Great Britain in 1968 to take up his post as Consultant Child and

Adolescent Psychiatrist. His research interests have covered the fields of children in residential care, the impact of secure accommodation upon young people and the outcome of Section 53 serious young offenders. From 1984 to 1987 he was involved in an extensive DHSS Research project when he was Research Director of the Avon Drug Abuse Monitoring Project looking at the extent of drug misuse in a city population and identifying key indicators of drug misuse within the local community.

Dr Eilish Gilvarry

Dr Eilish Gilvarry is Clinical Director and Consultant Psychiatrist in the Northern Regional Alcohol and Drug Service in Newcastle upon Tyne. Her particular interests are in the fields of preventive and treatment interventions for substance use among young people. She was instrumental in the re-establishment of the Centre for Drug and Alcohol Studies in Newcastle and helped to establish the North East Addiction Services Alliance in conjunction with Leeds Addiction Unit and the economics department at York University. Both these organisations foster research, emphasising audit and evaluation. In particular, she has developed services for young people in conjunction with child and adolescent mental health services and the voluntary sector. In collaboration with child psychiatrists, she has published work on epidemiology in the field of youth and substance use.

Mrs Zena Muth

Mrs Zena Muth is the present Deputy Director of the NHS Health Advisory Service (HAS). Zena Muth is a Department of Health civil servant and is responsible for the day to day management of the HAS. Since taking up appointment in 1993, she has held particular responsibility for the management and organisation of the NHS Drug Advisory Service, which is a component of the HAS. She has also undertaken a number of HAS visits and managed the team that conducted a review of Ashworth Special Hospital.

Dr Richard Williams

Dr Richard Williams is the present Director of the NHS Health Advisory Service (HAS). Upon appointment in 1992, he was required to reposition the HAS so that it worked in accordance with the reformed health service. One of the new activities of the HAS, which he has developed, are the Thematic Reviews. Four of these have been completed and another seven are either close to completion or in progress. Richard Williams is also a Consultant Child and Adolescent Psychiatrist at the Bristol Royal Hospital for Sick Children, where he developed an extensive liaison and consultation service, with other community childcare workers and the child health services. His particular clinical interests include the psychological impacts and treatment of life-threatening and chronic physical disorders and he has extensive experience of working with families which have experienced psychological trauma. He has been involved in service management over a number of years and has a particular interest and experience in the theory and practice of leadership and the selection and development of leaders. Along with the Director of the Institute of Health Services Management, he inspired the creation of a Leadership Development Programme for Top Managers in Mental Health in 1994. Consequent on his work with the HAS, he has developed particular experience in the challenges posed to health authorities in purchasing comprehensive health services for mentally ill and elderly people.

THE AUTHORS

In addition to the editors, the authors of this report are:

Mr Niall Coggins

Niall Coggins, a Senior Lecturer in the Department of Pharmaceutical Sciences at the University of Strathclyde, was responsible for the national evaluation of drug education in Scotland. His research interests include health promotion, health-promoting schools, drug and alcohol education, and alcohol and aggression.

Mr Mike Farrar

Mr Mike Farrar is the mental health strategy manager for the Northern and Yorkshire Regional Health Authority. He is currently seconded to the Performance Management Directorate, in the National Health Service Executive in Leeds. He is a social sciences graduate from Nottingham University, who has pursued a varied career in both the public and private sector undertaking managerial, research and development and strategic planning roles. He has focused particularly on services for people with mental health or addiction problems and has been based predominantly in the north of England. In recent years, he has also been a member of the Director's advisory panel for the NHS Health Advisory Service Thematic Review of Child and Adolescent Mental Health Services and, in 1993, a member of the NHS Health Advisory Service/Mental Health Act Commission/Social Services Inspectorate Review Team on Adolescent Forensic Psychiatry Services.

Mr Finlay Graham

Finlay Graham is a Consultant Forensic Psychologist employed currently by Newcastle City Health NHS Trust in a Department of Adolescent Forensic Psychiatry formed in the wake of the Reed Committee. He has worked with young offenders for over 20 years and in a range of settings including the Police, Prison Service and Social Services in addition to the NHS.

Mr Richard White

Mr Richard White is a partner in White and Sherwin, solicitors of Croydon. The practice specialises in the law relating to children. He is co-author of a Guide to the Children Act, 1989, and the Concise Guide to the Children Act 1989, and editor of Clarke Hall and Morrison, an encyclopedia on child law. He was a member of the NHS Health Advisory Service/Mental Health Act Commission/ Social Services Inspectorate Team which reviewed Adolescent Forensic Psychiatry Services in 1993-94.

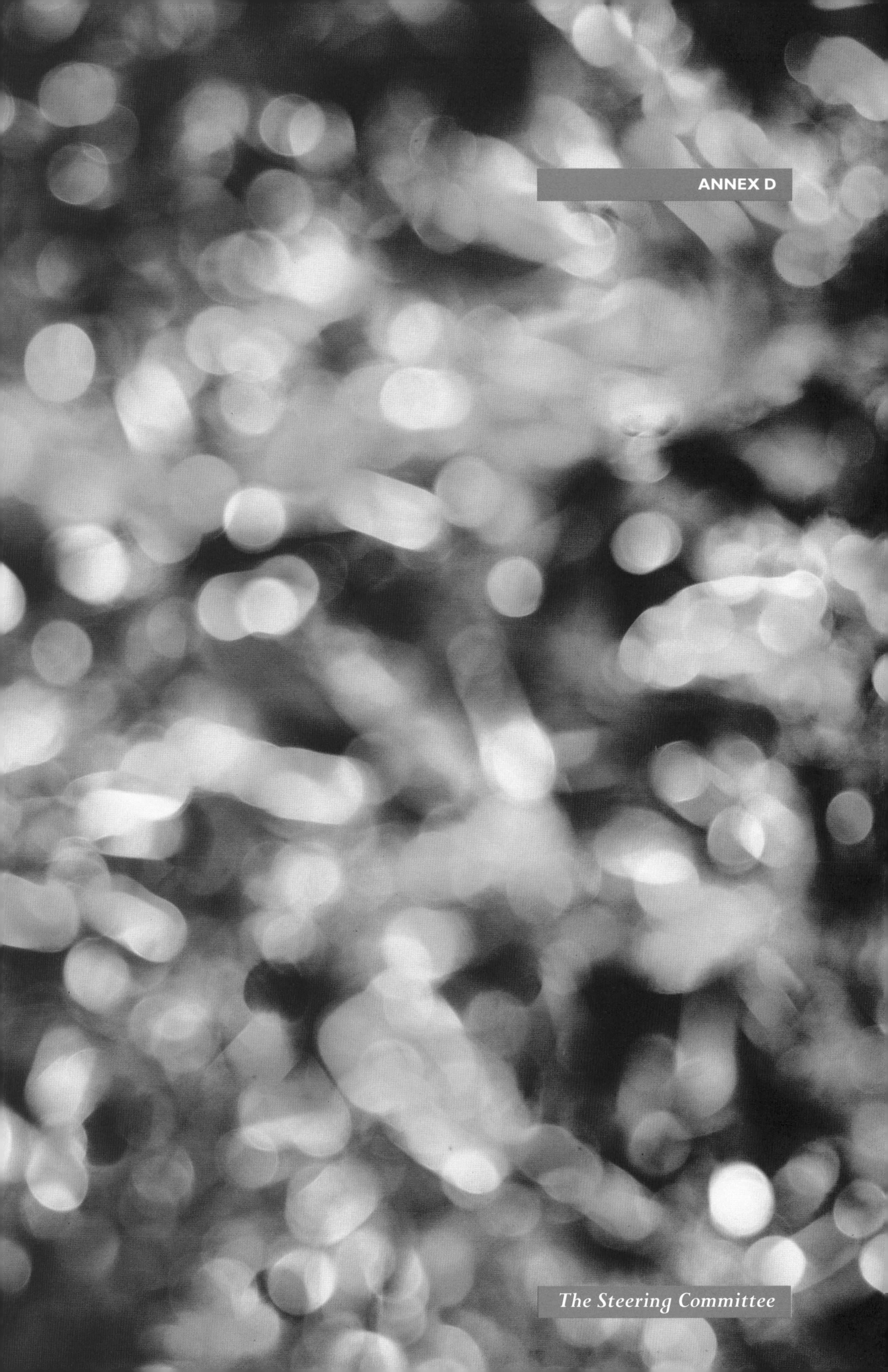

ANNEX D

The Steering Committee

In addition to the editors, the steering committee for this review included Mr Mike Farrar, Mr Richard White and the following people.

Mr Roy Atkinson

Roy Atkinson was educated at Bolton County Grammar School and followed graduate and postgraduate studies at the Universities of Leeds, Nottingham and Birmingham. His main studies have been in psychology and he is a holder of the Diploma in Management Studies. Following teaching experience at Colne Valley High School, further professional training at Birmingham University and experience in the counties of Durham and Gwent, he became principal educational psychologist to the County of Staffordshire in 1976. During his service with Staffordshire he moved into educational administration, being first principal assistant education officer for Special Services and then for Schools in the Northern part of the County. In November 1984, he moved to Northamptonshire to the post of deputy county education officer and succeeded Michael Henley to the post of county education officer, now the director of education and libraries, in September 1986.

Dr Hugh Barnes

Dr Hugh Barnes is a consultant child and adolescent psychiatrist in the United Bristol Healthcare NHS Trust and is based at the Bristol Royal Hospital for Sick Children. Presently, he is consultant in charge of the Lumsden Walker House children's psychiatric day and inpatient unit and resource centre. His clinical commitments also include paediatric liaison, and outreach sessions from a clinical base in the south of Bristol. His special interests include consultation and family therapy.

Mr Paul Bates

Mr Paul Bates is currently divisional manager for special needs within South Tees Community & Mental Health NHS Trust. Paul Bates' clinical background is in mental health nursing. He completed his registered mental nurse training in Newcastle, and then qualified in child and adolescent mental health nursing at the Nuffield unit, in Newcastle. After a short period working with children and teenagers in a social services department, Paul Bates was a charge nurse for Burnley, Pendle and Rossendale Health Authority, and was then the Senior Nurse in Child, Adolescent and Family Mental Health in York Health Services for seven years.

Dr Wendy Casey

Dr Casey is head of the Clinical Psychology Service for Children in the West Herts Community Health (NHS) Trust and is responsible for the development and provision of all child clinical psychology services in that Trust. She graduated from Queen's University Belfast and took her Ph.D. at London (Birkbeck) in 1974, and her Diploma in Clinical Psychology in 1975. Originally working in learning disability, she moved on to work with children with special needs in Haringey and Barnet, finally settling in Hertfordshire in 1988. Her main professional interest is children under five years old and she is a firm believer in the prevention of later problems through early intervention.

Dr John Coleman

Dr John Coleman trained as a clinical psychologist at the Middlesex Hospital, London and worked for 14 years as a senior lecturer in the department of psychiatry in the Royal London Hospital. Since 1988, he has been the Director of the Trust for the Study of Adolescence, an independent research and training organisation based in Brighton. He is currently the editor of the *Journal of Adolescence* and the editor of the Routledge book series, *Adolescence and Society*. He has published a number of books, the most well-known being *The Nature of Adolescence*, now in its second edition. He is a Fellow of the British Psychological Society and acts as a consultant for many organisations, including the World Health Organisation and the Prince's Trust.

Dr Stuart Cumella

Dr Stuart Cumella is senior research fellow and director of the Centre for Research and Information in Mental Disability (CRIMD) at the University of Birmingham. His academic background is in economics, politics, and social administration, and he has worked as a qualified social worker, a researcher in central government and with the Medical Research Council, and as a manager in the NHS. Stuart Cumella's current research interests are the impact of the internal markets for health and social care on mental health services, the development of outcome measures for learning disability services, primary care and social work, and the development of techniques for analysing the clinical process in community mental health services.

Professor Ron Davie

Ron Davie, consulting child Psychologist, is visiting professor at Oxford Brookes University and honorary research fellow at UCL. His work, as recent past president of the National Association for Special Educational Needs and, until 1990, as director of the National Children's Bureau, have given him a very close familiarity with current legislation and practice in the child care and special needs fields. He has particular expertise on children's emotional and behavioural problems. He now writes and lectures extensively in these areas and draws on this knowledge for his forensic practice and in consultancy for a range of statutory agencies.

Ms Mary Hancock

Ms Mary Hancock, works for the Sainsbury Centre for Mental Health Development. She was previously a social services inspector within the policy division of the Social Services Inspectorate of the Department of Health. After a brief career teaching in New Zealand and England, Mary Hancock qualified as a psychiatric social worker, and worked in Islington and Southwark as a mental welfare officer, and, subsequently, a generic social services team leader. Later, she took a joint appointment with Goldsmiths College, as a senior lecturer in social work, and a training officer in Lambeth, where she specialised in mental health, staff and student supervision, handicap, and organised field and residential placements. In the Department of Health, she covers mental health policy, including that relating to adult and child and adolescent mental health services and mental health legislation.

Dr Michael Kerfoot

Dr Michael Kerfoot is a senior lecturer and co-director of the Mental Health Social Work Research and Staff Development Unit in the Department of Psychiatry of the University of Manchester. He has 16 years experience of working in child and adolescent mental health services in Liverpool, Newcastle, and Manchester. His main research interest has been in adolescent suicidal behaviour. He has published widely in this field, both nationally and internationally, and has been a regular contributor to conferences both in the UK and abroad. He has twice been a visiting research associate at the Los Angeles Suicide Prevention Centre, and is an honorary consultant to the Samaritans.

Ms Olga Kurtianyk

Ms Olga Kurtianyk qualified as a Registered Sick Children's Nurse (RSCN) in 1974. In 1988, after holding posts in neonatal intensive care and general paediatrics, she was appointed as director of nursing services at the Queen Elizabeth Hospital for Children in London. Her interests include the effects of cultural influences on the approach of individuals to health services and education. In particular, she is interested in how this affects the psychological and physical well-being of children.

Dr Zarrina Kurtz

Dr Zarrina Kurtz is a paediatric epidemiologist and, until 1995, she was a consultant in public health medicine at South Thames Regional Health Authority and honorary senior lecturer at St George's Hospital Medical School. Formerly a paediatrician and medical advisor to the Inner London Education Authority, she is honorary advisor in child health to the National Children's Bureau. The main focus of Dr Kurtz' research and policy development is on children and young people with chronic disorders and the respective roles of the health, social and education services. She acted as the representative for purchasing on the multi-disciplinary group that produced the Quality Review of Services for the Mental Health of Children and Young People, *With Health in Mind*, for Action for Sick Children and edited that report. In 1993, she completed, with colleagues, a survey of provision and purchasing of mental health services for children and young people throughout England, funded by the Department of Health, and is currently carrying out a related project to develop models of services to meet differing population needs.

Professor William Ll. Parry-Jones

William Ll. Parry-Jones is professor of child and adolescent psychiatry at the University of Glasgow. Previously, he was consultant in charge of the Oxford Regional Psychiatric Adolescent Unit and Fellow of Linacre College, Oxford. His clinical and academic interests include psychological traumatisation, adolescent psychiatry, chronic illness and adolescent health care. He was a member of the HAS Steering Committee responsible for the Report, *Bridges Over Troubled Waters*, (1986). Recently, he directed a European Community project to develop child and adolescent psychiatry in Hungary and, currently, he is involved in establishing psycho-social programmes for traumatised children in former Yugoslavia.

Dr Gregory Richardson

Dr Gregory Richardson led the NHS Health Advisory Service Thematic Review on The Commissioning, Role and Management of Child and Adolescent Mental Health Services. He is a consultant in child and adolescent psychiatry in the York Health Services NHS Trust. Prior to becoming a consultant, he worked in Sudan and Canada. He is particularly interested in the management of mental health services and has published works on management topics relating to mental health services. He is also chairman of the Royal College of Psychiatrists' Management Special Interest Group. He is also the deputy regional advisor in psychiatry for the Yorkshire part of the Northern and Yorkshire Regional Health Authority, and is an honorary lecturer at the University of Leeds.

Dr Michael Shooter

Dr Michael Shooter came late to medicine via a history law degree and years spent as a newspaper reporter and a secondary school teacher. He is currently a consultant in child and adolescent psychiatry for the Gwent Community Health NHS Trust and was formerly the clinical director of the sister service in South Glamorgan. He is deputy registrar of the Royal College of Psychiatrists and a member of its Child and Adolescent Psychiatry Section's Executive Committee. Dr Shooter has an interest in working with children who have a chronic physical illness, in liaison with paediatricians. He has run hundreds of experimental workshops for people who are in front-line contact with dying and bereaved people, both in the UK and abroad, and has written extensively on the subject.

Dr Martin Smith

Dr Martin Smith trained at the universities of Cambridge and Birmingham. He has been a GP in Toxteth in Liverpool for the last seven years. His special interests are working with problem drug users and working with children and adolescents.

Dr Eddy Street

Dr Eddy Street is consultant clinical psychologist with Llandough Hospital NHS Trust and honorary senior research fellow in the Department of Child Health, of the University of Wales College of Medicine in Cardiff. His clinical work is focused on the provision of services to abused children and their carers. He has published widely on issues related to the theory, practice and service development of family therapy.

Mr Peter Wilson

Mr Peter Wilson started work as an unattached youth worker for the National Association of Youth Clubs, and then trained to be a social worker at the London School of Economics. He worked in New York, USA, from 1964-67 as a psychiatric social worker in a residential treatment centre for emotionally disturbed children and, subsequently, returned to England and trained as a child psychoanalyst at the Anna Freud Centre. Qualifying in 1971, he spent many years practising as a child psychotherapist in child guidance clinics in London and a walk-in centre for adolescents, and occupied the role of a senior clinical tutor at the Institute of Psychiatry and Maudsley Hospital Children's Department. During the 1980s, he was director of the Brandon Centre and consultant psychotherapist to the Peper Harow Therapeutic Community. Since April 1992, he has been the director of Young Minds.